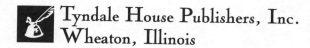

GOD'S STORY and Me

Karyn Henley

Tyndale House Publishers, Inc.
Wheaton, Illinois

Visit Tyndale's exciting Web site at www.tyndale.com

Copyright © 1998 by Karyn Henley. All rights reserved.

Exclusively administered by the Institute of Child Sensitive Communication, LLC.

For permission to copy excerpts from this book, contact Tyndale House Publishers, Inc., P.O. Box 80, Wheaton, Illinois 60189.

Cover illustration by Corbert Gauthier. Interior illustrations by Marlene Ekman.

Illustrations copyright © 1998 by Karyn Henley. All rights reserved.

Exclusively administered by the Institute of Child Sensitive Communication, LLC.

Bible story excerpts and weekly Scripture verses are taken from God's Story, copyright © 1998 by Karyn Henley. All rights reserved. Exclusively administered by the Institute of Child Sensitive Communication, LLC.

Edited by Betty Free

Designed by Beth Sparkman

Library of Congress Cataloging-in-Publication Data

Henley, Karyn.
   God's story and me / Karyn Henley.
      p.   cm.
      Summary: Presents daily devotional readings and prayers arranged by weekly themes covering such topics as unfailing love, forgiveness, patience, and God's promises.
      ISBN 0-8423-4361-X (pbk. : alk. paper)
      1. Children—Prayer-books and devotions—English.   [1. Prayer books and devotions.   2. Devotional calendars.]   I. Title.
BV4870.H45   1998
242'.62—dc21   98-19020

Printed in the United States of America

04   03   02   01   00   99   98

7   6   5   4   3   2   1

CONTENTS

Now and Always

I'll never leave you. *Hebrews 13:5*

MONDAY

Read "From Children's Mouths," page 200 in *God's Story*. Or read this part of the story:

Lord, our Lord, your name is great all over the earth! I see the sky that you made with your hands. I see the moon and stars that you put up there. Then I wonder why you even think about people. I wonder why you care about us. But you made us only a little lower than the beings from heaven. You made us important to you.

You put people in charge of everything you made.
Psalm 8:1, 3-6

Watch the deep, dark night sky. Look at the tiny pin points of winking light. Wonder at the stars and the moon and the planets. Do they make you feel small? King David felt small when he looked at the night sky. That's why he told God, "I see the moon and stars that you put up there. Then I wonder why you even think about people."

But God does think about people. God loved David and took care of him. God loves you and takes care of you, too. You may sometimes feel very small. You may feel that you're not important. But you are important to God. He says, "I'll never leave you."

What important job does David say that God gave people to do? What are some ways people do this job? How do you help with this job?

"Dear Father God, you are so great. Thank you for seeing me and hearing me. Thank you for caring about me. Help me to know that you are always near."

TUESDAY

Read "A Ladder up to Heaven," page 25 in *God's Story*. Or read this part of the story:

Jacob left his home and began his trip to Laban's. The sun went down before he got there. So Jacob stopped to rest. He took a stone and used it as a pillow. He lay down for the night.

That night Jacob had a dream. He saw a ladder that went all the way up to heaven. God's angels were going up and down the ladder.

God stood at the top of the ladder. God said, "I am the Lord."

God also said, "I'll be with you. I will watch over you everywhere you go. I won't leave you. I will keep all my promises to you."
Genesis 28:5-13, 15

Laughing and playing with friends can be fun. Being with your family can be fun too. But when no one is around, it's easy to get lonely and sad. Jacob felt lonely until God showed him that he wasn't really alone.

When do you feel lonely? What do you do to help yourself feel better? Are you really alone? What can you do to remind yourself that you are never alone?

God told Jacob, "I'll be with you. I will watch over you everywhere you go. I won't leave you." Jacob was not alone, and you are not alone. God will be with you. He will watch over you everywhere you go. He won't leave you.

"Dear God, thank you for being with me. Thank you for watching over me everywhere I go. Help me to remember that I'm never alone."

WEDNESDAY

 Read "Hiding on the Roof," page 95 in *God's Story*. Or read this part of the story:

God told Joshua, ". . . Now get ready to go across the Jordan River. You'll go into the land that I'm giving my people. I'll give you the land you walk on. This is what I promised to Moses. Nobody will be able to come against you all your life. I will never leave you. I will never forget about you.

"So be strong. Be very brave. Be careful to obey the laws Moses gave you. Think about the laws day and night. Then you'll do what they say. You'll do a good job in whatever you do." *Joshua 1:1-3, 5-8*

SOME THINGS YOU CAN DO THIS WEEK

☐ **Look at old pictures** of you and your family. Talk about some of the good times and hard times you've had together. Think about how God has been with you all the time.

☐ **Make moon cookies.** Use a roll of sugar-cookie dough from the food store. Put a spoon of dough on some waxed paper. Pat it flat into a circle. This makes a full moon. Cut the circle in half to make half moons. Shape them into C shapes for fingernail moons. (Or make star cookies with star-shaped cookie cutters.) Bake them the way it says on the cookie package. Think about the moon and stars David saw in the sky. *(See Monday's reading.)*

☐ **Get a big rock** and clean it. Write today's date on it with paint or a marker that won't come off. Jacob stood up the rock he slept on. Set your rock in a place where you can see it often. It will help you remember that God has been your helper, just as he was Jacob's helper. *(See Tuesday's reading.)*

☐ **Play "Hide-and-Seek."** Think about how Elijah hid. Was he all alone? *(See Thursday's reading.)*

☐ **Play "Turning Wind"** outdoors or in a big room with nothing to bump into. One person is the wind. He carefully holds another person's arm. He swings that person around and then lets go. The other person falls away and has to freeze still wherever he lands. Think about the wind that took Elijah to heaven. *(See Friday's reading.)*

Picking up toys can be a hard job. Washing dishes can be a hard job. Even saying you're sorry can be a hard job. It's not as hard if someone helps. But did you ever have to do a hard job all by yourself? Joshua had a hard job to do. He had to lead God's people into a new land. They had to fight for their land.

But Joshua did not have to do his hard job all by himself. God was with him. God told him, "I will never leave you. I will never forget about you."

What hard jobs do you have to do? How can you do those jobs? Will you have to do them by yourself? God will never leave you. He will never forget about you.

"Dear Father God, thank you for helping me do hard jobs. Help me remember that you will never leave me or forget me."

THURSDAY

 Read "Afraid in the Desert," page 283 in *God's Story*. Or read this part of the story:

"Go stand on the mountain," said God. "I'm going to pass by."

A strong wind blew. It was so strong, it broke rocks. But God was not in the wind.

The earth began to shake. But God was not in the shaking earth.

A fire came. But God was not in the fire.

Then Elijah heard a soft, quiet voice.

Elijah pulled his coat over his face. He stood at the opening to the cave.

Then God spoke. "Why are you here, Elijah?"

"I've worked hard for you, God," said Elijah. "But your people have turned away from you. They tore your altars down. They killed your prophets. I'm the only prophet left. Now they're trying to kill me."

"Go back," said God. "Make Jehu king of Israel. Make Elisha the next prophet after you."

Then God said, "I have saved 7,000 people for myself in Israel." *1 Kings 19:11-16, 18*

God's soft, quiet voice told Elijah that he wasn't alone. Did you ever feel like Elijah? Did you ever think you were the only one choosing to do what's right? How did that make you feel?

Elijah thought he was the only one who followed God. He felt scared. So he ran away and hid. But he found out that he was not alone. God was there. God had saved lots of other people who followed him too.

When have you felt as if you were the only one? What made you feel that way? What can you do about it? How can you remember that God is with you?

God was with Elijah. God is with you, too. He said, "I'll never leave you."

"Dear Father God, sometimes I feel alone. Sometimes I think no one else feels the way I do. Help me to remember that you are with me no matter what."

FRIDAY

Read "A Chariot and Horses of Fire," page 294 in *God's Story*. Or read this part of the story:

All of a sudden, horses of fire appeared. They pulled a chariot of fire. It went between Elijah and Elisha. Then a wind came, turning around and around. It took Elijah up to heaven.

Elisha saw it. He cried, "My father! Israel's horses and chariots!"

Elisha didn't see Elijah anymore. He tore his own coat apart. Then he picked up Elijah's coat. It had fallen from Elijah.

Elisha walked back to the Jordan River. He hit the water with Elijah's coat. He said, "Where is Elijah's God?"

The water moved apart for him. Elisha walked across on the dry ground. *2 Kings 2:11-14*

Horses of fire pulling a fast chariot must have surprised Elisha. How would you have felt? Maybe Elisha stood there with his eyes wide and his mouth open! Then the wind rushed past, and his friend was gone. Elisha was all alone.

But do you think Elisha was really alone? He hit the river with his friend's coat. He asked, "Where is Elijah's God?" Where *was* Elijah's God? Elijah's God was Elisha's God. Elijah's God is your God too. God was with Elijah and Elisha. God is with you, too.

You may sometimes feel very small. You may sometimes feel alone. You may think you have a hard job to do all by yourself. But God says, "I'll never leave you." You are never alone.

"Dear God, thank you for being with me all the time. Thank you for going with me everywhere. Thank you for helping me and taking care of me. Help me to always remember that I am never alone. Help me to remember that you will never leave me."

A Keeper of Promises

God keeps all his promises. *Psalm 145:13*

MONDAY

Read "A World under Water," page 6 in *God's Story*. Or read this part of the story:

Noah made a big pile of rocks. It was an altar for worshiping God. Noah put some fresh meat on it as a gift to God.

God said, "I'll never get rid of all living things again. There will always be a time to plant. There will always be a time to pick the crops. There will always be cold and heat. There will always be summer and winter. There will always be day and night. These will be around as long as the earth lasts."

God said, "Have children and fill the earth. You are in charge of the animals now. I'm making a promise to you and all the animals. It's a promise that will last forever. I'll never get rid of everything by flood water again.

"Here is the sign that shows my promise is true," said God. "I am putting a rainbow in the clouds. I will remember my promise when I see the rainbow." *Genesis 8:20-22; 9:1-2, 11-15*

Have you ever seen a rainbow? The sun shines through drops of water in the sky. The water breaks the sun's light into colors: red, orange, yellow, green, blue, and purple. We can think of the rainbow as God's watercolors painted across the sky. But there is something even more special about rainbows. They help us remember that God keeps his promises.

Rainbows don't stay around very long. But God's promises do. God remembers his promises. And God always keeps his promises.

What are some of God's promises to you? Here are two of them. God promises, "I will teach you how you should live. I will watch over you" (Psalm 32:8). God also says, "Call on me when you are

SOME THINGS YOU CAN DO THIS WEEK

☐ **Color a rainbow** on a piece of white paper. Press down hard on your crayon so the color is dark and shiny. Then paint over the paper and the rainbow with watercolor paints. The rainbow will keep shining right through the paint. Think about what the rainbow means to God. (See Monday's reading.)

☐ **Go outdoors at night.** Look at the night sky. If you have an encyclopedia, ask someone to help you look up astronomy. See if you can find some pictures (constellations) in the sky. God told Abraham, "Count the stars if you can. That's how many people will be in your family someday" (Genesis 15:5). Abraham's family became the whole nation of Israel. (See Tuesday's reading.)

☐ **Draw a picture** of something God promised you. Or draw a picture of a promise from one of the stories. Hold the paper in front of a mirror. Look in the mirror to see what God sent to keep his promise. God sends exactly what he promises.

☐ **Make a promise shoe box.** Decorate the shoe box with stickers, markers, paint, or self-stick paper. Print or draw pictures of some of God's promises to you. Put each promise on a piece of paper. Then place the papers in the box. When you need something to cheer you up, look at a promise from your box.

☐ **Play a promise game.** Print God's promises on index cards, using one card for each promise. Print each promise twice, so you'll have matching cards. Mix them up and turn them over so you can't see what they say. Choose two cards. If they match, keep them and choose two more. If they don't match, turn them over again. Then let someone else try to match two cards.

in trouble. I will save you" (Psalm 50:15).

"Dear God, thank you for keeping all your promises. Thank you for teaching me and watching over me. Thank you for saving me."

TUESDAY

Read "A New Name," page 12 in *God's Story*. Or read this part of the story:

Then God said, "Sarai's name will now be Sarah. She will have a son. She will be the mother of nations."

Abraham laughed. "Will I have a son after I'm 100 years old? Will Sarah have a baby after she is 90? Maybe you can do these good things for Ishmael instead."

"Sarah will have a son," said God. "Name him Isaac. My promise is for him and his family forever. But I hear what you say about Ishmael. I will do good things for him. He will have a big family, too. But my promise is for Isaac." *Genesis 17:15-21*

Abraham could hear the wind shaking the leaves. He could hear

---

God's Promises

Here are some of God's promises for you to use with the **promise shoe box** and the **promise game.**

God will never leave you. (Joshua 1:5)
God watches over people who do what's right. (Psalm 1:6)
God helps you to be safe. (Psalm 4:8)
God holds your hand. (Isaiah 41:13)
God will help you. (Isaiah 41:13)
God will not remember your sins. (Isaiah 43:25)
God shows you the way you should go. (Isaiah 48:17)
God will not forget you. (Isaiah 49:15)
God will give you food and clothes. (Matthew 6:25, 33)
God's Son, Jesus, will give you rest. (Matthew 11:28)
Jesus gives you his peace. (John 14:27)

Jesus will come back. (Acts 1:11)
God makes everything turn out for our good. (Romans 8:28)
Believe in Jesus, and you will be saved. (Romans 10:9)
God will give you all you need. (Philippians 4:19)
God puts power and love in your spirit. (2 Timothy 1:7)
God puts self-control in your spirit. (2 Timothy 1:7)
You will live with Jesus. (2 Timothy 2:11)
God will come close to you. (James 4:8)
God cares about you. (1 Peter 5:7)
You will be like Jesus. (1 John 3:2)
Love comes from God. (1 John 4:7)

owls calling. He could even hear God talking to him. But he could not hear what God had promised to give him and Sarah: a baby.

Abraham could see the gold sun and the silver white stars. But he could not see what God had promised to give him and Sarah: a baby. God had promised. But God had not kept his promise yet.

Did anyone ever make you a promise and then not keep it? When that happens, we feel sad. Sometimes people forget their promises. Sometimes people make promises they can't keep. But God never forgets his promises. He will always do what he says.

God kept his promise to Abraham and Sarah. They "had a son, even though they were old. The baby came just when God said it would. Abraham named the baby Isaac. Abraham was 100 years old when Isaac was born" (Genesis 21:2-3, 5). For the complete story, read "Two Sons," page 16 in *God's Story*.

God kept his promise to Abraham and Sarah. God will keep his promises to you, too.

"Dear Father God, thank you for keeping your promises. Show me your promises. Help me wait for them to come true."

WEDNESDAY

Read "A Great Light," page 342 in *God's Story*. Or read this part of the story:

Someday, people who were sad will be glad. Someday, God will make Galilee great. People walking in the dark see a great light. . . . A child is born. A son is given to us. He will rule. People will call him Wonderful Guide, Powerful God, Father Forever, Prince of Peace.
Isaiah 9:1-2, 6

Think about a place where wind sweeps over the trees. It blows down the hills and out across the lake shaped like a harp. That's Galilee. It's a place where God's people lived. God promised to send someone special to his people there. Someone wonderful. Someone who would guide them. Someone powerful. Can you guess who it was? It was Jesus. A long time before Jesus was born, God promised to send Jesus someday.

Lots of prophets from long ago told about this promise. Did God keep his promise? Yes. God always keeps his promises.

What does God promise to you? This is one of his promises: "I'm your God. I hold your right hand. I tell you not to be scared, my little people. I will help you myself" (Isaiah 41:13).

How has God helped you? How do you need him to help you? He will help. He has promised.

"Dear God, thank you for keeping your promises. You made me. Take care of me, Father. Help me and save me."

THURSDAY

Read "Another Leader," page 632, and "Wind, Fire, and Different Languages," page 633 in *God's Story*. Or read this part of the stories:

Once Jesus said to his friends, "Don't leave Jerusalem. Wait for the gift my Father promised to give you. You heard me talk about it. John baptized people with water. But soon you'll be baptized with the Holy Spirit."

Now Jesus had gone back to heaven. After he left, his best friends went back to Jerusalem. It wasn't even a mile away from the place where Jesus left them. . . . They kept praying together.

It was time for the Holiday of Weeks. Jesus' friends got together at someone's house.

All of a sudden, they heard a sound. It sounded like a strong wind blowing. The sound came from heaven. It filled the whole house.

Then they saw something that looked

like fire. The fire broke into different parts. It came to sit on each of them.

Then God's Holy Spirit filled them. They started talking in different languages. God's Spirit made them able to do this. *Acts 1:4-5, 12-14; 2:1-4*

You worked very hard in class this week," said the teacher. "So on Friday, we will have a pizza party. I promise!"

"You can't go on my business trip with me," said Dad. "But I promise to bring back a surprise for you."

Do you remember a promise that someone made to you? When people promise you something, it means they want you to believe them. They know you will have to wait for it to happen. So they want you to know that they plan to do what they said.

Jesus' friends had to wait for the gift God had promised. The special gift was God's Holy Spirit. God kept his promise to Jesus' friends. God has promised to give you his Holy Spirit too. Peter said, "This gift is for . . . anybody God calls into his

kingdom" (Acts 2:39). That means you. What a special promise!

"Dear Father God, thank you for keeping your promises. Thank you for sending your Holy Spirit to me, too. You are a great God!"

FRIDAY

Read "Going into the Clouds," page 630 in *God's Story*. Or read this part of the story:

Then Jesus went up off the ground. His friends watched until a cloud hid him. They peered up into the sky.

Suddenly, they saw two men standing by them. The men were dressed all in white.

"Men from Galilee!" said the two men. ". . . Why are you peering into the sky? Jesus has gone up into heaven. He will come back the same way you saw him go." *Acts 1:9-11*

Clouds. Sometimes they are puffy and white like whipped cream. Sometimes they are dark gray and full of rain. Sometimes they are thin and wispy.

Did you ever wonder what kind of cloud Jesus went into as he left the earth? The angels said that Jesus will come back the same way he left. Jesus' friend John wrote, "Look, he is coming in the clouds. Everyone will see him" (Revelation 1:7). That's a promise. Jesus will come back. Then he will take us to be with him where there is no hurting, no sickness, and no dying.

When John heard about heaven, he was ready to get that promise. He said, "Come, Lord Jesus!" One day, Jesus will come. We know he will, because he always keeps his promises!

"Dear Father God, you give wonderful promises. Thank you for being so good to me. Thank you for keeping your promises! And come, Lord Jesus!"

Keep Following God

Don't get tired of doing good things. *Galatians 6:9*

MONDAY

Read "The King in the Winter House," page 393 in *God's Story.* Or read this part of the story:

God told Jeremiah, "Get a roll of paper. Write on it everything I told you."

So Jeremiah called his helper, Baruch. Jeremiah told his helper what to write. Baruch wrote it on the roll of paper.

King Jehoiakim sent a helper to get the roll of paper. The helper brought it back and read it to the king. All the leaders were standing there too.

Now the king was in his winter house. Fire was burning in a pot in front of him. His helper would read part of the paper roll. Then the king would cut that part off with a knife. He'd throw it into the fire pot.

At last the whole roll of paper was burned.

Then Jeremiah gave another roll of paper to Baruch. Jeremiah told Baruch what to write. Baruch wrote it. He put in even more of God's words.

Jeremiah 36:1-2, 4, 21-23, 32

Dip, dip. Draw a letter or two. Dip, dip. Draw a letter or two. Baruch wrote what Jeremiah told him. His pen may have been cut from a reed. That's a grass that grows in the water. His ink may have been made from berry juice. His roll of paper may have been made of sheep skin, called parchment. It took a long time to write anything. Dip, dip. Draw a letter or two. Dip, dip. Write again.

How do you think Baruch felt when he heard what the king did to his writing? Then God gave Jeremiah more words! And Baruch wrote them down. He also wrote the first words over again. Dip, dip. Draw a letter or two. Dip, dip again.

Did you ever have to do something over again? How did that make you feel? God wants us to keep on doing what's right. He promises to bring good to us when we keep following him.

"Dear God, I want to follow you and do what you want. Help me to keep doing what's right."

TUESDAY

 Read "Tools in One Hand, Swords in the Other," page 491 in *God's Story*. Or read this part of the story:

We built the wall back up again. We got it half as high as we wanted. The people were working as hard as they could.

Our people said, "The workers are getting tired. There are so many piles of sticks and stones! We can't build the wall."

Our enemies said, "We'll go in there with them. They won't know we're coming. We'll kill them. Then their work will end."

Our enemies found out that we knew about their plan. Then we all went back to work on the wall.

After that, half of my men did

the work. The other half held swords and bows.

So we kept working. We started every morning when the sky first got light. We worked until the stars came out. *Nehemiah 4:6, 10-11, 15-16, 21*

It was dusty work. It was dirty work. It was hard work building a wall all the way around a city. The people got thirsty and hungry and tired. They said, "We can't do this!" But they didn't give up. They kept on working. And they finished that hard job!

Did you ever do hard work? Did you ever get thirsty and hungry and tired? Working outside in the yard can be hard. Cleaning the house can be hard. Did you ever think, *I can't do this?* Don't give up. When a hard job is finished, God will give you a good feeling. You did it!

Paul was one of Jesus' followers. He wrote, "I can do everything with Jesus' help. He makes me strong" (Philippians 4:13).

"Dear Father God, help me not to give up when work gets hard. I'll work with your power. Thank you for making me strong."

WEDNESDAY

Read "The Judge," page 587 in *God's Story.* Or read this part of the story:

"Once there was a judge," said Jesus. "He didn't worship God. He didn't care about people.

"There was a lady who lived in his town. Her husband had died. The lady kept coming to see the judge. 'My enemies aren't treating me right,' she would say, 'Help me, please.'

"Time after time she came. But the judge wouldn't listen to her.

"At last the judge thought, 'I don't worship God. I don't care about people. But this lady keeps bothering me. So I'll make sure she is treated fairly. Then she won't wear me out by coming so much.'" *Luke 18:2-5*

The judge heard footsteps coming to his door. He looked up. It was the same lady. Here she was, back again. What do you think the judge thought? He may have thought, *Here she comes again. This must be very important to her. She doesn't give up.* Finally, he gave her what she asked for.

Jesus told this story to let us know that we should keep on praying. He is telling us not to give up. We might not see God's answer to our prayers right away. But God doesn't want us to stop talking to him. He wants us to tell him everything. We can even tell him the things we think about deep down inside. We can tell him things we never tell anyone else. We can do it because God cares. He hears our prayers, and he will answer.

"Dear Father God, thank you for listening to me. I know you will answer my prayers. Help me to keep following you. Help me not to give up. I trust in you."

SOME THINGS YOU CAN DO THIS WEEK

☐ **Play "Follow-the-Leader"** with your family or friends. Talk about following God. How do we know we're following God?

☐ **Bake refrigerator cookies.** Get a roll of your favorite flavor of cookie dough from the food store. Let a grown-up help cut the dough into circles. Remember the story of the king who cut the roll of paper. Remember how Baruch wrote another message and didn't give up. Bake the cookies the way the directions on the package of dough tell you. *(See Monday's reading.)*

☐ **Build a city wall.** Turn paper cups upside down. Line up about 10 of them. Stack nine cups on top of the 10 to make a second row. To do this, rest the rim of each second-row cup on the bottoms of two first-row cups. Keep building up as high as you can go. Then begin adding more cups to the end of each row. Add more rows, too. See how high and wide you can make the wall. Remember the story of the people building the wall and not giving up. *(See Tuesday's reading.)*

☐ **Play "Over the Wall."** Get two people to hold a rope across the floor. Jump over it while it's low. Let them raise it higher and higher. See how high you can get it and still jump over it. Think about the people who built the high wall. *(See Tuesday's reading.)*

☐ **Make a flashlight campfire.** Lay a flashlight on the floor or ground. Stack sticks, blocks, or cardboard tubes on top like logs. Turn the flashlight on so it looks like there is fire on the logs. Tell some of the stories you read this week.

THURSDAY

Read "Snakes and Blood" and "Frogs, Bugs, and Flies," pages 52 and 53 in *God's Story*. Or read this part of the second story:

The king called Moses and Aaron. "Pray to God," he said. "Ask him to take the frogs away. Then I'll let your people go."

"Tell me when," said Moses.

"Tomorrow," said the king.

"All right," said Moses. "Then you'll know there's nobody like God. The frogs will leave. They will only be in the river."

. . . The king saw that the frogs were dead. So he got angry. He let his heart get hard again. He wouldn't listen to Moses and Aaron. It was just like God had said. *Exodus 8:8-11, 15*

Rivers full of blood. Houses full of frogs. Bugs and flies everywhere. But did all of that make the king of Egypt let God's people go? No. How would you have felt if you had been Moses?

Maybe Moses felt like saying, "The king will never let them go. I give up." But Moses didn't say that.

He just kept doing what God said. He went back to the king again and again. The next three Bible stories in *God's Story* tell what happened (Exodus 9–12).

Moses followed God no matter what happened. God wants us to do that too. Do you know what "following God" means? It means doing what God wants you to do. It means going where God wants you to go. And it means saying what God wants you to say. What does God want you to do to follow him?

"Dear God, show me how to follow you. I want to keep following you no matter what happens. Thank you for leading me."

FRIDAY

Read "Trying to Scare God's People" and "God Sends His Angel to Fight," pages 355 and 356 in *God's Story*. Or read this part of the first story:

Assyria's army leader . . . shouted so everyone could hear. "Listen to what the great king of Assyria says! Don't believe Hezekiah. He can't save you. Don't let him talk you into trusting God."

The leaders from Assyria tried to scare the people. They wanted to take over the city. They talked about God as if he were a fake god.

But the people kept quiet. King Hezekiah had told them, "Don't answer."

2 Kings 18:19, 28-30, 34-36

The water bobbed softly up and down in the Upper Pool. Nearby on the road, the enemy army leaders stood shouting. "Follow us. We'll give you what you need. Don't believe Hezekiah. He is lying. God can't help you." They were trying to make God's people give up.

Sometimes people work hard at something. But they see that it's not going to happen. So they give up. Is it ever all right to give up? When? Is it ever all right to give up following God? People might tell us that God won't help us. But that's not true. God *will* help us.

Do you sometimes think you might stop following God? Then remember the story of Hezekiah. Keep following God no matter what happens. You never have to give up on God.

"Dear God, thank you for always helping me. I won't give up. I will follow you no matter what happens. You are a wonderful, powerful God."

Coming Near to God

Come close to God. Then he will come close to you. *James 4:8*

MONDAY

 Read "Saul's Shepherd Tells," page 146 in *God's Story*. Or read this part of the story:

David ran away to a cave. . . . People who didn't like King Saul went with David. He was their leader. There were about 400 men.

David wrote this prayer.

I cry out loud to God.
I tell him my troubles.
My spirit gets weak inside me.
But you still know my way, God.
People have set a trap for me.
No one seems to care about me.
There is no safe place.

So I cry to you, God.
I say, "You are a place to be safe."
Listen to my cry.
I need you very badly.
Save me from those who chase me.
They are too strong for me.
Set me free from my jail
*   so I can praise you.*
1 Samuel 22:1-2; Psalm 142

How did David feel about God? He loved God with all his heart, didn't he? He wanted to be close to God. And he wanted God to be close to him.

To get close to God, David talked with God. The psalms that David wrote let us know when he talked to God. We can read them to learn what he talked about. He talked with God when he was sad and when he was happy. He talked with God when he was afraid or angry. He talked with God when he was thankful. He talked with God about everything.

Perhaps you want someone to be your good friend. But what if you never talk with that person? What if you never try to be with your friend? It's the same with God. To get to know God and be close to him, you need to have some time with him. You need to talk with him. "Come close to God. Then he will come close to you."

"Dear Father God, I want to know you better. I want to come close to you. Thank you for wanting to come close to me."

TUESDAY

Read "Animals in a Big Sheet," page 646 in *God's Story*. Or read this part of the story:

There was a Roman army captain named Cornelius. . . .

One afternoon around three o'clock, Cornelius saw one of God's angels. He saw it very clearly. . . .

"Your prayers have been a gift to God," said the angel. "Your gifts to poor people have been gifts to God. Now send some men to Joppa. Ask them to bring Peter back. . . ."

The next day Peter was praying. As Peter was praying . . . he saw a picture in his mind. It was a picture God was showing him. . . . Something that looked like a big sheet came down. . . . Different kinds of animals were in the sheet. . . . A voice said, "Get up, Peter. Choose one of these to eat. . . . God says it's all right."

Peter went to see Cornelius at his house. . . . Peter saw many people there. . . . Peter began to talk to them. " . . . We're not supposed to visit someone who is not Jewish. But God showed me that it's all right with him. . . .

"Jesus told us to teach people," said Peter. "He told us to say he is the one God chose.

God chose Jesus to judge people. All the prophets tell about him. They say he forgives the sins of everyone who believes in him."

Suddenly, the Holy Spirit came on Cornelius and the others. They talked in other languages. They praised God.

The Jews with Peter were surprised. That's because Cornelius and his friends were not Jewish.

"Can we stop them from being baptized?" asked Peter. "They got the Holy Spirit just like we did."

Acts 10:1-47

An angel was standing right there in the room with Cornelius! In the middle of the afternoon! Cornelius was scared. How would you have felt?

Cornelius had been coming close to God. He had prayed to God often. He had tried to do what was right. Now God was coming close to Cornelius. First, God sent an angel. Then God sent Peter to help Cornelius learn more about God. After that, God sent his Holy Spirit. That's when Peter found out

something very important. God will come close to anyone who comes close to him.

You can do what Cornelius did. You can learn more about God by reading about him. You can talk with him often. You can try to do what's right. You can come close to God.

"Dear God, help me learn more about you. Help me talk with you often and do what's right so I can be close to you."

WEDNESDAY

 Read "Getting the Dirt Out," page 347 in *God's Story*. Or read this part of the story:

Hezekiah opened God's worship house again. He fixed the doors. He brought the priests back.

"Listen," said Hezekiah to the priests. "Take all the dirt out of here."

So the priests and their families got to work. They cleaned out every part of the worship house. Then they told King Hezekiah they had done the job.

The next morning King

Hezekiah got up early. He got the city leaders together. They went to the worship house. They offered gifts of meat on the altar. They asked God to forgive their sins. Priests came with cymbals, harps, and lyres. They did what God had said to do long ago. Priests also got their horns ready.

King Hezekiah told them when to offer the gifts on the altar. Then they began singing. Priests played music.

When the gifts had been given, they all bowed down. They worshiped God. *2 Chronicles 29:3-5, 12, 15, 18-21, 25-28*

The people opened up the doors and lit all the lamps. They swept out the dirt and dusted off the dust. Everyone worked hard to get the

SOME THINGS YOU CAN DO THIS WEEK

☐ **Write a psalm.** Write about things you are thankful for. Or draw pictures of these things. Then write something that tells how great God is. Say this as a prayer to God. *(See Monday's reading.)*

☐ **Play "Jumping Animals"** outdoors. Ask friends to stand around a sheet and hold the edges. Put a stuffed animal on the sheet. Toss it up and try to catch the animal. Try it with two stuffed animals. Add more animals. See how many you can toss and catch. Do you remember Peter's dream about the sheet and the animals? Why did God send him that dream? *(See Tuesday's reading.)*

☐ **Collect clothes or food** for needy people. Or bake a treat for someone who is sick or old. Part of being a living gift is doing things that share God's goodness with others. *(See Wednesday's reading.)*

☐ **Make a tent.** Put a sheet over a table or across chairs. You can read your Bible in your tent. Sing and pray. You can even "camp out" in this tent in your house. Think about how Joshua stayed in the worship tent to be close to God. *(See Thursday's reading.)*

☐ **Make a calendar.** Lay plain paper on top of an old calendar. Trace the squares. Make one page for each month. Draw pictures on the special days. Count the weeks (or the days) until Christmas. Remember how long Anna and Simeon waited for Jesus to be born. They stayed close to God. How can you stay close to God? *(See Friday's reading.)*

worship house clean. It was a way to let God know that he was the most important.

Then the people played music and sang. They bowed down in worship to God. They gave gifts to God on the altar.

We can play music and sing to God. We can bow and worship. But we don't have altars where we give gifts to God. Do you know what we can give God? The most important thing we can give God is ourselves. God says we are living gifts for him. That is part of our worship.

God gave himself to us. He came close to us. Now we can give ourselves to him. We can come close to God. How did God give himself? How can we give ourselves?

"Dear Father God, I will sing to you. I will bow down and worship you. But most of all, I will give myself to you."

THURSDAY

Read "Moses Sees God's Back," page 71 in *God's Story*. Or read this part of the story:

Now Moses had a special tent outside the camp.

He called it the meeting tent. People who wanted to ask God something would go there. When Moses went there, people would stand in their tent doors. They would watch Moses go into the tent. Then the tall cloud would come down in front of the tent. It would stay there while God talked to Moses. The people would see the cloud. Then they would worship at their tents.

God talked to Moses as a friend. They talked together. Then Moses would come back to camp. But Joshua, his helper, wouldn't leave the meeting tent. *Exodus 33:7-11*

Think about what it might have been like.

You live in the camp with God's people. "Here he comes," says your dad. Your whole family moves to the door of your tent. You all peek out. You see Moses pass by. Then you stand outside your tent and watch Moses. He walks outside the camp and goes into a special tent. Now a wonderful thing happens. A tall cloud comes down out of the sky. It covers the door of the special tent. You know God is talking to Moses. So you worship God.

Later, Moses comes back from the tent. But Joshua, his young helper, stays there. Joshua wants to stay as close to God as he can.

God and Moses were friends. Do you know how they got to be such good friends? Moses took a lot of time to talk with God. He listened to God. He obeyed God. He loved God.

How can you get to be a good friend of God's?

"Dear Father God, I want you to be my good friend. I want to stay as close to you as I can. I love you, God. Thank you for loving me."

FRIDAY

 Read "No More Waiting," page 507 in *God's Story*. Or read this part of the story:

The Spirit told Simeon to go to the worship house. That's when Joseph and Mary brought Jesus there.

Simeon held baby Jesus and praised God. "God, you promised this," he said. "Now you are letting me die in peace. I have seen the one who will save."

Another person was at the worship house. She was a woman prophet. Her name was Anna. She was very old. She had been married when she was very young. But her husband had died after seven years. After that, she had no husband. Now she was 84 years old.

Anna stayed at the worship house. She worshiped night and day. She prayed. Sometimes she even went without food to worship God.

Right at that moment, Anna came up to Mary, Joseph, and baby Jesus. She thanked God. And she talked about Jesus. She talked to everyone who was waiting to be saved.
Luke 2:27-30, 36-38

There was a smoky fire smell from the meat on the altar. Then there were animal smells. There were animal sounds, too: cows mooing, sheep baaing, birds cooing. And as always, there were the pat-pat-pat sounds of feet walking across the floor. Busy priests walked this way and that. People talked and prayed. The worship house was a place that Anna knew very well.

Why do you think Anna knew so much about God and his Son, Jesus? Every day she was at the worship house. She worshiped night and day. Sometimes she even stopped eating food for a day or more to worship God. She was showing God that he was more important to her than food. She was coming close to God. So God came close to Anna. He let her see baby Jesus.

How can you come close to God?

"Dear God, teach me how to pray. Teach me how to worship you. You are wonderful, God. You are important to me. I want to be close to you. Thank you for being close to me."

I'm a Letter from Jesus

Seeing you is like reading a letter from Jesus. This letter wasn't written with ink. It was written with God's living Spirit.

2 Corinthians 3:3

MONDAY

Read "Salt and Light," page 530 in *God's Story*. Or read this part of the story:

"You're like salt here on earth," said Jesus. "But what if the salt stops being salty? Can it get salty again? No. It's not good for anything. It has to be thrown out. It's only good for walking on.

"You're like a light to this world," said Jesus. "You're like a city high on a hill. It's up where everyone can see it.

"People don't put a lamp under a bowl," said Jesus. "Instead, they put it out where it will shine. It lights up the house. So let your light shine where people can see it. They'll see the good things you do. Then they'll cheer for God your Father."

Matthew 5:13-16

Did you ever eat salty chips? What does salt do? It makes us thirsty! Salt also makes some foods taste better. And it keeps meat from rotting, or "going bad."

So what does it mean when Jesus says we are like salt? We make life better for others by what we do. We show people how to keep from doing wrong, or "going bad." And we help them get thirsty for God.

What does light do? It helps us see. What did Jesus mean when he said we are like a light? He meant that we help people see how good God is. How do we do that? By doing good things.

It's as if we were a letter from Jesus to the world. He uses us to show the world what he is like. He uses us to tell people what he has done for them.

"Dear God, I will be your letter to the world. I will be like salt and light. Thank you for shining through me."

Tuesday

Read "Good Fruit and Bad Fruit," page 536 in *God's Story*. Or read this part of the story:

"People don't pick grapes from weeds," said Jesus. "They don't pick figs from weeds. Good trees make good fruit. Bad trees make bad fruit. A good tree can't make bad fruit. A bad tree can't make good fruit.

"Trees get cut down if they don't make good fruit. They get burned up," said Jesus. "So you will know trees and people by their fruit. You can tell what they are like by what they do.

"Good things happen when good people are around," said Jesus. "That's because they have good stored up in their hearts. 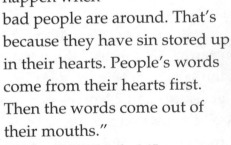 But bad things happen when bad people are around. That's because they have sin stored up in their hearts. People's words come from their hearts first. Then the words come out of their mouths."
Matthew 7:16-20; Luke 6:45

Did you ever grow tomatoes or strawberries? Did you ever grow weeds? When you want good fruit to eat, do you get it from the weeds? No! It's the same with people. Bad things come from bad people. Good things come from good people.

We show people what Jesus is like by doing what Jesus would do. That's why we are like a letter from Jesus. It's as if Jesus is saying, "Dear world, look at my friend here. See how loving and kind I am. See how good it is to be saved from sin. Don't you want to be my friend too?"

"Dear Father God, I want to be like the good tree that has good fruit. Help me choose to do good. Help me to show people how kind and loving you are."

SOME THINGS YOU CAN DO THIS WEEK

☐ **Draw the shadow of your face.** Tape a piece of paper to a wall. Place a bright light in the room so that it shines on the piece of paper. Turn sideways, and stand out from the wall beside the paper. The bright light makes a shadow of the side of your head. Ask a friend to draw around the shadow that your head makes. Think about how you can be a light to the world. *(See Monday's reading.)*

☐ **Write a letter** to a friend or someone in your family. Write, "You are like a letter from Jesus to the world. Thank you for letting Jesus show in your life." Also write how the person shows Jesus' love. Then send the letter.

☐ **Give a surprise basket** to a neighbor. Use a real basket, or cut down a paper sack and staple a strip of paper on it to be a handle. Decorate it. Put cookies in it, or soaps and sweet-smelling candles, or flowers. Think of other things to do to show God's love to others.

☐ **Play flashlight tag.** After dark, go outside or into a large room. If you're outside, you can run around. Inside, you may want to crawl or tiptoe. The person who is "it" must tag people by shining a flashlight on them. Think about what it means to "let your light shine" for Jesus. *(See Monday's reading.)*

☐ **Taste different fruit** with your eyes closed. Ask friends or family to help you. They can give you little bites of different kinds of fruit. Try to guess what the fruits are without looking. Then let your friends or family try it. *(See Tuesday's reading.)*

WEDNESDAY

Read "Rich Man, Poor Man," page 763 in *God's Story*. Or read this part of the story:

You believe in Jesus. So don't treat some people better than others.

God's Word says, "Love your neighbor like you love yourself." That's the law of our King. If you do this, you're doing the right thing.

But what if you treat some people better than others? Then you are sinning. You're breaking the law.

What if a person says he believes? But he doesn't obey. Then what good does it do for him to believe? Can that kind of believing save him?

Let's say one of God's people has no clothes. Or the person has no food. You say, "Go on your way. I hope the best will come to you. Stay warm! Get plenty to eat!" But you don't do anything to help the person stay warm. You don't share any of your food. What good is your faith?

If all you do is believe, it won't do any good. You also have to do what God wants. Faith by itself is nothing. It's dead. *James 2:1, 8-9, 14-17*

Let's say you have a friend who says, "I'm a good artist. I draw great pictures." But your friend never shows you any pictures. You never see your friend drawing anything. At last, you ask your friend, "Do you ever draw?" "No," says your friend. "But I'm a good artist." What do you think about that friend?

It's the same when someone says, "I believe in Jesus." But that person doesn't obey God. Is that person a letter from Jesus to the world?

People who believe and obey are very good letters from Jesus. What are some ways you can obey God?

"Dear God, thank you for choosing me to be a letter from your Son, Jesus. I believe in you. Help me to obey you."

THURSDAY

Read "A Bright Light and a Voice," page 644 in *God's Story*. Or read this part of the story:

Saul headed for Damascus. All of a sudden, a

bright light came from heaven. It shone down on Saul.

Saul fell down. He heard a voice. "Saul, Saul, why are you hurting me?"

"Who are you?" asked Saul.

"I'm Jesus," said the voice. "I'm the one you're hurting. Get up. Go into the city of Damascus. . . ."

Saul got up and opened his eyes. But he couldn't see anything. So his friends . . . led him into the city. . . .

Jesus called to [Ananias] . . . . "Go to Straight Street," said Jesus. ". . . Ask for a man named Saul. . . . He saw a man with your name in a dream. In his dream, you put your hands on him. Then he could see again. . . .

"Go!" said Jesus. "I chose this man to serve me. . . ."

Ananias found the house. He went in and put his hands on Saul. "Saul," he said. "The Lord Jesus . . . sent me here so you can see again. He sent me so you can be filled with God's Holy Spirit."

. . . Saul stayed in Damascus for a few days. Right away, he started teaching in the town's worship houses. He told everyone that Jesus is God's Son. . . .

Many days passed. The Jews made plans to kill Saul. Every day and night, they watched the city gates. The gates were in the wall around the city. The Jews were going to kill Saul when he left.

Saul found out about their plan. So one night, Saul's friends took him to the city wall. Saul got into a big basket. His friends put the basket through an open place in the wall. Then they let it down to the ground. *Acts 9:3-25*

Darkness. That's all Saul could see. Darkness. But he could hear a voice. It was someone he didn't know. This person was telling him about Jesus. It was Ananias. Ananias was like a letter that Jesus had sent to Saul. Ananias was showing Saul how much Jesus loved him.

Some other people in this story were like a letter that Jesus sent to Saul. Jesus' followers in Damascus showed Jesus' love to Saul. What did they do to help him?

Who can you show Jesus' love to? How?

"Dear Father God, I want to show other people how good you are. Show me how I can help people. Help me to be a good letter from Jesus."

FRIDAY

Read "Teaching Us to Say No," page 755 in *God's Story*. Or read this part of the story:

Teach older men not to overdo things. They should act right so people can speak well of them. They should control themselves. They should have a strong faith. They should love others. They should keep believing even in hard times.

Teach older women to show that they look up to God. They shouldn't say bad things about others. They shouldn't drink too much wine. They should teach good things.

Teach servants that they should always obey their masters. They should try to make their masters happy. Teach them not to talk back to their masters. They shouldn't steal from their masters. Their masters should be able to trust them. That way, the teaching about God will look good.

God's kind love saves people. It's for everyone. His kind love teaches us to say no to bad things. It teaches us to say no to things the world loves. It teaches us to have self-control. God's kind love teaches us to do what's right. It teaches us how to be good. *Titus 2:2-3, 9-12*

Who would you rather be around: Someone who lies or someone who tells the truth?

Someone who controls himself or someone who doesn't control himself? Someone who steals or someone who can be trusted?

We say we are Jesus' followers. So the way we act helps other people choose whether they want to follow Jesus too. We can make the teaching about God look bad.

Or we can make the teaching about God look good.

You are a letter from Jesus to the world. What do you think he is telling people through you?

"Dear God, I want to follow your Son, Jesus. I want to make you look good. Why? Because you are good. You are good to me. Thank you."

Love Is . . .

Love never fails. *I Corinthians 13:8*

MONDAY

 Read "God's Children," page 793 in *God's Story*. Or read this part of the story:

Here's the message. You heard it from the start. Love each other.

Here's how we know what love is. Jesus gave up his life for us. We should give up our lives for God's people too.

Let's say someone owns lots of things. He sees one of God's people who needs something. But he doesn't feel sorry for that person. How can we say God's love is in him?

Let's show love not just by what we say. Let's show love by what we do. That's how we know we belong to God.
1 John 3:11, 16-19

(This is part of a letter John wrote to some of God's people.)

John remembered. He remembered a night many years before, when Jesus was on the earth. Jesus' friends had come together to eat dinner. Jesus said, "I have a new rule for you." The rule had just three words: "Love each other."

But what is love? "I *love* ice cream!" Is that the kind of love Jesus was talking about? Or is it the love between a man and woman? Is it when they want to be with each other all the time? No, those are different kinds of love.

John said to look at Jesus to find out what love is. Jesus stopped thinking about himself. Instead, he thought about us. He knew our sins would keep us away from his Father in heaven. So he took our sins as if they were his. And he died for them. Now *that's* love!

"Dear Father God, thank you for your love. Thank you for Jesus' love. Help me to love others."

TUESDAY

Read "Love," page 687 in *God's Story*. Or read this part of the story:

Let's say I can tell you what God wants people to know. Or I can understand all kinds of mysteries. Let's say I know everything. Let's say I have faith big enough to move mountains. But I don't love people. Then I'm nothing.

What if I give everything I have to poor people? What if I give up my whole life for Jesus? But I don't love people. Then it doesn't do me any good.

Love waits quietly. Love is kind. It doesn't want what others have. It doesn't brag. It isn't proud. It has good manners. It doesn't think of itself ahead of others. It doesn't get angry very fast. It doesn't try to remember who was wrong.

Love isn't happy with sin. Instead, it's happy to know the truth.

Love always takes care of people. It always trusts. It always hopes. It always keeps going. Love never fails.

Three things will always be with us. They are faith and hope and love. But love is the best.
1 Corinthians 13:2-8, 13

(This is part of a letter that Paul wrote to some of God's people.)

Do you remember the Christmas story about Scrooge? Scrooge gives

Bob Cratchit the day off. But Scrooge is gruff. He does something good, but he does it with a frown.

Did you ever do something good, but you frowned when you did it? Paul wrote that doing good without love doesn't do us any good. What did Paul say love is?

Jesus said, "Everyone will know you're my friends if you love each other." That's still the way people know we're Jesus' friends. We love each other. There are lots of good things in the world. But love is the best! How can you show love?

"Dear God, help me to have a loving heart when I do good things. Help me to show that I'm your friend."

WEDNESDAY

Read "An Eye for an Eye," page 532 in *God's Story*. Or read this part of the story:

"You've heard that you're to love your neighbor and hate your enemy," said Jesus. "I say, love your enemies. Pray for people who hurt you.

Then you will be children of your Father in heaven. . . .

"What if you love just the people who love you? What good does that do?" said Jesus. "Even sinners love people who love them. What if you're friendly just to people you like? How is that different from what other people do? Even people who don't believe in God do that.

"Love your enemies," said Jesus. "Do good to them. Lend to them. Don't look for anything back. Then God will plan good things for you. You will be his children. God is kind to people who are not even thankful. He is kind to sinful people. So be kind like your Father."
Matthew 5:43-47; Luke 6:35-36

If your teacher asked you to draw any picture you wanted, what would you draw? Most boys and girls draw fun things that they have seen. Or they draw fun pictures of something they make up. In a land far away, a teacher asked the children to draw pictures. They drew airplanes dropping bombs. They drew houses on fire. They drew people dying. Why? Because that is what they had seen in a war in their land. That is what happens when enemies come against each other. Fighting. Hurting.

When someone treats us badly, what do we feel like doing? Most of the time, we want to fight back. But Jesus said a strange thing. He said, "Love your enemies. Pray for people who hurt you." Is that easy to do? It's not easy for children. And it's not easy for grown-ups. But that's the way to show God's love. Why? Because God loves people even when they do wrong.

"Dear Father God, it's hard to love people who treat me badly. Help me to show them your love. Thank you."

SOME THINGS YOU CAN DO THIS WEEK

☐ **Make valentine cards** for friends. (Do this no matter what time of the year it is!) Make valentine cards for older people in your neighborhood or church. Make a card for someone who has treated you badly.

☐ **Make cookies** shaped like hearts. Decorate them, and share them with other people. Remember what love is.

☐ **Go for a hike** around a park, nature center, or your neighborhood. Look for things that show God's love. God made the world for all people to enjoy, even people who don't believe in him. That shows what a good, loving God we have.

☐ **Play a ball-toss memory game** with 1 Corinthians 13:4-8. "Love waits . . . is kind . . . doesn't want what others have . . . doesn't brag . . . isn't proud . . . has good manners . . . doesn't think of itself ahead of others . . . doesn't get angry very fast . . . doesn't try to remember who was wrong . . . isn't happy with sin . . . is happy to know the truth . . . always takes care of people . . . always trusts . . . always hopes . . . always keeps going . . . never fails." After you learn this with family or friends, toss a ball. Whoever catches the ball says one thing that love is. Then that person tosses the ball to someone else. *(See Tuesday's reading.)*

☐ **Make a hobo bag.** Tie a bandanna on the end of a stick. Carry it by putting the stick over your shoulder so the bandanna hangs behind you. That's one way people used to carry things before they had backpacks. Think about how much Ruth loved Naomi. Ruth carried all of her things to a new home so she could live with Naomi. *(See Thursday's reading.)*

THURSDAY

Read "Going Home," page 111 in *God's Story*. Or read this part of the story:

When Naomi's sons were old enough, they got married. One married a young woman named Orpah. One married a young woman named Ruth. But about 10 years later, both of Naomi's sons died. So Naomi was left alone with Orpah and Ruth.

One day Naomi heard there was food in Judah. That's when she decided to go back home.

So Naomi and Orpah and Ruth packed up. They got ready to go back to Naomi's home. Then they started down the road to Judah.

But Naomi turned to Orpah and Ruth. "Go back home," she said.

Then Orpah kissed Naomi. She said good-bye and went home. But Ruth kept hugging Naomi.

"Don't tell me to leave you," said Ruth. "I'll go where you go. I'll stay where you stay. Your people will become my people. Your God will be my God."

Naomi could see that Ruth really wanted to go with her. So she didn't ask her to go back anymore. *Ruth 1:4-8, 14, 16, 18*

They had just begun their trip. The road ahead was long and dusty and bumpy. It went around hills and through valleys. And it led to a place where Ruth had never lived before. It led to new people, new ways of doing things, new kinds of food.

Did you ever move to a new place? It's not easy to leave old friends and make new friends. It's not easy to leave the old house you knew.

Naomi told Ruth she didn't have to go. How do you think Ruth felt? What did Ruth say? Ruth loved Naomi. So Ruth stopped thinking about herself. She would live at Naomi's house, meet Naomi's neighbors, and worship Naomi's God.

Love means thinking about other people and doing what's best for them. Sometimes we give up what we want so they can have what they want.

If you know the rest of Ruth's story, tell about other ways that Ruth showed her love for Naomi. Or read about it. Name some people you love. How can you show your love?

"Dear Father God, help me to think about others instead of just myself. Help me to show love. Thank you for loving me."

FRIDAY

Read "Stick with Each Other," page 712 in *God's Story*. Or read this part of the story:

Your love should be real. Hate sinful things. Hang on to good things. Stick with each other. Love each other like brothers and sisters. Treat other people as if they're better than you.

Always be in a hurry to do what's right. See that your spirit keeps wanting to serve the Lord.

Be happy because of the hope you have. Wait in peace when you have troubles. Keep praying. Share with God's people who need things. Welcome people into your house.

Pray for good things to happen to people. Pray for people even if they treat you badly.

Be happy with people who are happy. Be sad with people who are sad. Live at peace with each other. *Romans 12:9-16*

Dillon loved to play baseball. He practiced a lot. Still, he struck out a lot. His cousin Travis hardly ever practiced. But Travis always seemed to be able to hit the ball. Sometimes it made Dillon angry. It was hard to feel loving toward Travis.

Dillon told Travis, "I wish I were a good batter like you."

"I wish I were a good catcher like you," said Travis.

Dillon was surprised. "Then we need to stick with each other," he said. "And we'll have a great team!"

Sometimes it's hard to love people who do things better than we do.

Sometimes it's hard to love people who don't do things as well as we do. What does God tell us to do?

How can you show love to someone who does things better than you do? How can you show love to someone who doesn't do as well?

"Dear God, thank you for loving all kinds of people. Show me how to love all kinds of people too."

With All My Heart

Love God with all your heart. Love him with all your soul. Love him with all your strength. *Deuteronomy 6:5*

MONDAY

Read "A New Self," page 735 in *God's Story.* Or read this part of the story:

You have a new self now. You are being made like new so you'll be like Jesus. It doesn't matter if you're Jewish or not. It doesn't matter if you're a slave or a free person. Jesus is the important one.

God chose you to be his people. You are special to him. He loves you dearly. So be kind. Don't be proud. Treat other people with care. Be glad to wait.

Work with each other. Forgive each other. Forgive like Jesus forgave you.

Do everything in Jesus' name. It may be what you say. It may be what you do. But do it in Jesus' name, giving thanks to God.

Whatever you do, do it with your whole heart. Do it as if you were working for Jesus. He has good things planned for you. It's really Jesus you're serving. *Colossians 3:10-13, 17, 23-24*

Put your hand over your heart. *Pa-dum, pa-dum, pa-dum.* The muscle is pumping away, night and day, keeping you alive. But it's not the heart muscle that Paul wrote this letter about. The heart he wrote about is the thinking, feeling part of you. It's who you really are, deep inside.

So how do you work at something with your whole heart? You do the best job you can. You do it with a smile. Why do you do that? Think about who you are really working for. You are working for Jesus! And he is helping you do your best.

What kinds of jobs do you have to do? How can you show that you are working with all your heart?

"Dear Father God, whatever I have to do, I'll do it with my whole heart. I'll do it that way because I'm working for Jesus. Help me to do my very best."

TUESDAY

Read "A Whole Heart," page 188 in *God's Story*. Or read this part of the story:

Hear me, God, and
   answer me.
I'm poor, and I need you.
Keep my life safe,
   because I am all yours.
Be kind to me, God,
   for I call to you all day long.

Teach me your way, God.
I will follow you.
Give me a heart that is all yours.
Then I'll cheer for you, Lord my
   God.
I will praise you with all my heart.
I will always tell how great you are.
Your love for me is great.
Psalm 86:1-3, 11-13

Have you ever watched people getting into a swimming pool? Some people walk to the edge and stick just their big toe in the water. Some people wade in, step-by-step. Other people go for the diving board and jump right into the deep end.

That's the way people follow God. Some people want to follow him just a little. Other people want to follow God in some ways but not in others. But David wanted to jump right into the deep end! He wanted to give his whole heart to God.

What things did David say to show he was giving his whole heart to God? You can give your whole heart to God too.

"Dear God, I give you my whole heart. I will praise you with all my heart like David did. Thank you for loving me."

WEDNESDAY

Read "The Big, Burning Oven," page 431 in *God's Story*. Or read this part of the story:

Now King Nebuchadnezzar made a gold idol in Babylon. The speaker called, ". . . You will hear the music. Then you must bow down and worship the gold god. If you don't, you'll be thrown into a big, burning oven."

"King Nebuchadnezzar," said Shadrach, Meshach, and Abednego. "We don't need to tell you we're right. Our God can save us if we're thrown into the burning oven. Even if he doesn't save us, you should know this. We won't obey your gods. We won't worship the gold idol you set up."

The king wanted the guards to move fast. So they

SOME THINGS YOU CAN DO THIS WEEK

☐ **Make a heart mobile.** Cut hearts from different colors of paper. Punch a hole in the top of each heart. Cut strings, some long and some short, to tie through the holes. Tie the other end of each string to the bottom part of a clothes hanger. Hang your heart mobile in your room. It can remind you to give your whole heart to God.

☐ **Do a job around your house** or a neighbor's house. Get your whole family together to do it. Or get friends together to do it. Remember to work for Jesus as you do the job. *(See Monday's reading.)*

☐ **Record the story about "The Big, Burning Oven"** on a blank tape. You can make the sounds for all the voices, or friends and family can help. To make fire sounds, crush paper or plastic wrap or bags from inside a cereal box. *(See Wednesday's reading.)*

☐ **Build a city** out of blocks or paper cups. Build it on top of a sheet or tablecloth. Then make the earth shake by shaking the sheet. Remember the story of Paul and Silas. *(See Friday's reading.)*

☐ **Make a trick picture** of Paul and Silas in jail. Fold an index card in half. Open it. Draw jail bars on the left half, using a dark marker or crayon. Draw Paul and Silas on the right half, near the fold. Keeping the card open, look at the fold in the middle of the card. Slowly bring the card closer and closer to your eyes. Stop when Paul and Silas seem to move into the jail. *(See Friday's reading.)*

threw the men into the burning oven. . . .

"Look!" said the king. "I see four men walking around in the fire. They aren't tied up! Three of them are the men we threw in. The other one looks like a son of the gods."

Then the king went to the door of the oven. He called, "Shadrach, Meshach, and Abednego! Servants of the Most High God! Come out!"

So Shadrach, Meshach, and Abednego came out. All the leaders gathered around them.

The fire had not hurt the three friends at all.
Daniel 3:1, 4-6, 16-18, 21, 25-27

The orange and white fire licked around the wood. It snapped and roared. Even people who stood far away from the fire could feel its heat. Shadrach, Meshach, and Abednego could have bowed to false gods and walked away. But they would not worship false gods. How do you think you would have felt if you had been there?

Solomon wrote, "Trust in God with your whole heart. Don't count on the way you understand things. Always remember to let God be in charge. Then he will show you what to do" (Proverbs 3:5-6).

That's just what Shadrach, Meshach, and Abednego did. They each trusted God with their whole heart. Is there something that makes you worry? Trust God with all your heart. He will take care of you.

"Dear Father God, I give you my whole heart. I trust you. You are in charge. Show me what to do."

THURSDAY

Read "Paul Visits Many Towns,"
page 665 in *God's Story*. Or read
this part of the story:

Paul waited for Silas
and Timothy in Athens. He was
upset to see so many idols in
that city. So he went to the city's
worship house. He talked to the
Jews about it. He talked to
Greeks who believed in God. He
went to the market place every
day. He talked with whoever
was there.

"We are God's children," said
Paul. "So we shouldn't think
God is made of gold. He is not
made of silver or stone. He is not
a figure that people made."
Acts 17:16-17, 29

The Greek people had many false
gods. Zeus was the ruler of the gods.
The Greeks thought he fought with
thunder and lightning. Apollo was the
god of music. Poseidon was the god
of the sea. Some of their false gods
were women. Athena was the
goddess of wise thinking and war.
Even now you can read stories about
these false gods in storybooks.

But Paul told the people that the
true God isn't made of silver or
gold. He doesn't live in worship
houses.

Then how can a person find God?
"You'll find me when you look with
all your heart" (Jeremiah 29:13).
And how do you look for God with
all your heart? You read about him
in your Bible every day. You look
around you to see what he has given
you every day. And you talk with
him about anything and everything.
Every day.

When do you like to read about
God? When do you like to talk with
him? Whenever you look for him,
he is there.

*"Dear God, thank you for letting me
find you when I look for you. I want to
know you better and better. So I will
look for you with my whole heart!"*

FRIDAY

Read "The Earth Shakes," page 663
in *God's Story*. Or read this part of
the story:

So the jailer put Paul
and Silas in the inside jail room.

He chained their feet in holes on a wooden board.

At midnight, Paul and Silas were praying. They were singing songs to God. The other people who had been put in jail were listening.

All of a sudden, the earth began to shake hard. The floors of the jail shook. Everybody's chains fell off.

The jailer took Paul and Silas out of jail. "How can I be saved?" he asked.

"Believe in Jesus," they said. "Then you'll be saved. Your family can be saved too." Paul and Silas told him the Good News about Jesus. Everyone in his house listened.

The jailer washed the two men's hurt places. Then right away, he and his family were baptized. *Acts 16:24-26, 30-33*

It's midnight. It's dark. Listen. Chains rattle on the floor as the men in jail move a little. Just a little. They can't move much. But now there's another sound. Two men are praying and singing. Then there's a low roar. It gets louder. Metal chains fall to the ground. Jail doors bang open.

Paul and Silas were in trouble. But they trusted God with all their hearts. They didn't know what was going to happen. But they knew God would make everything turn out all right. So they talked to God. They sang to God. What happened to the two men then? And what happened to the jailer? He ended up giving *his* whole heart to God, didn't he?

Do you have a problem that you need God to take care of? How can you get God to take care of it? How can you show others that you trust God with your whole heart?

"Dear God, I trust you to take care of all my troubles. My whole heart trusts you. So I thank you and praise you. You are a great, wonderful God."

Thinking, Thinking, Thinking

Think about things that are true and good. Think about things that are right and clean. Think about beautiful things. Think about things you can look up to. If anything is the best, think about it. If it's something to cheer for, think about it. *Philippians 4:8*

MONDAY

Read "Riches for a Wise King," page 228 in *God's Story*. Or read this part of the story:

Solomon wrote 3,000 wise sayings. He wrote 1,005 songs. He wrote about big trees and little plants. He taught people about animals, birds, fish, and snakes.

People from all around the world came to hear Solomon's wise words. Kings had heard how wise he was. So they sent people to see him.

Every year Solomon got about 25 tons of gold.

Solomon had 1,400 chariots. He had 12,000 (twelve thousand) horses. He had to have 4,000 pens for his horses.

Solomon also built ships. *1 Kings 4:32-34; 2 Chronicles 1:14; 9:13, 21, 25*

What would you do if you were as rich as Solomon was? He had ships and horses and gold. He didn't even have to work to take care of his things. His servants did the work. But there was one thing Solomon had to work at: learning. God made Solomon wise. But Solomon wanted to know more and more. So he looked at plants. He watched animals. He learned about them. Then he taught other people about them.

God made your mind to think and wonder like Solomon did. God made your mind to ask questions. And just look at all God made for you to learn about! God made wonderful things to watch and hear and smell and taste and touch. God is glad when you learn about the things he made. What do you like to learn about?

"Dear God, thank you for all that you made. And thank you for giving me a mind that wants to think and know. Help me to learn what you want me to learn. Make me wise."

TUESDAY

Read "Plans of the Heart," page 237 in *God's Story*. Or read this part of the story:

Even children show what they're like by how they act.

You can tell they are good if what they do is right.

God looks inside people to see their spirits.
He sees what they are thinking.

When you look into water, you can see your face.
When you understand someone's heart, you see what that person is really like.
Proverbs 20:11, 27; 27:19

Sometimes when water is very still, a pond or a lake looks like a mirror. If the sky is bright blue, the water is bright blue. If the sky is sunset pink and orange, the lake is sunset pink and orange. And if you look into it, you'll see yourself in this watery mirror.

Your heart and thoughts are a mirror too. What do they show? They show what kind of person you are. That's why it's important to think good things.

What are some good things that you can think about?

"Dear Father God, I want my thoughts to show that I'm your child. Help me to think good thoughts."

WEDNESDAY

Read "Early Morning Light," page 231 in *God's Story*. Or read this part of the story:

When I was a boy, my father told me,

"Take my words into your heart.
Obey me, and you'll live.
Wise thinking will keep you safe.
* So love it.*

Listen, my child.
Do as I say, and you will live many
* years.*

SOME THINGS YOU CAN DO THIS WEEK

☐**Make an "in-my-head poster."** Draw a picture of your head. Get some old magazines and cut out pictures of things that are good to think about. Glue those inside and around the head you drew. Write this week's verse underneath it.

☐**Make "animal pizzas."** Put pizza sauce on top of an English muffin. Decorate it with cheese and other toppings to make it look like an animal face. Think of how Solomon learned about animals. *(See Monday's reading.)*

☐**Play "Who's Got the Heart?"** Cut a small heart out of paper, or use a candy heart. Choose one person to be "it." The rest of the players sit in a circle with their hands held out. Go around the circle, and pretend to drop the heart into each person's hands. The players must close their hands as if they are holding the heart. But give the heart to only one person. When you've been around the circle, the person who is "it" must try to guess who is really holding the heart. *(See Tuesday's reading.)*

☐**Make a mystery picture.** Use a computer, a typewriter, or a pencil and paper to make a pattern. Try a pattern like this:

Row One: 7 spaces, 12 *X*'s, 7 spaces, 1 *X*
Row Two: 5 spaces, 14 *X*'s, 4 spaces, 1 *X*
Row Three: 3 spaces, 18 *X*'s
Row Four: 1 space, 4 *X*'s, 2 spaces, 13 *X*'s

Row Five: 20 *X*'s
Row Six: 1 space, 20 *X*'s
Row Seven: 5 spaces, 14 *X*'s, 4 spaces, 1 *X*
Row Eight: 7 spaces, 12 *X*'s, 7 spaces, 1 *X*

Try making other mystery pictures. Remember that what you put in is what comes out. This is true for your mind and heart, as well as for your computer. *(See Wednesday's reading.)*

☐**Look at ads** in magazines, in newspapers, and on TV. Ask yourself what these ads are trying to make you think. How can you tell whether something would be bad or good to think?

More than anything, be careful of
*   what you let into your mind.*
Look ahead. Think about what you
*   should do.*

Follow the ways that are sure and
*   right.*
Stay away from things that are
*   sinful."*
Proverbs 4:3-4, 6, 10, 23, 25-27

Have you worked or played on a computer? A computer shows you the words and pictures that somebody put into it. If bad things were loaded into it, bad things come out. If good things were loaded into it, good things come out.

Brains are kind of like computers. If we let bad things in, we think about bad things. If we let good things in, we think about good things. And

what we do and say shows what we've been thinking about.

David knew it was important to put good things into his mind. He wrote, "I won't let my eyes see anything bad" (Psalm 101:3). He chose not to let bad things into his mind. That's because he wanted to think about good things. He wanted to please God. How do you control what goes into your mind?

"Dear God, I want to think about good
things. So help me to be careful of what
I let into my mind. Help me to choose
the right things to watch and hear so I
can have good thoughts."

THURSDAY

Read "In the Secret Place," page 212 in *God's Story*. Or read this part of the story:

God, you know me.
You know when I sit down and
*   when I get up.*
You know what I'm thinking.

Look into me, God.
Know what's in my heart.
Test me, and know what I think
*   about.*

See if there is anything bad in me.
Lead me in the way that lasts
    forever. Psalm 139:1-2, 23-24

There's so much to think about!
School. Friends. Family. Work. Play.
Things to watch and read and listen
to. God knows that we have lots to
think about. But he knows that if we
are going to be wise, we need his
help. Psalm 10 says that sinful
people don't have room in their
thoughts for God. If we want to be
wise, we must make room in our
thoughts for God.

God knows that we want to be
happy. And God wants us to be
happy. He knows that we can't be
happy if we're thinking bad things.
So he tells us to think things that are
true and good and right. What is
something true that you can think
about? Name something good to
think about. What's something clean
to think about? What's something
beautiful? What is something that
we can cheer for?

Something else happens when we
think of good things: We have good
dreams! Did you ever have a hard
time going to sleep? Or do you

sometimes have bad dreams?
Thinking about good things when
you get into bed at night can help.
Sweet dreams!

"Dear Father God, you know what I
think about. Help me to think about
things that are good and right and
true."

FRIDAY

Read "Trees Will Clap," page 369
in *God's Story.* Or read this part of
the story:

    "My thoughts aren't
  your thoughts.
My ways aren't your ways," says
  God.
"The sky is higher than the earth.
  And my ways are higher than
    your ways.
My thoughts are higher than
  your thoughts."
"You'll go out with joy and peace.
Mountains and hills will start
  singing right in front of you.
All the trees in the field will clap!
  Pine trees will grow instead of
  weeds.
This will show everyone that God is
  the Lord." Isaiah 55:8-9, 12-13

What happened before the world began? Why do some people get well and others stay sick? Why do bad things happen? There are many questions we can't answer. There  are many things we don't understand. Some people say, "I don't understand it. It doesn't make sense. So I don't believe in God."

It's true that we can't figure God out. But that's all right. His thoughts are greater than ours. He knows more than we do. He is wiser than we are. If we could figure God out, he wouldn't be much of a god. Solomon wrote, "God can hide how he does things. That shows God is great" (Proverbs 25:2).

Paul wrote, "No eye has seen what God has planned. No mind has thought of God's plans. His plans are for people who love him" (1 Corinthians 2:9). You are in God's thoughts. God has wonderful plans for you. So keep on loving him, and he will keep on working out his plans.

"Dear God, there are many things I don't understand. But I'm glad your thoughts are greater than my thoughts. I will love you and trust you to work out your plans for me."

I Forgive You

Forgive each other. Forgive like Jesus forgave you. *Colossians 3:13*

MONDAY

Read "Pig Food," page 583 in *God's Story*. Or read this part of the story:

"Soon after that, the younger son left home. He took his part of the money. He moved to a land far away.

"He lived a wild life there. He used up all his money. . . . The only job he could get was feeding pigs. By that time, he was very hungry. He even wanted to eat the pigs' food. But no one would let him.

"At last he started getting smart. He said, 'People who work for my father have plenty to eat. Here I sit, dying of hunger! I'm going home. I'll tell my father that I've sinned against heaven and against him. I'll say that I'm not good enough to be called his son.'

"So the young man got up. He went back home. He wasn't even close to his house yet. But his father saw him coming. His father was full of love for his son. He ran to his son. He hugged and kissed him."
Luke 15:13-20

The young man was a mess. No more money. No more friends. No more food. He sat in a pig pen, hungry and dirty. He felt dirty on the outside and dirty on the inside. He could go home and wash the dirt off of his body. But how could he get rid of the dirty feeling in his heart? He could say, "I'm sorry."

Sometimes it's hard to say, "I'm sorry." But sometimes it's even harder to forgive. When people have done wrong to us, we get angry. Sometimes we don't want to forgive them, even if they say they're sorry. That's what the young man was afraid of. Maybe his dad would still be angry.

But Jesus told this story to show us what God is like. The dad forgave his son. And God forgives us for the wrong we do. Now God wants us to forgive others.

"Dear Father God, thank you for forgiving me. Help me to forgive other people when they do wrong to me."

TUESDAY

Read "Meeting Esau," page 30 in *God's Story*. Or read this part of the story:

Esau ran up to Jacob. He hugged and kissed him.

"Why did you send all the goats ahead of you? Why did you send sheep and cows?" asked Esau.

"They are a gift for you," said Jacob. "So you will be kind to me."

"I have enough goats and sheep and cows," said Esau. "You may keep them."

"No," said Jacob. "I am so happy to see your kind face. Please keep the animals as my gift to you. For God has been very good to me."

So Esau kept them.
Genesis 33:4, 8-11

Jacob and Esau's mother loved Jacob best. Esau could hunt, but Jacob could cook. When Esau came in hungry one day, Jacob got him to pay for his soup. And Jacob told his father a lie to get what belonged to Esau. Esau was so angry, he said he would kill Jacob. So Jacob ran away.

Jacob was away for a long time. Esau could have thought about the mean things he would do to Jacob someday. He could have gotten madder and madder. Would that have hurt Jacob? No. Jacob was gone. Getting madder and madder would have hurt only Esau.

When Jacob came back, Esau "hugged and kissed him."

We can choose. We can stay mad. That hurts us inside. Or we can forgive, even if the other person isn't sorry the way Jacob was. Forgiving gives us peace in our hearts. And God will deal with the wrong that the other person did.

"Dear God, I forgive the people who have treated me badly. I'll let you deal with them. I want peace in my heart."

SOME THINGS YOU CAN DO THIS WEEK

☐ **Make a jigsaw puzzle.** You can do it by writing this week's verse on a piece of cardboard or paper. Draw and color around the verse. Then cut the cardboard or paper into a few large pieces. Mix them up and see if your friends or family can put the puzzle together.

☐ **Color a sheet of paper** with lots of different colors. Then color over your whole drawing with black crayon, rubbing hard. Now get a toothpick, a plastic picnic knife, or a pair of scissors that are not sharp. Scratch through the black to write the word *forgive*.

☐ **Bake cupcakes** and frost them. Decorate with balloons and streamers. Have a "Homecoming Party" to remember how the young man in the story came home. Remember that God forgives us like the father forgave the young man. *(See Monday's reading.)*

☐ **Play "Lost and Found."** Choose someone to hide an object while everyone else is out of the room. When it's hidden, call out, "Lost!" Then the other players come in and look for it. Whoever finds it calls out, "Found!" The father who forgave said his son "was lost, but now he is found." What did he mean? *(See Monday's reading.)*

WEDNESDAY

Read "The Servant Who Would Not Forgive," page 568 in *God's Story.* Or read this part of the story:

"God's kingdom is like a king," said Jesus. "This king wanted his servants to pay what they owed him. One man owed him millions. But he couldn't pay the money back. . . .

"The king felt sorry for the man. So he told the man not to worry about what he owed. The king wouldn't make him pay it back. He let the man go.

"So the servant left. He didn't owe all that money anymore! But the servant met a man who owed him just a little money. He caught this man and started choking him. 'Pay me what you owe me!' he said. . . .

"The king called the servant. '. . . I was kind to you. So shouldn't you have been kind to this other man?'

"The king was angry. He sent his servant to jail."

Matthew 18:23-34

It's not fair," said the king. "It's not fair when I forgive you but you don't forgive someone else."

God forgives us. Now he wants us to forgive the people who hurt us.

Look carefully at the word *forgive.* Do you see two other words inside it? *For give.* Make those two words trade places. *Give for.* When you forgive someone, you are choosing to stop being angry at them. You *give* up the anger in your heart *for* peace in your heart. It also helps to *give* other things *for* those people. *Give* prayer *for* them. *Give* kindness *for* them. *Give* help *for* them. Who do you need to *give for*? How will you do it?

"Dear God, thank you for forgiving me. Help me to give for the people who have done wrong to me. I pray that you will bring good things to them."

THURSDAY

Read "Perfume," page 539 in *God's Story.* Or read this part of the story:

Now there was a sinful woman in town. She heard that Jesus was having dinner at

Simon's house. So she went there. She took a beautiful stone jar with her. The jar was filled with sweet-smelling perfume.

The woman went into the house. She stood close to Jesus, at his feet. Then she began to cry. Her tears dripped on Jesus' feet. They made his feet wet. So she wiped his feet with her long hair. Then she kissed Jesus' feet. She let perfume flow out of the jar onto his feet. . . .

Jesus . . . said to Simon . . . , "You didn't even give me water to wash my feet. You didn't welcome me with a kiss when I came. . . . You didn't put oil on my head.

"This woman has lots of love," said Jesus. "She had many sins. But they have been forgiven. Some people haven't been forgiven for very much. So they don't love very much."

Then Jesus said to the woman, "Your sins are forgiven."
Luke 7:37-38, 44-48

Simon thought he was a pretty good man. He tried to keep all of the laws. He gave money at the worship house. He didn't work at all on the worship day. The Jewish leaders had made laws about how to wash hands. So he washed his hands in just the right way.

Simon was pretty proud of himself for keeping the laws. That's why he was upset when he saw this woman with Jesus. He knew she was a sinner. But Jesus said she loved him more than people like Simon did. Why? Because she knew she had done lots of bad things. So she knew how much Jesus loved her when he forgave her. Simon didn't think about how he needed to be forgiven.

Sometimes we look at all the good things we've done. We forget that we sometimes do bad things, say bad things, or think bad things. We forget how much Jesus loves us and forgives us. Then it's easy for us to forget to love and forgive others.

"Dear Father God, thank you for loving me and forgiving my sins. Help me to love and forgive other people."

FRIDAY

 Read "Stephen Sees Jesus," page 640 in *God's Story*. Or read this part of the story:

"Long ago, people from your families hurt God's prophets," said Stephen. "They killed people who said Jesus would come. And now you have killed Jesus. . . ."

The leaders were so angry they couldn't stand it. But Stephen was full of the Holy Spirit. He looked up to heaven. There he saw God's shining greatness.

"Look!" said Stephen. "I see heaven! It's open. Jesus is standing at God's right side!"

The leaders . . . started throwing rocks at him.

The rocks were hitting Stephen. But he prayed, "Lord Jesus, take my spirit." He bowed down. He called, "Lord, don't blame them for this sin." After he said that, he died.

Acts 7:52, 54-60

How do you feel when someone hurts you? What is the first thing you want to do? Most of us want to hurt the person back. But Paul wrote: "Don't try to get back at people. Let God do it. In God's Word the Lord says, 'It's my job to pay people back. I'll take care of it'" (Romans 12:19).

Do you remember Joseph? Joseph's brothers made fun of him. They hurt him. Then they sold him. Much later, they asked Joseph to forgive them. He did. He said, "You meant to hurt me. But God planned for good things to come from it." (See "A Trip to the Cave," page 44, or Genesis 50:20.)

When we don't forgive, we don't leave room for God to work. What did Stephen say just before he died? He asked God to forgive the people who were killing him. Do you remember who else did that? Jesus. When we forgive people who are hurting us, we are being like Jesus.

"Dear Father God, I will let you deal with the people who are mean to me. Help me to forgive them. Help me to be more like Jesus."

Talking with God

Always pray. *1 Thessalonians 5:17*

MONDAY

Read "Fire on Carmel Mountain," page 281 in *God's Story*. Or read this part of the story:

Baal's prophets called from morning until noon. But there was no answer. . . . So they called louder and louder. . . . But there was no answer.

Then Elijah prayed. "God, show that you are God in Israel. Show that I'm your servant. Show that I'm obeying you. Answer me, God. Let these people know that you are God."

Then fire came down from God onto the altar. It burned up the meat. It burned up the wood. It burned up the stones. It burned up the dirt. And it burned up the water in the pit!

The people were watching. They bowed down with their faces to the ground. "The Lord is God!" they shouted. "The Lord is God!" *1 Kings 18:26-39*

A light, cool wind moved through the trees. Flowers dipped their pretty petals as it passed. The sunset painted the sky red-orange. Leaves glowed in its light. Birds sang evening songs. Lions yawned with loud purrs. Monkeys chattered and jumped from branch to branch. And footsteps came softly across the grass. God came to the Garden of Eden. God came and talked with Adam.

God has always wanted to talk with the people he made. But somehow, the people he made got busy with other things. Some of them even forgot they could talk with God. They began to talk to false gods like Baal, who couldn't even hear them.

When Elijah prayed on Carmel Mountain, God heard him. The false god Baal could not answer prayer. But God could. And he did. God wants to talk with you, too. He will hear and answer.

"Dear God, thank you for wanting to talk with me. Thank you for hearing and answering my prayers."

TUESDAY

Read "The Broken Wall" and "Burned Gates," pages 489 and 490 in *God's Story*. Or read this part of the stories:

One of my brothers from Judah came to see me. I asked him about Jerusalem. . . .

He said, ". . . Jerusalem's wall is broken down. . . ."

I sat down and cried. . . . Then I said, "Lord! Great, wonderful God. You keep your loving promises to people who obey you. Listen. Open your eyes. Hear my prayer. . . . Remember what you told Moses. You said that . . . if your people came back to you, you'd bring them back. You'd bring them back to the land you gave them. . . . Be kind to me. May things go well."

One day I took the king's wine to him.

The king had never seen a sad look on my face before. So he asked, "Why are you sad?"

"It's because of Jerusalem. It's

the city where my people lived. It's a pile of sticks and stones. . . ."

"What do you want to do about it?" asked the king.

I prayed to God. Then I answered the king. "If you're happy with me, let me go to Jerusalem. Let me build the city back up."

God was with me. So the king did what I asked.
Nehemiah 1:2-11; 2:1-5, 8

What do you do when you get bad news? The first thing Nehemiah did was cry. Then he prayed. He praised God for his greatness. He said he was sorry for the sins of his people. He reminded God of his

SOME THINGS YOU CAN DO THIS WEEK

☐ **Make a phone** from tin cans. You'll need two empty, clean cans. Have an adult help punch a small hole in the bottom of each can. Cut a long piece of string. Put one end through the hole going into one can. Put the other end through the hole going into the other can. Tie the ends to metal paper clips to keep the strings from coming out. Hold the string tight between the cans. One person can talk in one end while another person listens at the other end. Think about how you talk to God.

☐ **Start a family prayer journal.** Write down the things you pray about. Watch to see how God answers those prayers. When God answers a prayer, write it on a praise list and thank God for it. Sometimes when you pray, you can remind God of what he has done.

☐ **Make prayer hand prints.** Make play dough by mixing three cups of flour, one cup of salt, and one cup of water. If it's too dry, add more water. If it's too wet, add more flour. Make a circle of dough, and press your hand onto it. Keep all your fingers together so it looks like your hand is folded to pray.

☐ **Take a prayer walk.** Walk with your family or friends around your neighborhood. Pray about the things you see. Thank God for things. Ask him to be good to your neighbors. Pray for people to come into God's kingdom.

☐ **Play "Pharisee."** The proud man who prayed was called a "Pharisee." Get a deck of Old Maid cards. Ask Mom or Dad if it's OK to draw a mustache and beard on the old maid. Turn her into the Pharisee. Then play the game like you'd play Old Maid. *(See Wednesday's reading.)*

promises. And he asked for God's help.

Later, Nehemiah took wine to the king. The king asked Nehemiah what he wanted. And Nehemiah prayed right then and there. He didn't even have to pray out loud. He didn't have to pray for a long time.

We can pray like Nehemiah did. Sometimes we say long prayers. We praise God. We say we're sorry for our sins. We remind God of his promises. And we ask for God's help. At other times, we say quick, quiet prayers. God hears all our prayers.

"Dear Father God, help me remember to pray. Thank you for hearing all my prayers, big ones and little ones."

WEDNESDAY

Read "The Proud Prayer," page 587 in *God's Story*. Or read this part of the story:

"Once there were two men," said Jesus. "They went to the worship house to pray. One man was a leader of God's people. The other man was a tax man.

"The leader stood up tall. He prayed about himself. 'God, thank you that I'm not like other men. I'm not a robber. I don't sin. I'm not like this tax man. . . .'

"The tax man stood a little way off. He wouldn't even look up. He pounded his chest. 'God, be kind to me,' he said. 'I'm a sinful person.'

"God forgave the tax man," said Jesus. "It was just as if he'd never sinned. But God didn't forgive the leader."
Luke 18:10-14

He stood up tall and proud. People looked up to him. And he made sure they saw the good things he did. The other man bowed his head. Nobody looked up to him. People didn't like him. They fussed at him and called him a sinner.

The first man prayed as if he were the greatest. He wasn't really praying so he could talk with God. He just wanted to make himself look good. The other man treated God as the greatest. He knew he needed

God. He asked for God's help. Do people pray like these men today? Which man do you want to pray like?

"Dear God, you made the sky and earth. You take care of me. You are the greatest. Be kind to me and help me."

THURSDAY

Read "Your Secret," page 533 in *God's Story.* Or read this part of the story:

"This is how you should pray," said Jesus.

"Our Father in heaven,
  your name is wonderful.
Bring your kingdom here to earth.
We pray that what you want
    will be done on earth
    like it is in heaven.
Give us the food we need each day.
Forgive us for our sin.
  Forgive us as we forgive people
    who sin against us.
Don't let anyone try to make us do
    wrong.
Save us from Satan, the enemy."
Matthew 6:9-13

Did you ever wonder, "What should I say when I pray?" Jesus' friends wondered. So Jesus told them.

First, Jesus praised God. He showed that he was putting God first. He prayed that whatever God wanted would be done on earth. You can praise God too. And you can pray that what he has planned will be done.

Jesus asked God for the food he needed to eat. You can ask God to give you whatever you need too. Jesus said we should ask God to forgive our sins. You can do that when you pray. And you can ask God to help you not to sin. You can ask him to keep you safe from the devil and his plans.

God is Jesus' Father. God is your Father in heaven too. So you can talk to him about anything. Sometimes our own dads and  moms are too busy to listen to us. But God is never too busy. He loves to have you talk with him.

"Dear Father God, you are great. I pray that what you have planned will be done. Give me what I need. Forgive my sins. Keep me safe from the devil and his plans. Thank you for listening anytime I pray. I love you."

FRIDAY

 Read "The Angel in the Jail," page 649 in *God's Story.* Or read this part of the story:

One night, Peter was sleeping in jail. . . . All of a sudden, an angel was there. A light shone into the jail room. The angel tapped Peter's side and woke him up.

"Hurry!" said the angel. "Get up!"

Peter's chains fell off. . . .

Peter went to the house where John Mark's mother lived. That's where lots of people were praying that night. Peter tapped on the door. . . . At last they opened the door. They saw that it really was Peter. They were very surprised.

Peter held his hand up to show they should be quiet. He told them how God had saved him. *Acts 12:6-17*

Peter was in trouble. Big trouble. One of his friends had already been killed for following Jesus. Now he was going to be killed too. What were his friends doing? Praying.

Some people pray to God only when they are in trouble. When things are going great, they forget about God. But Peter's friends knew they could pray anytime, anywhere. And they did. Now they all got together to pray for Peter.

What do you do when you have problems? Some people try their own ideas to get out of trouble. If that doesn't work, then they pray. They say, "The only thing left is to pray." Other people pray first. They make room for God to work. They ask God to show them how to handle their problems. Which way do you think is better?

"Dear God, thank you for letting me pray anytime, anywhere. I will tell you my troubles. I'll talk with you about all the other things going on in my life too. Thank you for being such a loving, listening God."

A Special Place of Worship

Your body is the Holy Spirit's worship house. The Holy Spirit is in you. *1 Corinthians 6:19*

MONDAY

Read "Kingdom of Light," page 733 in *God's Story*. Or read this part of the story:

God wants me to tell about a mystery. It's been hidden for a long time. But now God's people see what the mystery is. God even shows it to people who aren't Jewish. The mystery is that Jesus lives in you. This is your hope of being part of his greatness. *Colossians 1:26-27*

Did you ever read a mystery book? Have you ever seen a mystery movie? What is a mystery? It's a question that you don't know the answer to. It's something that's hidden. Paul wrote about a mystery. The mystery is that Jesus lives in us. Jesus said so himself. (See the last line of "Out of the World," page 614 in *God's Story*—John 17:26.) How can that be? The answer is that God sent his Holy Spirit to live in us. Still, it is a mystery.

Long ago, people went to the worship house. They worshiped God there. But now our bodies are worship houses. So we worship God wherever we are. We can worship God with our whole lives, showing how good and great God is. How do you worship God?

"Dear Father God, I want Jesus to live in me. I will be your special place of worship. I will show how great you are!"

TUESDAY

Read "Who Can Open the Roll of Paper?" page 804 in *God's Story*. Or read this part of the story:

I heard many angels' voices. There must have been thousands and thousands. Ten thousand times ten thousand. . . . The angels sang loudly,

"Jesus is good enough.
He was killed.
So now he has power.
He has riches.
He is wise.
He is strong.
We worship him.
His greatness shines.
We praise him!"

Then I heard all the living beings in heaven and earth. . . . They were singing.

"We worship the King and Jesus,
the Lamb.
We praise them.
Their greatness shines.
They have power forever and
ever!" Revelation 5:11-13

The rainbow looked like a beautiful, shiny green stone. It circled around a throne. Thunder rolled, and lightning flashed from the throne. And four living beings called out, "Holy, holy, holy. God is clean, sinless, and holy. . . . He lived before. He lives now. He will always live." (See "An Open Door," page 803 in *God's Story*—Revelation 4:8.)

Then what did the angels sing? What did all the other beings sing?

Worship is praising God for who he is. Why do you think everyone bowed down in front of God? God must look great and wonderful. He must look so awesome that whoever sees him as he really is bows down. Can you think of what that must be like?

Thinking about God helps us worship. Who is God? What can you do and say to worship him?

"Dear Father God, you are the maker of the sky and earth. You are the giver of everything good. You are the one who takes care of me. You are good and powerful! I worship you!"

WEDNESDAY

Read "Open Graves," page 623 in *God's Story*. Or read this part of the story:

Jesus knew his time on earth was finished. . . . He cried out in a loud voice. He said, "Father, I give my spirit to you." Then he bowed his head. And he died.

Inside the worship house there hung a big, long cloth. It hung in front of the Most Holy Place. It kept people out of that room. But at the moment Jesus died, it tore in half. The tear started at the top. It ripped all the way down to the bottom.

The earth shook. Rocks broke. Graves came open. Dead people came back to life!

Matthew 27:50-53; John 19:28, 30

SOME THINGS YOU CAN DO THIS WEEK

☐ **Make a worship banner.** Get an old sheet or pillowcase. Use markers to write "God is _____." You choose the word or words to fill in the blank. You can put the banner on a wall to help you think about worshiping God.

☐ **Play "God Is."** Go through the alphabet, saying words that tell about God. If you do this with family or friends, take turns with the letters of the alphabet.

☐ **Make a pasta necklace.** Cut a piece of yarn. Make it 24 inches long. Get five medium-sized pieces of tube-shaped pasta. On each one, print a letter: J-E-S-U-S. Put the yarn through the pieces of pasta to spell Jesus' name. Let your necklace remind you that Jesus lives in you. *(See Monday's reading.)*

☐ **Wrap a small gift box.** First wrap the sides and bottom of the box. Then wrap the lid. On a card, write *JESUS*. Put it in the box. Give the box to someone. Tell the person that inside is the best gift of all. Say that Jesus is the gift that God sent to pay for our sins. *(See Wednesday's reading.)*

☐ **Take a hike to explore nature.** Take a magnifying glass with you. Look at leaves, tree bark, rocks, and other things. Think about what we mean when we say we "magnify" God. *(See Friday's reading.)*

Long ago, God's people worshiped him at one worship house. They brought gifts for God. Priests gave these gifts on an altar. Priests talked to God for the people. But there was one room that no one could go into. Not even the priests. It was the Most Holy Place. Only the high priest could go in there. And he went in only one time a year. It was a special place because God's ark box was in there. So the priest went inside to be close to God for the people. The gift he gave was to pay for the people's sins.

But then God sent Jesus. Jesus became the gift that paid for people's sins. When Jesus died, what happened to the cloth that kept people out of the Most Holy Place? It tore right down the middle. That means we don't need a priest to talk to God for us anymore. We can go right to God ourselves. We go in Jesus' name, because Jesus was the gift that paid for our sins. God did all this for us! How can you thank and worship God for being so good?

"Dear God, thank you for sending Jesus to pay for the wrong things I do. Thank you for letting me come right to you. You are a good God, and I worship you."

THURSDAY

Read "Water from a Well," page 518 in *God's Story.* Or read this part of the story:

Jesus was on his way to Galilee. He went through the land of Samaria. He was tired. So he stopped at a well and sat down. . . .

It wasn't long before a woman came to the well. She was coming to get water. . . .

"You're a prophet!" said the woman. "So what do you think? Here on this mountain is where my people worship. You Jews say we have to worship in Jerusalem."

"Someday you won't worry about where to worship. . . . Someday true worship will come from the spirit," said Jesus. "In fact, the time is already here. God is spirit. So worship must come from the spirit. It must be true. That's the way the Father wants it." *John 4:3-23*

Up the mountain the people of Samaria went. They went up the mountain to worship God. Down the road the Jewish people went. They went to the worship house in Jerusalem to worship God. But Jesus told the woman at the well about true worship. He said that someday worship wouldn't happen only on a mountain. Worship wouldn't happen only in the worship house in Jerusalem. Then how would people worship? Worship would happen in their spirits.

Jesus knew that people could go to the worship house. They could sing and pray. But if their spirits didn't love God, they weren't really worshiping at all. People who love God worship him wherever they are. They don't need to go to a special place.

Long ago, there were no church buildings. The church was the people. They worshiped in their own homes. Lydia and her friends worshiped by the river. Paul and Silas worshiped in jail. Where do you worship?

"Dear God, you are great and wonderful. You are with me everywhere. So I will worship you wherever I am."

FRIDAY

Read "Tell about God," page 202 in *God's Story*. Or read this part of the story:

Tell how great and strong
   God is.
Worship God.
Think of how beautiful he is, how
   special, how holy.
He is the best.

God's voice thunders over the sea.
His voice is great and full of
   power.
God sits on his throne.
He is the King forever.

He makes his people strong and
gives them peace.
Psalm 29:1-4, 10-11

Have you ever looked at something with a magnifying glass? What if you looked at a leaf through a magnifying glass? What would the magnifying glass do? It would help you see the leaf better. It would help you see what the leaf is really like.

Sometimes when we worship God, we say we magnify him. That means we help people see him better. We help people see what God is really like.

That's what David did when he wrote songs about God. He magnified God. His songs help us see God better. They help us see what God is really like. That's part of the way David worshiped.

How can you magnify God? If you wrote a song about God, what would you say about him?

"Dear God, thank you for David's songs. They help me see what you are like. I will magnify you. I'll show others that you are powerful! You are wise! You are great! You are loving! You are kind! I'm glad I'm your child!"

God Gave Himself

God loved the world very much. He loved it so much that he gave his only Son. *John 3:16*

MONDAY

Read "Getting Ready for God to Pass Over," page 58 in *God's Story.* Or read this part of the story:

God told Moses and Aaron what to do. He said, ". . . On that day each family should get a lamb to eat. But let's say a family is too small to eat a whole lamb. Then they should share with a neighbor.

"Keep the lamb for 14 days. That night, kill the lamb. Paint some of its blood around the door. Paint it on the sides and top. . . .

"That night I will go through Egypt. . . . I will see the blood.

Then I will pass over your houses. Nothing will hurt you.

"You should remember this time from now on. It will become a special holiday for God." *Exodus 12:1-14*

Long ago, when God's people sinned, they had to kill a lamb. That would pay for their sins. Then God wouldn't be angry about their sins anymore. In Egypt, God told his people to paint the lamb's blood over the doors. This showed that the people belonged to God. When the death angel passed over, God's people would be safe.

Why did God use blood? Blood is life. When an animal or a person loses its blood, it dies. Killing the lamb showed that sin is not just something small. It's a big deal. When we sin, someone always gets hurt.

But God's people had to keep giving lambs again and again. That's because they sinned again and again. So God sent his Son, Jesus. He became the lamb for everyone. He gave his blood one time to pay for everyone's sins. Now when death comes, we're not afraid. We're safe, because we have a life with God that lasts forever.

"Dear Father God, thank you for sending Jesus to pay for my sins. Thank you for giving me life with you that lasts forever."

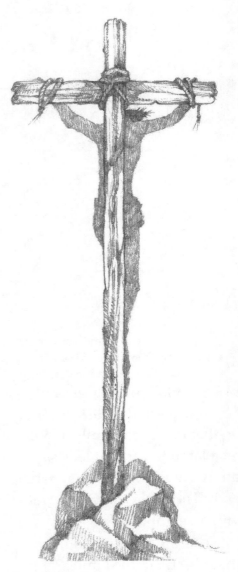

TUESDAY

Read "Shining like Stars," page 746 in *God's Story*. Or read this part of the story:

You should look at things the same way that Jesus does.

He was God.
  But he didn't hold on to being God.
He made himself into nothing.
  He became a servant.
  He became a human.

He looked like a man.
He put himself in a low place.
  He obeyed, and he died on a
    cross.
So God made him great. . . .
All people will bow down when they
    hear Jesus' name. . . .
Every voice will say that Jesus
    Christ is Lord. Philippians 2:5-11

Before he came to earth, Jesus lived in heaven with God. What do you think heaven is like? There is no night, no crying, no hurting, no dying. It's full of love and peace and joy because God is there. It must be a wonderful place.

Think about what Jesus gave up. Why would he leave the peace in

SOME THINGS YOU CAN DO THIS WEEK

☐ **Play "Sheep out of the Pen."** One person is the shepherd. The sheep gather at one side of the room or yard. The shepherd calls, "Sheep out of the pen!" The sheep try to run to the other side without being tagged. The ones who are tagged help catch the sheep on the next run. How is Jesus like a lamb? *(See Monday's reading.)*

☐ **Make sponge-print crosses.** Cut a sponge into a cross shape. Pour a little paint onto a paper plate. Press the sponge into the paint until one side of the sponge is covered. Then press the sponge onto a piece of paper to make a cross. Jesus gave up a lot when he came to die on a cross, didn't he? *(See Thursday's reading.)*

☐ **Be a news reporter.** Ask friends or family to play like they are people from Bible times that Jesus forgave. Some of the people might be the man who couldn't walk (Mark 2), the woman who put perfume on Jesus' feet (Luke 7), the man Philip talked to as he rode in his chariot (Acts 8), the woman who prayed by a river (Acts 16). Ask the Bible people about their lives before and after believing in Jesus. Record their answers on tape.

☐ **Tell riddles about Bible people.** Think of a person who was in the story of Jesus' death and coming to life. Give clues about that person. Friends or family can guess who it is.

☐ **Make popovers.** Beat one cup of milk, one cup of flour, and one-half teaspoon of salt for one and a half minutes. Beat in one tablespoon of melted butter and two eggs. Fill muffin cups half full. Bake at 400 degrees for 40 minutes. Then use a fork to make small holes in the sides of the popovers. Lay them on their sides for five minutes to dry inside. Open a popover. What's inside? It's empty. Think about Jesus' grave. It was empty too.

heaven for the hurts on the earth? Why would he leave the riches in heaven for the poor life on earth? Why would he leave the love in heaven for the hate on earth? He did it because he loved you. He wanted you to have heaven's peace and riches and love. So he died for you. Now you can have it all because you can be God's child.

"Thank you, Jesus, for giving up so much for me. Thank you, God, for letting me be your child."

WEDNESDAY

Read "Nothing Dark," page 792 in *God's Story*. Or read this part of the story:

God is light. There is nothing dark in him. If we keep sinning, we are living in darkness. We might say we are God's friend. But that would be a lie.

If we follow God in his light, we are friends with each other. Jesus' blood cleans the sin from our hearts.

If we say we don't sin, we are lying. But what if we say we

sin, and we're sorry? Then God keeps his promise. He forgives us. He cleans our hearts from the wrong we've done.
1 John 1:5-9

There's good news and bad news. The good news is that God is all good. Nothing sinful can be around him. The bad news is that we have all sinned.

Our sins would keep us away from God. But there's more good news. Jesus took our sins. Jesus never sinned. So he was always close to God, even on earth. We had lots of sins. Jesus had none. So Jesus traded with us. He took our sins and let us have none.

Sins bring hurts and death. That's what happened to Jesus because he took our sins. He was punished for our sins by being put on a cross to die. We sometimes say that Jesus' blood washes away our sins. So now when God looks at someone who believes in Jesus, he sees a person who has no sins.

"Dear Father God, thank you for letting Jesus take my sins. Thank you for washing my sins away!"

THURSDAY

Read "At the Right Time," page 706 in *God's Story*. Or read this part of the story:

You see, we could not save ourselves. We had no power. But at the right time, Jesus came. He died for people who sin. Sometimes a person will die for someone who does what's right. Sometimes a person will die for another good person. But we were sinners. Jesus died for us anyway. That shows just how much God loves us.

Now it's just as if we'd never sinned. It's all because of Jesus' blood. What's more, we'll be saved from God's anger! We were God's enemies. But now he lets us be his children, because Jesus died. His life saves us.
Romans 5:6-10

Have you ever seen a cart pulling a horse? Have you ever seen a baseball player start at third base, then run to second, then first, then home? Have you ever read a book by starting at the last page and going to the first page? All of these things would be backward.

Here's another question: Do you have to get rid of your sins before you ask Jesus to save you? That would be backward too. Some people think they're not good enough to be saved. But nobody is ever good enough. That's why we need Jesus. He loves and saves people who are sinful. He is the only one who can make us good!

"Dear God, thank you that I don't have to make myself good enough for you. Thank you for loving me and saving me."

FRIDAY

Read "The World's Light," page 572 in *God's Story*. Or read this part of the story:

Many people believed in Jesus. "Keep believing what I'm teaching," Jesus told them. "Keep obeying me. Then you'll really be my followers. You'll know the truth. The truth will set you free."

"We've never been anybody's

slaves," they said. "So how could we be set free?"

"Anybody who sins is a slave to sin," said Jesus. "A slave is not one of the family. Only a son belongs to the family forever. If the Son sets you free, you really are free." *John 8:30-36*

They worked hard. If they didn't do it right, somebody would hit them. They couldn't rest when they were tired. They never got a day off. They had to do what they were told to do. They had to sleep where they were told to sleep. They had to eat whatever they were given. And they couldn't fuss about it. They were slaves. They belonged to their master. He had bought them.

Jesus said that if we sin, we are slaves to sin. What did Jesus mean? Jesus meant that when we choose to do wrong, it leads to doing more wrong things. We get into bad habits. Then it's very hard for us to change. Pretty soon we find out that sin controls us. We follow sinful ways. We become slaves to sin.

But Jesus said that he can set us free. How? We tell Jesus we know we are sinners. We ask him to save us and set us free. We put him in charge of our lives. Right then, Jesus gets rid of our sins. He sets us free! So we stop choosing sin, and we start choosing Jesus' ways.

What if we sin again after Jesus saves us? He erases those sins too. We tell Jesus we're sorry and ask him to help us choose to do what's good and right.

"Dear Father God, I want Jesus to set me free from sin. I will let Jesus be in charge of my life. I will follow you. Help me to choose what's good and right. Thank you for setting me free from sin."

What Is Grace?

God's kind love saves you when you believe. *Ephesians 2:8*

MONDAY

Read "Coming Back to Life," page 689 in *God's Story*. Or read this part of the story:

I want to help you remember the Good News about Jesus. I told you about it. You believed it.

I taught you the most important thing I ever learned. Jesus died for our sins. . . . He came back to life on the third day.

I'm not an important apostle. I really shouldn't even be called an apostle. That's because I used to hurt Jesus' followers. But I am what I am because of God's kind love.

God's kind love changed me. I worked hard. But it wasn't me. It was God's kind love that was with me. *1 Corinthians 15:1, 3-4, 9-10*

Paul remembered the day people tossed their coats at his feet. That was just before they began throwing rocks at Stephen. They did it because Stephen had been telling them about Jesus. Paul cheered them on. That was when Paul didn't believe in Jesus.

When he remembered that time, Paul felt bad. Now that he was a follower of Jesus, he wrote to the people in Corinth. He said, "I really shouldn't even be called an apostle. . . . I am what I am because of God's kind love." Paul had been mean to other people. But that didn't stop God from being kind and loving to Paul.

Grace is being treated kindly when you have been mean to others. Grace is being loved when you haven't been loving. Grace is being treated better than you have treated others. How has God shown his grace to you?

"Dear Father God, you are kind to me, even when I have not been kind to others. I am not good enough for you to love me. But you love me anyway. Thank you for your grace."

TUESDAY

 Read "The King's Order," page 320 in *God's Story*. Or read this part of the story:

Jonah called out, "Nineveh has only 40 more days. Then the city will be destroyed."

The king of Nineveh heard what Jonah said. The king . . . put on clothes made from sack cloth.

Then the king gave an order. ". . . Pray to God. Stop doing wrong. Stop hurting others and being mean. Maybe God will change his mind. Maybe he will be kind. Maybe he will stop being angry, and we won't die."

God saw what the people were doing. He saw how they had stopped sinning. So he felt loving and kind toward them. He didn't get rid of them.
Jonah 3:4, 6-10

The enemy's city was huge. There were wide, tall walls around it. And it took three days to go through it.

Jonah knew how mean and hateful the people of Nineveh could be. So he didn't want God to be kind to them. But God gave the people of Nineveh his grace. He was loving and kind to them, even though they had treated others badly.

God gives his grace to us. He treats us with love and kindness. We have done things that have not been kind and loving. But God forgives us and loves us. He makes things turn out to be good for us. What a wonderful God we have!

"Dear God, I have done many things wrong. Sometimes I'm not loving or kind. Thank you for loving me anyway."

WEDNESDAY

Read "If I Die" and "Haman Brags," page 479 in *God's Story*. Or read this part of the stories:

Then Esther sent another message to Mordecai. "I can't go see the king about this. Everyone knows that you can't choose when to see the king. The king has to ask you to come. If you go without being asked, you'll be killed. There's only one way to go in if you aren't asked. That's if the king holds out his gold rod to you. . . .

SOME THINGS YOU CAN DO THIS WEEK

☐**Jump the vine.** Have each of two friends hold one end of a green streamer. The streamer should be about six feet long. Jump over it as your friends hold it close to the ground. Ask them to raise it little by little. Jump over it each time. See how high you can jump. Then let your friends try jumping. Read about the vine that God sent for Jonah (page 320 in *God's Story*—Jonah 4). And remember how God showed grace to the city of Nineveh. *(See Tuesday's reading.)*

☐**Make a throne.** Use markers to draw and color an old pillowcase to look like the back of a king's throne. Glue sequins and beads on it if you want. Then pull the pillowcase over the back of a chair to make your throne. Remember the story of Esther. *(See Wednesday's reading.)*

☐**Play "King, May I?"** Line up across the room from the person who is king. The king tells each person how to walk forward (three baby steps, one giant step, two hops, and so on). Before moving, the person must ask, "King, may I?" The king says, "Yes, you may." The one who reaches the king first wins and gets to be the next king. Remember the story of Esther.

☐**Make paper-plate puppets.** Turn one paper plate upside down on top of another paper plate. Staple the edges together, but leave an opening to stick your hand in. Draw a face on one plate. You can use yarn for hair if you want. Make several puppet people, and use them to act out one of this week's stories.

☐**Beat the clock.** Before cleaning your room, set a timer for three minutes. Try to pick up everything made of paper before the timer rings. Keep timing yourself as you pick up plastic. Then cloth. Then wood. Keep going until your room is clean. Remember the farmer who was kind even to the workers who worked only for a while. *(See Friday's reading.)*

Mordecai sent a message back to Esther. ". . . Maybe the reason you became queen is so you can help our people now."

After three days, Esther put on the robes she wore as queen. She went to the inside hall of the palace. It was in front of the king's hall.

The king was sitting on his throne. He was facing the door to the hall. He saw Queen Esther standing there. He was glad to see her. He held out his gold rod.

Esther walked up and touched the end of the gold rod.

"What do you want, Queen Esther?" asked the king. "I'll give you whatever you want. I'll even give you half of my kingdom if you want."
Esther 4:10-14; 5:1-3

How do you think Queen Esther felt before she went to see the king? Esther was not supposed to go to see the king. But the king showed grace to Esther. He didn't have to be kind to her, but he was. He didn't have to love her, but he did.

God gives us grace. God is the king over all that he made. He can tell the sun where to shine and the wind where to blow. He is in charge. And he doesn't have to be kind to us, but he is. He doesn't have to love us, but he does. Jesus didn't have to die for us, but he did. We are sinful people. But God treats us like his children. That's grace!

"Dear Father God, you are the great, powerful King. But you have made us your children. Thank you for your grace."

THURSDAY

Read "A King Gets Out of Jail," page 437 in *God's Story*. Or read this part of the story:

We had been in Babylon for 37 years. Jehoiachin, Judah's king, was still alive there. There was a new king in Babylon. He let Jehoiachin out of jail. He was kind to Jehoiachin. He treated him better than the other kings.

Jehoiachin got to take his jail clothes off. He ate at the king's table the rest of his life. The king even gave Jehoiachin money to live on for the rest of his life.

Jeremiah 52:31-34

God's people saw lots of fighting. Kings from other countries wanted more land. Or they wanted power over God's people. Or they wanted riches. So they would send their armies to fight. Most of the time, the winning king would kill the king who lost. Or the winning king would put the other king in jail for the rest of his life.

Jehoiachin was the king who lost the fight. He had been put in jail. But the new king in Babylon gave Jehoiachin grace. He let Jehoiachin out of jail. He even let Jehoiachin eat at the king's table.

God should let many bad things happen to us, because we often say and do bad things. But God does not treat us like sinners. Instead, he cares for us like a father. And he has moved our sins away as far as the east is from the west. (See "As High As the Sky," page 206 in *God's Story*—Psalm 103.) Isn't God's grace wonderful?

"Dear God, thank you for throwing my sins away. Thank you for treating me with grace."

FRIDAY

Read "Workers Who Fussed," page 588 in *God's Story*. Or read this part of the story:

"Here's what the kingdom of heaven is like," said Jesus. "It's like a farmer who had a grape field. He went to town early in the morning. He got men to come and work in his field. He told them what he'd pay them for the day. Then he sent them out to work in his field.

"The farmer got more workers at noon. He got more workers at three o'clock in the afternoon. At five o'clock, the farmer still found people standing around. . . .

"The farmer said, 'You can work in my field.' So they did.

"It wasn't long until evening came. 'Call the workers,' said the farmer to the head servant. 'Pay them. Start with the last men who came to work. Then go on to the first men.'

"The workers who went to work at five o'clock came. Each one got paid for a whole day's work.

"Then the early morning workers came. They thought they would get more money. But the farmer paid each worker for one day's work." *Matthew 20:1-2, 5-10*

They started work as the sun was coming up. After a while, more workers came to help them. They all worked and worked while the sun rose high. Later in the day, more workers came to help. They all worked and worked in the hot afternoon sun. A few more workers came to help. They all worked and worked as the sun sank low. Then more workers came to help. They all worked and worked until evening. Which ones worked hardest and longest? Which ones got paid the most?

The workers who worked only for a while got grace from the farmer. That means he gave them something they didn't work for. God gives us something we don't work for. He gives us a place in his family. He lets us be his children. He forgives our sins. He gives us life forever with him. That's not something we worked for. It's not our pay for being good. It's God's gift to us. It's grace.

"Dear Father God, thank you for letting me be your child. Thank you for forgiving my sins. Thank you for letting me live with you forever. Thank you for your grace."

I Believe

So say it with your mouth. "Jesus is Lord." Believe that God made him come back to life again. Then you will be saved.

Romans 10:9

MONDAY

Read "A Wedding Party," page 515 in *God's Story*. Or read this part of the story:

Two days later, there was a wedding in Galilee. It was in the town called Cana. Jesus and his friends went. Jesus' mother went too.

But the people who were having the party ran out of wine. . . .

"Fill those jars with water," Jesus told the servants.

The servants filled them all the way to the top.

"Now," said Jesus, "dip some of it out. Take it to the man in charge of the party."

The servants did just what Jesus said.

The man in charge took a drink. He didn't know it had been water. That's because it had turned into wine! But the servants knew! . . .

This was the first wonder Jesus did. It showed how great he was. Then Jesus' followers believed in him. *John 2:1-11*

One minute it was water. The next minute it was wine! Jesus' friends saw it. They had been told that Jesus was the one God had promised to send. Now they really believed it.

What is believing? It's knowing deep inside yourself that something is true. Even if you can't see it, you know it's true.

Do you know what gravity is? Gravity pulls you back down after you jump up. Gravity is like a big magnet pulling things down toward the ground. You can't see gravity. But you know it's real. You can see what it does.

Can you see God? Do you believe he is real? He is. You can see what God does. He is there even though you don't see him.

"Dear God, I believe in you. I know you are with me even though I can't see you. Thank you for helping me believe."

TUESDAY

Read "Keys," page 563 in *God's Story*. Or read this part of the story:

"Who do you think I am?" asked Jesus.

"You're the one God promised to send," said Peter. "You're the Christ. You're the Son of the Living God."

Jesus said, "God will be good to you, Peter. My Father in heaven showed you who I am. You're Peter. You are like a rock. I'll build my church on this rock. The power of hell will never get rid of it.

"I'll give you the keys to God's kingdom," said Jesus. *Matthew 16:15-19*

Where is your family from? Joseph and Mary would say that Joseph's family was from Bethlehem. Peter, Andrew, and Philip would say, "We're from the town of Bethsaida." Jesus would say, "I'm from heaven." But some people did not believe that.

Jesus also said, "I'm the way." Jesus is the way to get to God. He is the way to be saved from sin. Jesus said, "I'm the truth." Everything Jesus says is true. He is real. He keeps his promises. Jesus said, "I'm the life." He gives us life with God that will last forever (John 14:6).

Peter told Jesus, "You're the Son of the Living God." Peter knew deep down inside himself that Jesus is God's Son. Do you believe that too?

"Dear God, I believe that Jesus is your Son. I believe that he is the Way, the Truth, and the Life."

SOME THINGS YOU CAN DO THIS WEEK

☐ **Take a blind walk.** Close your eyes. Ask a friend to stand behind you and guide you by talking. This person can tell you when to walk straight ahead, when to stop, and when to turn. Do you believe what your friend says? Why or why not? Now trade places so you can guide your friend.

☐ **Open an empty paper sack.** Place it upside down on the floor next to a firm chair. Which will hold you up when you sit on it? How can you show that you believe it? Do you believe Jesus will take care of you? How can you show that you believe?

☐ **Get some old magazines and newspapers.** Cut out pictures of things people believe will make them happy. Glue the pictures onto a piece of paper. Why should you believe in Jesus and not in these things?

☐ **Snack on grape drink** and "wedding" cookies. Talk about what Jesus did at the wedding. Why did his friends believe in him? *(See Monday's reading.)*

☐ **Play "I Doubt It"** with dominoes. *Doubt* means not believing. Put all the dominoes face down. Give each player the same number of dominoes. The first player looks for a domino with one dot to place on the table face down. Or he can lay another domino down and pretend it has one dot. Say, "One." The next person lays down a domino with two dots. The next person lays down a domino with three dots, and so on. If someone thinks the domino is not what a player says it is, that person can say, "I doubt it." If he or she is right, the player has to pick up all the dominoes. If the one who doubted is wrong, that person has to pick up all the dominoes. Keep playing until someone runs out of dominoes. What did Thomas doubt? *(See Thursday's reading.)*

WEDNESDAY

Read "The Men Who Could Not Believe," page 575 in *God's Story*. Or read this part of the story:

So the leaders called again for the man who had been made well. They said, "Tell us the truth. We know the man who made you well is a sinner."

"I don't know if he is a sinner or not. I do know one thing. I couldn't see before," said the man. "But now I can see."

"What did he do to you?" they asked. "How did he make you see?"

"I told you already," said the man. "You didn't listen. Do you want to hear it again? Do you want to follow him too?"

Then the leaders made fun of the man. *John 9:24-28*

When he was born, he could not see. When he got big enough to walk, people had to lead him around. When he got big enough to go to work, nobody had a job for him. So he couldn't make money to buy food and clothes. He had to ask people to give him money. He had to beg.

But now he could see! "Jesus made me well," he said. The Jewish leaders did not believe him, no matter what he said.

God lets people choose. They see and hear about the things he has done. And they can choose to believe or not to believe. Which do you choose?

"Dear Father God, I've seen and heard about great things you've done. I choose to believe in you and your Son, Jesus."

THURSDAY

Read "In a Locked Room," page 628 in *God's Story*. Or read this part of the story:

Jesus' special friends . . . were together in a locked room. . . . All of a sudden, there was Jesus! He was standing right there with them.

"Be at peace!" Jesus said.

Thomas wasn't there that night. Jesus' other friends told him, "We saw the Lord!"

Thomas said, "I don't believe

it. I'm not going to believe. First I'd have to see the nail marks in his hands. I'd have to touch the places where the nails were. I'd have to put my hand on his side where the spear went in."

A week later, Jesus' friends were in the same house. Thomas was there too. They still kept the doors locked.

Jesus came again. He stood with his friends. "Be at peace!" he said.

Then he turned to Thomas. "Thomas, put your finger here," he said. "Touch my side. Look at my hands. Stop thinking that this is just a story. Believe!"

"My Lord and my God!" said Thomas. *John 20:19, 24-28*

How would you have felt if you had been one of Jesus' friends? You knew Jesus had been killed. You heard that Jesus was alive again. But you hadn't seen him. What would you think?

Thomas would not believe that Jesus was alive. He had not seen Jesus with his own two eyes. So he would not believe. Not believing is

called "doubting." Jesus' brother James wrote about people who doubt. He said they are like sea waves that the wind blows around. They don't know what to believe in. First they believe one thing. Then they believe another thing.

People choose what to believe in. When people don't believe in Jesus, what are some things they believe in? Will those things help them? What do you believe in?

"Dear God, I choose to believe in your Son, Jesus. Help me not to doubt. Help me to follow Jesus no matter what happens."

FRIDAY

Read "Close to the Cross," page 622 in *God's Story*. Or read this part of the story:

Jesus' mother stood close to the cross. His aunt was there too. Another Mary and Mary Magdalene were also there. Jesus looked out. He saw his mother. He saw his friend John there too.

"Dear woman!" Jesus said to

his mother. "John will be like your son now."

"Take care of her," he told John. "Care for her like you'd care for your own mother."

After that, John let Jesus' mother stay at his house. He took care of her. *John 19:25-27*

Someone who sees something happen is called a witness.

A man named John dipped people in water to baptize them. He told about Jesus. He was a witness. He told what he heard and saw. And he said, "I saw it. So I know this is God's Son" (John 1:34).

One of Jesus' 12 special friends was also named John. He wrote a book of the Bible called "John." He wrote about many wonders that Jesus did. John saw what happened at the cross, so he was a witness. He told what happened so others could believe it. He wrote, "Jesus did many other wonders that his followers saw. They are not written about in this book. But these things were written so you will believe that Jesus is God's Son. If you believe, you can live forever because of him" (John 20:30-31).

Many people who wrote books of the Bible saw Jesus. They were witnesses. By reading the Bible, we can learn about Jesus too. And we can believe in him. Then we can ask him to be our Lord. We will get to know him even better. That's because he will work in our lives. Then each of us can be a witness for him. And others can believe.

"Dear Father God, I believe in you and your Son. Show me how to tell others about you so they can believe in you too."

Nothing Can Take God Away

Nothing in the world can keep God's love from us. *Romans 8:39*

MONDAY

Read "A Seed," page 598 in *God's Story*. Or read this part of the story:

"A wheat seed falls to the ground," said Jesus. "It dies. It's just a little seed. But it will make many other seeds. It will send out roots and grow. It will live again.

"It's time to chase away Satan, the world's sinful prince. I'll be lifted up from the earth. Then I'll draw all people to me." Jesus was talking about how he would die.

"You have the light just a little while longer," said Jesus. "Walk while you have the light. The dark is going to come. People in the dark don't know where they're going. Trust in the light while it's here. Then you can be children of light."
John 12:24, 31-33, 35-36

Look around you. What do you see? There is another world around you too. It's a world you can't see. And in that world there are two kingdoms. One kingdom is a good kingdom. God sometimes calls it "the kingdom of light." The other kingdom is a bad kingdom, "the kingdom of darkness."

Try something. Get a flashlight and turn it on. Go to the darkest room you can find. Does the darkness block out the light? Can you put enough darkness in the room to get rid of the light? Darkness can never get rid of light. But light can get rid of darkness. Light is stronger.

God's kingdom is stronger than the kingdom of darkness. God is stronger than Satan. And when his Son, Jesus, lives in you, nothing can take his love away. Jesus "is great. He is greater than Satan, the sinful one in the world" (1 John 4:4).

"Dear Father God, keep me in your kingdom of light. Thank you that you are stronger than darkness."

TUESDAY

 Read "More than Winners," page 708 in *God's Story*. Or read this part of the story:
Jesus died. What's more, he came back to life. Now he is at God's right side. Jesus prays for us too.

So who can take us away from Jesus' love? Can trouble take us away? Can hard times? . . . Can danger take us away? No. These things will never take us away from Jesus' love. We are more than winners because he loved us.

I am sure of this. Death can't keep us from God's love. Life can't. Angels can't. Bad spirits can't. Nothing with us right now can keep God's love away. Nothing that can happen will keep God's love away. No power can keep God's love away, nothing high or low. Nothing in the world can keep God's love from us. We'll always have this love from Jesus. *Romans 8:34-39*

Did you ever get a postcard from someone who went on a trip? What picture was on the front? What did the person write on the back? Maybe the card said, "I'm having fun. I wish you were here." Your friend was miles away. The miles kept you apart.

Did you ever have the chicken

pox? You had to stay home, away from your friends. The sickness kept you apart from your friends.

But do miles keep you apart from God and his love? Does sickness keep you apart from God's love? No. Nothing can keep God and his love away from you.

"Dear Father God, thank you for being with me all the time. Thank you that nothing can take your love away from me."

WEDNESDAY

Read "My Eyes Look Up," page 190 in *God's Story*. Or read this part of the story:

My eyes look up to the hills.
Where does my help come from?
My help comes from God.
He made heaven and earth.

God is the shade at your right hand.

SOME THINGS YOU CAN DO THIS WEEK

☐ **Glue two pieces of paper together.** Let the glue dry. Now try to pull the two pieces apart. What happens? When you belong to God, nothing can pull him away from you.

☐ **Make waffles.** Let a grown-up help you. First get two egg yolks apart from the egg whites. Do this by carefully breaking each egg into a large spoon. Use another spoon to hold the yolk from the first spoon. Then tip the spoon and let the white go into a small bowl. Mix one cup of flour, two teaspoons of baking powder, and one-half teaspoon of salt. In another bowl, mix two cups of milk and the two egg yolks. Beat the two egg whites until they are stiff. Mix the milk and yolks into the flour. Mix in one-fourth cup of vegetable oil. Fold the egg whites in. Cook the batter in a waffle iron. It makes about four waffles. Think about how God is with you and nothing can take him away. When you made waffles, you had to *separate* the egg yolks from the whites. But *nothing* can separate you from God.

☐ **Play "Kitty Wants a Corner."** One player is "Kitty." Choose a "corner" for all the other players. When Kitty says, "Kitty wants a corner," everyone has to trade corners. Kitty tries to get a corner too. The player left without a corner becomes the next Kitty. Talk about how God never leaves you out. You always have a place in God's heart.

☐ **Learn Romans 8:39:** "Nothing in the world can keep God's love from us." To help yourself learn it, make up actions that go with each part.

*The sun won't hurt you in the
daytime.
The moon won't hurt you at night.*

*God will keep you safe.
God will watch over you when you
go out.
He will watch over you when you
come in.
He will watch over you now and
forever.* Psalm 121:1-2, 5-8

It's a sunny summer day. You
are playing outside. You get very
hot. You want to cool off and
rest. Where do you go? You
might rest in the shade. The
shade keeps you safe from the
heat of the sun.

God keeps you safe. He takes
care of you when you come and
when you go. He takes care of
you now and forever. He does it
because he loves you. And
nothing can take you away from
his love.

*"Dear God, thank you for taking care
of me when I come and when I go.
Thank you for loving me now and
forever."*

THURSDAY

Read "A Picture on God's Hands,"
page 366 in *God's Story*. Or read
this part of the story:

*God called me before I
was born.
He said, "You are my servant.
I'll use you to show how great I
am."*

*"Can a mother forget her baby?
Can she stop being kind to her
own baby?
Even if a mother might forget,
I won't forget you," said God.
"See? I drew your picture on the
inside of my hands.
I always see you."*
Isaiah 49:1, 3, 15-16

There was once a man who was a
good singer. He played guitar, too.
He was going to stand up in front of
a lot of people and sing his songs.
But he was afraid he wouldn't
remember what songs to sing. So he
wrote the names of the songs on his
hand. That way, he could look at
them and remember what to sing.

You are so special to God! It's as
if he has written your name on his

hand. So he remembers you.
Always. Jesus talked about people
who follow him. He said, "Nobody
can take them out of my hand.
That's because my Father gave them
to me. He is greater than anyone or
anything (John 10:28-29). That
means no one can take you away
from God. And no one can take
God away from you.

*"Dear Father God, you are the greatest.
Thank you for taking care of me. Thank
you that no one can take you away
from me. And no one can take me away
from you."*

FRIDAY

Read "A Quiet Life," page 669 in
God's Story. Or read this part of the
story:

Try to live a quiet life.
Mind your own business. Work
with your hands. . . .

What if someone dies? Then
don't be sad like people who
don't have any hope. Here's what
we believe. Jesus died and came
back to life again. So God will
bring people back to life again
too. They'll get to be with Jesus.

What if we're still alive when Jesus comes back? . . .

Jesus will come down from heaven. The angel in charge will shout with a loud voice. He will tell us what to do. God's horn will call us. Jesus' followers who died will go up first. Then people who are alive will go up with them. We'll go up in the clouds. We'll meet Jesus in the air. Then we'll live with Jesus forever. *1 Thessalonians 4:11-17*

The football teams had been playing. But now the half-time show was starting. The people who had been watching the game began talking. A band marched out onto the football field. Then the horns began to play. *Ta-da!* Everybody looked. The sound was so loud and bright and wonderful! The horns seemed to be saying, "Look, everybody!"

What do you think it will be like when Jesus comes back? The angel in charge will shout! A horn will blow! "Look, everybody!" And everybody will look! Then Jesus will take us to be with God forever.

God's love for us is deep and strong. Nothing can take his love away from us. Not now. Not ever. God loves us so much that one day he will take us to live with him. God is with us now. And God will be with us forever! Praise God!

"Dear God, thank you for your love. Thank you for being with me now and forever!"

New Every Day

If anyone follows Jesus, he has been made new. The old is gone. The new is here! *2 Corinthians 5:17*

MONDAY

Read "Our Tent," page 696 in *God's Story*. Or read this part of the story:

Our bodies are like tents we live in on earth. What if a body dies? Then we have a house in heaven. It's built by God, not by people. Until we get it, we think about it. We want very much to have our heavenly tent.

It's not that we want to get rid of this body. We'll trade our dying bodies for bodies that live forever.

We don't look at people the way the world does. If anyone follows Jesus, he has been made new. The old is gone. The new is here!

God brought us to himself through Jesus. Our job is to bring people to God. *2 Corinthians 5:1-2, 4, 16-18*

Way back in the corner of the refrigerator sits an old orange. It has been sitting there for a long time. Now it's not orange anymore. It's green! And it's fuzzy! It's moldy. Yuck!

Things on this earth get old and worn out and broken. But in God's kingdom, things become new. God even makes you and me new. When we choose to follow Jesus, we say good-bye to sin. Now we want to obey Jesus. We want to live the way Jesus wants us to live. Instead of wanting more and more things for ourselves, we want to share. Instead of saying bad things, we say good things. The old part of us is gone. The new part of us is here. It's like being born again! Happy birthday to the new me!

"Dear God, I want to follow your Son, Jesus. I want to obey you. I say good-bye to my old self. Make me new! Thank you!"

TUESDAY

Read "Into the Water," page 706 in *God's Story*. Or read this part of the story:

Being baptized is like going into the grave with Jesus. We go into the water. Then we come out again. We can live a new life. It's just like Jesus did when he came back to life again.

We were dipped in water. So we shared Jesus' "grave." Our old self died with him. Now sin is gone from us.

Sin doesn't control Jesus. When he died, the power of sin died. He is alive now, living for God. You're like that too. You're dead to the power of sin. Now you live for God.

The pay for sin is death. But God gives us a gift. It's life that lasts forever. It comes to us because of Jesus.
Romans 6:3-6, 9-11, 23

When Jesus died, his body was put into a grave. But he came back to life. His body came out of the grave. Now he will live forever.

We get to do something very special to show that we choose to follow Jesus. We get to be baptized. Just like Jesus' body was put into the grave, we can let our bodies be put into water. We can be dipped into water for just a few seconds. It's like putting our old selves into the grave. Then we come back up out of the water. It's like coming back to life. We are new!

Now, even if our bodies die someday, our spirits will keep living. And even our bodies will come back to life when Jesus comes again. We will live forever with God and his Son, Jesus!

"Dear Father God, thank you for making a way for us to live forever. Thank you that we can leave our old selves behind. Thank you that we can have a new self that loves and obeys you."

SOME THINGS YOU CAN DO THIS WEEK

☐ **Grow a small bean plant.** Fold a paper towel and put it around the inside of a clear plastic cup or jar. Put some dried beans between the cup and the paper towel. Put a little water on the paper towel. Make it wet around the spot where the beans are. But don't fill the cup with water. Keep the towel wet each day and watch the plant grow. The old part of the beans is left behind. The new part grows.

☐ **Make a growth chart.** Use adding-machine tape. Or cut typing paper into pieces that are two and one-half inches wide. Tape the pieces of paper together end-to-end until it's taller than you are. Stand or lie next to it, and mark how tall you are. Use a ruler or yardstick to measure how many inches that is. Think about growing up in Jesus. Think about saying good-bye to your old self and becoming new by following Jesus.

☐ **"Baptize" the dishes.** The word *baptize* means "dip" or "soak." Help your mom or dad wash the dishes. Fill the sink with soap and water. "Baptize" the dishes in it. Then rub them with a dish cloth. Rinse them off and dry them. Think about a person who hasn't given his life to Jesus. For that person, being baptized is no different from taking a bath. Just like the dishes. *(See Tuesday's reading.)*

☐ **Hide a surprise for someone.** Draw a map, or give hints about where to find the surprise. Then the person who finds the surprise can hide a surprise for you. Think about how God's kingdom is like special riches. *(See Thursday's reading.)*

WEDNESDAY

Read "Who Gets into God's Kingdom?" page 679 in *God's Story*. Or read this part of the story:

Sinful people won't get into God's kingdom. Don't be fooled. People who sin with sex won't get into God's kingdom. People who worship idols won't get in. People who rob others won't get in. People who want more and more things won't get in. Drunks won't get in. People who say bad things about others won't get in. People who lie to get money won't get in.

Some of you used to do those things. But your hearts were washed. Your hearts were made clean from sin. It was just as if you'd never sinned. It happened in Jesus' name. It came by God's Spirit. *1 Corinthians 6:9-11*

The food smelled good. It tasted good. People talked and laughed. Matthew was glad. It was his party. He gathered tax money for the king. But Jesus had asked Matthew to be one of his 12 special friends. Now Matthew was having a party to let all

his friends meet Jesus. (Read "A Party at Matthew's," page 525 in *God's Story*—Luke 5:27-35.)

Matthew's friends were not the best people in the world. They had done wrong things. The Jewish leaders wondered why Jesus would eat with those sinners.

"I came to save sinners," said Jesus. Jesus didn't come to the world to blame people for being bad. Jesus came to tell people that God loved them and would save them from their sins (John 3:17). Sinners can say good-bye to their old selves and be new again. They can follow Jesus and live with God forever!

"Dear Father God, thank you for loving us even when we've done wrong. Thank you for making us new!"

THURSDAY

Read "Seeds, Yeast, Pearls, and Nets," page 549 in *God's Story*. Or read this part of the story:

"God's kingdom is like a mustard seed," said Jesus. "A man took the seed and planted it. Now the mustard seed is the smallest seed of all. But it grows into the biggest plant in the garden. It becomes a tree. The birds fly to it. They sit in its branches.

"God's kingdom is like riches in a field," said Jesus. "The riches were hidden under the ground. A man who was digging found them. He covered them up again. He was very glad to find the riches. So he sold everything he owned to buy that field.

"God's kingdom is like a man shopping for fine pearls. One day, he found a very special pearl. There was no other pearl like it in the world. It was the best. It cost a lot of money. So the man sold everything he owned. He bought the pearl."
Matthew 13:31-32, 44-46

What is a kingdom? A kingdom is wherever the king rules. God rules his kingdom. His kingdom is a heavenly kingdom. But we can be in his kingdom, even though we live on earth right now.

God's kingdom is like riches hidden in the field. It's like the pearl that cost a lot of money. The man who found the hidden riches gave up all he had to buy them. The man who found the pearl gave up everything too. Do we have to give up anything to be in God's kingdom? Yes! We have to give up our sins.

Some sins feel good for a while, even though all sins end up hurting someone. But when we see how wonderful God's kingdom is, we give up our sins. We say good-bye to a life of sin. That's our old life. We get to have a new, sinless life with God. He is our king.

"Dear God, I am glad to give up my sins for you. Thank you for letting me live in your wonderful kingdom."

FRIDAY

Read "A Letter from Jesus," page 695 in *God's Story*. Or read this part of the story:

You are like a letter that tells how we've helped you. Everybody knows you. Seeing you is like reading a letter from Jesus. This letter wasn't written with ink. It was written with God's living Spirit.

God's Spirit will never fade away. He will shine even brighter.

We aren't like Moses. His face was shining. He covered it until the brightness wore off. But our faces are not covered. So we share the Lord's shining greatness. We are being changed. We are becoming like him. He shines brighter and brighter in us every day. This is a gift from the Lord. He is the Spirit. *2 Corinthians 3:2-3, 11, 13, 18*

Your old T-shirts go into the box. They don't fit anymore. Your old jeans go into the box. They are too small. Your old socks and shoes have to be put away. You can tell that your body is growing.

How can you tell that your spirit is growing? You put your sins away. You leave your old, sinful self behind. You are new because you belong to Jesus. You become more and more like Jesus every day. You show what Jesus is like by what you do and say.

Do you ever grow too big for Jesus, or too old for Jesus? You can never be too old to have Jesus for a friend. Your body may grow older, but your spirit can be made new every day (see 2 Corinthians 4:16).

"Dear Father God, help me to put away my old sins. Help me to become more and more like Jesus. Thank you for making me new every day."

The Fruit of God's Spirit Is Love

You can be like a good tree growing good fruit. Loving.
Galatians 5:22

MONDAY

Read "Spirits," page 794 in *God's Story*. Or read this part of the story:

Let's love each other. Love comes from God. People who love have been born into God's family. They know God. People who don't love don't know God. That's because God is love.

Here's how God showed us his love. He sent his only Son to the world. He did it so we could live. That's love. It's not that we loved God. It's that he loved us. So he sent his Son as a gift. He sent Jesus to die for our sins.

God loved us that much! So we should love each other.

God loved us first. So we love others. People might say that they love God. But what if they hate somebody? Then they're lying. They don't love someone they can see. So how can they love God when they can't see him? We have this rule from God: If we love him, we have to love his people, too.

1 John 4:7-11, 19-21

Granny has a big garden. She has grape vines and apple trees and blackberry bushes. In winter, branches on the fruit plants look bare and dead. But when spring comes, something happens deep inside the plant. Sap starts moving up into the trunks and branches. Sap looks like thick water inside the plant. It helps the plant to live. So buds begin to show on the branches. Soon there are leaves. Then tiny flowers. And later in the summer, there is yummy fruit to eat!

God loves us. His love for us is like sap coming into us and filling us up. When his love fills us up, then it's as if we grow fruit. Not fruit like grapes and apples and blackberries. It's a special fruit. It's a fruit from God's Spirit. It's called love. How does this fruit show? It shows in how we treat other people. God first loved us, so we love other people.

"Dear God, thank you for loving me. Fill me up with your love. And make love grow in me just like fruit on a tree!"

TUESDAY

Read "The First Days of King Solomon," page 222 in *God's Story*. Or read this part of the story:

One day two women came to King Solomon. One said, "We live in the same house. I had a baby there. Three days later, this other woman had a baby. We were all by ourselves in the house. In the night, she rolled on top of her baby, and he died. So she took my baby while I was sleeping. She put her dead baby by me. . . .

"No!" said the other woman. "The one that's alive is my baby! The dead baby is hers." . . .

Then the king asked for a long blade. . . . "Cut the baby in half," said King Solomon. "Each woman can have half."

The real mother loved her baby. She cried out, "Please don't kill the baby! Give him to the other woman."

"Cut him in half!" said the other woman. "I won't have him, and you won't have him."

"Don't kill the baby," said Solomon. "Give the baby to the first woman. She wants him to live. She is his mother."
1 Kings 3:16-27

Did you ever see a new baby? When a baby is first born, it's not very cute. Its skin may look a little baggy. Its face may frown. It cries a lot. But the baby's mom and dad love it very much. Why? They love it because it belongs to them. It is their very own baby. They love it no matter what it looks like.

The mother in the story loved her baby. She loved it so much, she would do anything to save it. God loves us that much. We may not be the cutest or the smartest. We don't even act nice all the time. But God loves us so much, he sent his Son to die to save us from sin. Now he wants us to treat others with love. Even if they are not the cutest or smartest or nicest. He wants us to love them because we know God made them and loves them.

"Dear Father God, thank you for making me and loving me. Help me to love others because you love me."

SOME THINGS YOU CAN DO THIS WEEK

☐ **Start a "fruit of the Spirit" mobile.** On white paper, draw and color a fruit of some kind. Write *love* on it. (You can read more about the Spirit's fruit in "A Good Tree Growing Good Fruit," page 661 in *God's Story*—Galatians 5.) Make a hole in the top of the paper fruit. Tie a string through it, and hang it on a clothes hanger. Hang it somewhere in your room. Start learning Galatians 5:22, this week's memory verse.

☐ **Act out the story of Jesus and the man with the skin sickness.** Put baby powder on your arms to make pretend skin sickness. Don't rub the powder in until Jesus heals you. *(See Wednesday's reading.)*

☐ **Make "hugging arms."** Tape the ends of typing paper together to make one long piece of paper. Lay one arm down on the paper, and ask a friend to trace around it. Do the same with the other arm on another piece of paper. Color these and cut them out. Draw a face on another piece of paper or on a paper plate. Use a pillow for the body, and pin the arms and the head onto the pillow with safety pins. Talk about different ways you use arms to show love.

☐ **Make a fruit salad.** Get different kinds of fruit that your family likes. Ask an adult to help cut the fruit into pieces. Mix the fruit pieces in a big bowl. Serve and eat. Talk about what the "fruit of the Spirit" is.

☐ **Plant some orange or grapefruit seeds.** Fill a pot with dirt or potting soil. Plant some of the seeds. Keep the dirt wet, but not soggy. Let the pot sit in a sunny place. Think about the kind of "fruit" that God grows in you.

WEDNESDAY

Read "Many Sick People" and "People from Everywhere," page 523 in *God's Story*. Or read this part of the second story:

People kept bringing sick friends and family to Jesus. Some people were hurting very badly. Some had bad spirits in control of them. Some people couldn't move. Jesus made them well.

One day a man with a skin sickness came to Jesus. "You can make me well if you want to," he said.

Jesus felt kind and caring toward this man. So Jesus touched him. "I do want to," said Jesus. "Be well."

Right away the sickness went away. The man was well.
Mark 1:32-34, 40-42

Sometimes when people are sick, they get fussy. And anyone who is near them could catch the sickness too. So it takes a lot of love to care for a sick person. Think about the people who take care of you when you are sick. Do they bring you special food and drinks? Do they put your pillows and covers around you so you feel better? They must love you very much.

In Bible times, a skin sickness could be very bad. Anyone who got this sickness had to stay away from people. That's because it was easy for other people to get this sickness. If you touched the sick person, people would say you were not clean. You would have to stay away from people for a while. Jesus knew that. But he touched the sick man anyway. Jesus loved all people. Even the sick ones.

How can you show your love for someone who is sick?

"Dear Father God, thank you for loving all people. Help me to love and help people, even the ones who are sick."

THURSDAY

Read "A Camel and a Needle," page 591 in *God's Story*. Or read this part of the story:

People started bringing little children to Jesus. They wanted Jesus to touch them and pray for them. But Jesus' friends got mad at the people.

Jesus saw this, and he was upset. He said, "Let the little children come to me. Don't stop them. God's kingdom belongs to those who are like these children.

"People must welcome God's kingdom like a child does," said Jesus. "If they don't, they won't get to go into it."

Then Jesus picked up the children. He held them in his arms. He touched them. He prayed that God would bring good things to them.
Mark 10:13-16

Do you have a little brother or sister? Do your friends have little brothers or sisters? Do they bother you sometimes? Little children can't sit still for very long. There are a lot of things they don't understand. Sometimes you have to tell them things over and over again. That's because they are so little.

Jesus loved children of all ages. He loves you. And he loves little brothers and sisters. Jesus said, "Let the little children come to me." They were not a bother to him. He wanted to take time to be with them. When you show kind love to little children, you are being like Jesus. You can take some time to be with little children, just like Jesus did. When you love little children, you may find yourself loved back!

"Dear God, thank you for loving me. Thank you for loving children. Help me to love little children like Jesus did."

FRIDAY

Read "The Vine," page 612 in *God's Story.* Or read this part of the story:

"I'm like a vine," said Jesus. "You are like the

branches. My Father is the one who takes care of the garden. He cuts off the branches that don't grow fruit. He trims the branches that do grow fruit. That way they will grow even more fruit.

"You can't do anything without me," said Jesus. "So what happens if you don't stay in me? You're like a broken branch. It dries up and gets thrown away. Then it gets burned up in the fire.

"Stay in me, and let my words stay in you. If you do that, you can ask for anything you want. And it will be given to you.

"Be like a branch that grows a lot of fruit. Show everyone that you are my followers. Then people will see what my Father is like. They will see how great my Father is." *John 15:1-2, 5-8*

Think of an apple tree. Where does the fruit grow? It grows out on the branches. It's the same way with a grape vine. The vine grows out of the ground, fat and twisty. Then branches come out. Grapes grow on the branches. Think about what would happen if you broke a branch off of the vine. Could it make grapes by itself? No. It has to stay on the vine if it's going to make fruit.

Jesus said he is like a vine. We are like branches. What is our fruit? Love is one. Joy is another. But can the fruit of the Spirit grow in us if we are not with Jesus? No. That would be like taking the branch away from the vine. Stay with Jesus. Love him. Follow and obey him. If you do, God promises that you will grow lots of his Spirit's special fruit!

"Dear God, thank you for your Son, Jesus. Thank you that he helps me grow loving and joyful. Grow all of your Spirit's fruit in me!"

The Fruit of God's Spirit Is Joy

You can be like a good tree growing good fruit. Loving. Showing joy. *Galatians 5:22*

MONDAY

 Read "Chased by the Army!" page 60 in *God's Story*. Or read this part of the story:

Then God's people walked across the sea on dry land. A wall of water stood on their right. A wall of water stood on their left.

Morning was coming. The sun was just starting to come up. Moses held his hand out over the sea. The water flowed back into place.

The army of Egypt tried to run away from the water. But God trapped them in the sea.

Moses and God's people sang this song to God.

"I will sing to God.
He is great!
He threw the horse and its rider
into the sea."

Moses' sister Miriam picked up a tambourine. She led the women. They played tambourines, and they danced. Miriam sang this song.

"Sing to God.
Tell how great he is.
He threw the horse and its rider
into the sea!"
Exodus 14:22, 27; 15:1, 20-21

What do you think it would have been like to cross the Red Sea with God's people? What would you have seen? What would you have heard? How would you have felt to see the enemy army coming after you? When God got rid of the enemy army, God's people were full of joy. They had been saved!

Satan and sin are our enemies. But God has saved us from our enemies. He sent Jesus. Jesus took the blame for all our sins. So he was killed as if he were a killer or a robber. Our enemy may have thought that he got rid of Jesus. But Jesus came back to life! Now we can always live with joy deep in our hearts. That's because no matter how bad things look, we know one thing. We get to live forever with Jesus! We have been saved!

How did Moses and Miriam show their joy? How do you show your joy?

"Dear God, thank you for saving me. Thank you for putting joy in my heart."

TUESDAY

Read "Reading from Morning until Noon," page 495 in *God's Story*. Or read this part of the story:

Then the people got together in front of the Water Gate. They told Ezra to bring out Moses' Law Book. It had God's laws for his people in it. So Ezra brought it out. He read it out loud. He read it from early morning until noon.

Then men from the family of Levi taught the people. They made the Law Book clear. They told the people what it meant.

All the people had been crying while they listened. But Nehemiah and Ezra talked to the people. "This is a special day to God. Don't cry," they said. . . . "God's joy makes you strong."

So the people . . . had a joyful holiday. That's because they understood the words of the Law Book. *Nehemiah 8:1-3, 7-10, 12*

Have you ever felt sad? When you are sad, your shoulders sag. You feel weak. You don't feel like doing much of anything. But when you feel joy, your whole body feels better. You feel stronger. You feel like doing something. Joy makes you strong.

But here is a mystery. We can have joy even if we are sad. How? Joy is different than just being happy. Joy is a feeling that we have deep down inside. It's knowing that God will make everything turn out for our good. That means we're looking to see the good that God will do.

And deep down inside of ourselves, we feel a joy from God's Spirit. It's a joy that nobody can take away.

How do you get that kind of joy? It grows inside you when you let Jesus be in control of your life.

"Dear Father God, I want Jesus to be in control of my life. Fill me with the joy of your Spirit, which nobody can take away."

SOME THINGS YOU CAN DO THIS WEEK

☐ **Make shakers.** Clean some empty soda-pop cans. Put a little bit of dried rice in one. Put a few dried beans in another. Put a little salt in a third one. Cover the opening of each can with tape. Shake the cans to hear the different sounds. Try other things in more cans. Shake them when you sing worship songs. Think of how Miriam worshiped God. *(See Monday's reading.)*

☐ **Add to your fruit mobile.** Draw another fruit on paper and color it. Cut it out and print the word *joy* on it. Hang it on the mobile that you started making last week. Say Galatians 5:22, and add the part about joy.

☐ **Write your own song of joy.** First write a letter to God, telling him that you are full of joy. Write why you are full of joy. Then look at the letter and begin singing the words. God doesn't mind if it doesn't sound just right. He loves to hear your own song of joy! If this is hard to do, sing to the tune of "Row, Row, Row Your Boat." Use the words, "Father, Father God, I am full of joy. You have given me (fill in the blank—your love, your care, good friends, and so on). Now I'm full of joy!"

☐ **Make a wall hanging** with alphabet-shaped cereal. Glue onto a paper plate letters that spell the fruit of the Spirit. Spray the plate with spray paint. Hang it on your wall.

☐ **Play J-O-Y.** Use a basketball and basket. Or use another ball and a box. Take turns with friends trying to throw the ball into the basket or box. If you make the basket (or box), you earn one letter in the word *joy*. The person who spells *joy* first wins.

WEDNESDAY

Read "The Ark Comes Back," page 162 in *God's Story*. Or read this part of the story:

So the priests put poles through the rings in the Ark. Then they carried the Ark with the poles on their shoulders. That's the way Moses had told them to carry it.

David told some of the people to be singers. He told them to sing happy songs. There was shouting. There was music from horns and cymbals and harps. . . . King David was jumping and dancing.

Then David talked to the priests who led the music. He told them to thank God with this song.

Give thanks to God.
Call his name.
Tell the nations what he has done.
Sing praise to him.
Tell about the wonderful things he
    has done.
Enjoy his name. It's the best.
Let people who trust God show their
    joy.
1 Chronicles 15:15-16, 28-29; 16:7-10

God's ark box was made of wood. It had gold all over it, inside and out. It was kept in the worship tent. Moses would go into the tent and meet with God at the ark box. So this box was very special to God's people. It was a sign that God was with them. But the enemy had taken the ark box. And it had been gone a long time. Now David was bringing it back to Jerusalem. All of God's people were full of joy! How was David showing his joy?

What gives you joy? Somebody once said that you can find true joy by looking at the letters in the word *joy*. The *j* means Jesus. The *o* means others. The *y* means yourself. If you want to find true joy, put Jesus first. Put others second. Put yourself last. How can you do that? Try it and see!

"Dear God, I want to have true joy. Help me to put your Son, Jesus, first. Then I'll put others second and myself last."

THURSDAY

Read "A Colt," page 596 in *God's Story.* Or read this part of the story:

Jesus' friends took the colt to Jesus. They put their coats on the little donkey's back. Then Jesus got on it. Off they went, down the road. . . .

Lots of people were in Jerusalem for the Pass Over holiday. They heard that Jesus was on his way to Jerusalem. So they got big branches from palm trees. Then they went to meet Jesus.

"God save us!" the people shouted. "May good things come to the King of God's

people! May good things come! He is coming in the Lord's name!" They began to follow him. *Matthew 21:7-9*

The Romans could be very mean. They ruled over God's people. These people wished they could be free. They wished they had their own king. And they knew that God had promised to send a king to them. They had heard about Jesus. He did wonderful things. He was a great teacher. Now he was coming to Jerusalem. They thought that he would be their king. So they were full of joy. They cheered for Jesus.

Jesus really is the King. But his kingdom is not a kingdom on earth. It's a heavenly kingdom. People all over the world can be in it. You can be in it too. Just believe in Jesus and ask him to be your King. That's easy, isn't it?

Jesus gives some wonderful gifts to the people in his kingdom. Joy is one of his gifts. The people who cheered for an earthly king may have thought they felt joy. But they didn't feel as much joy as people who cheer for a heavenly King! How do you show your joy for having a heavenly King?

"Dear Father God, I believe in Jesus. I want him to be my King! Fill me with the joy that comes from heaven."

FRIDAY

Read "A New Heaven and a New Earth," page 822 in *God's Story*. Or read this part of the story:

Then I saw a new heaven. I saw a new earth. . . . I also saw the Holy City. It was a new Jerusalem. It was coming down from heaven. It was like a bride with beautiful clothes on.

A loud voice came from where the King was. "Now God will live with people. . . . God will wipe all their tears away. They won't die anymore. They won't cry anymore. They won't hurt anymore. The old way of doing things is gone."

. . . The city doesn't need the sun or moon. God's greatness shines so bright, it lights up the city. Jesus is the city's lamp.

Nothing dirty or sinful will ever get into the city.
Revelation 21:1-4, 23, 27

The waiting room at the airport was crowded. Lots of people were looking out the big windows. They were watching for the jet to come to the gate. One person was holding some roses. Another person was holding a bunch of balloons. They were talking and laughing. At last the plane came to the gate. People began to get off the plane. Fat people and thin people came out. Tall people and short people came out.

Then a man and his wife came out. She was holding a baby. All at once, lots of people shouted, "Welcome home!" Someone handed them roses. Another person handed them balloons. Somebody else took pictures. They were full of joy. They were having a party right there at the airport!

Heaven will be full of joy. When

you get there, Jesus will say, "Welcome home!" And we will all have a great party! God says we can't even imagine the great things he has planned for us. So just think of the joy we can have now! We can have joy because God has great and wonderful plans for us.

"Dear God, thank you for planning wonderful things for me. I am full of joy because you love me so much!"

The Fruit of God's Spirit Is Peace

You can be like a good tree growing good fruit. Loving. Showing joy. Having peace. *Galatians 5:22*

MONDAY

Read "Peace from God," page 350 in *God's Story*. Or read this part of the story:

You'll keep giving peace to people who keep thinking about you.
They trust you.
Trust in God forever.
God the Lord is like a Rock.
He is strong, and he lasts forever.

My soul wants you in the night.
My spirit wants you in the morning.

God, you give us peace.
Isaiah 26:3-4, 9, 12

What is peace? Peace is a quiet feeling. It's being free from worry and fear.

Did you ever watch water boil? It jumps up and down and all around, faster and faster. It doesn't sit still or rest. Did you ever feel that way inside yourself? That's how it feels when you are angry or worried or afraid. Your body may be sitting still. But inside it feels like everything is jumping up and down and all around, faster and faster.

But peace is a quiet, still feeling. Your mind and spirit are resting, even if your body is moving. We get this peace by following God and trusting him. Why? Because then we know he makes everything turn out for our good!

"Dear God, thank you for making everything turn out for my good. Thank you for your still, quiet peace inside me."

Then the wind died down. Everything became still.
Mark 4:37-39

TUESDAY

Read "The Storm," page 550 in *God's Story*. Or read this part of the story:

A roaring storm blew in. Waves crashed over the boat. Water almost filled it. All this time, Jesus was in the back of the boat. He was sleeping on a pillow.

Jesus' special friends woke him up. "We're about to die in this water! Don't you even care?" they asked.

Jesus got up. He spoke firmly to the wind. He spoke firmly to the waves. He said, "Be quiet. Be still."

It was the middle of a hot summer afternoon in Texas. The sky grew dark. Wind began to blow hard. Rain started pounding on the roof of the house. Little round bits of icy hail tapped against the windows. Two little girls sat side by side on the bed, looking out the window. They were a little bit scared. But it was kind of fun, too. They knew they were safe indoors.

Did you ever feel like a storm was going on inside you? People sometimes feel like that when they are angry or worried or afraid.

Jesus told the storm, "Be quiet. Be still." And the storm stopped. Peace inside us comes from God's

Spirit in us. We can remember about peace when we start to be angry or worried or afraid. We can say, "Be quiet. Be still." And we can trust Jesus to help us and give us peace.

"Dear Father God, thank you for peace. Help me to trust Jesus so I can have peace when I'm angry or worried or afraid."

WEDNESDAY

Read "Choosing the Next King," page 137 in *God's Story*. Or read this part of the story:

Samuel put oil on David's head. Then God's Spirit came upon David. God's Spirit gave David power.

But God's Spirit had left Saul. A bad spirit had come on Saul instead.

Saul's servants told him, "A bad spirit bothers you. Why don't you get somebody who plays the harp? He can play when the bad spirit bothers you. Then you'll feel better."

So Saul sent a message to Jesse. "Send David here."

David played his harp when the bad spirit bothered Saul. Then Saul would feel better. The bad spirit would leave.
1 Samuel 16:13-16, 19, 23

King Saul felt stormy inside himself. He felt worried and upset. So he needed to hear David's music. It gave him a feeling of peace.

Did you ever listen to peaceful music? Sometimes peaceful music helps us settle down. It gives us a feeling of peace and quiet and rest. But what if we don't trust God? Then our stormy feelings come back when the music stops. The only way we can get real peace that lasts is to trust God. Then God's Spirit gives us peace inside ourselves.

"Dear God, thank you for music and other things that help me feel peaceful. But thank you most of all for giving me your Spirit. Thank you for the peace your Spirit gives me."

THURSDAY

Read "Birds' Food and Flowers' Clothes," page 534 in *God's Story*. Or read this part of the story:

"See the birds in the air?" said Jesus. "They don't

plant food. They don't bring in crops. They don't save food in barns. God your Father feeds them. You're more important than birds. Can anybody make his life last an hour longer by worrying?

"Why worry about clothes?" said Jesus. "Look at the flowers in the field. They don't work. They don't make their own clothes. King Solomon had beautiful clothes. But his clothes weren't as wonderful as one of these flowers. That's the way God dresses the grass in the fields. The grass is here today and gone tomorrow. So God will give you clothes too, won't he?

Put God first in your life. Then he will make sure you have everything you need.
Matthew 6:26-30, 33

What's for dinner? Bugs. Yummy! A dinner fit for a king! A kingbird, that is! What is there to wear today? Green leaves and pink flowers.

SOME THINGS YOU CAN DO THIS WEEK

☐ **Add another paper fruit** to your mobile. Color and cut out another fruit. Print *peace* on it. Hang it on your mobile. Try saying Galatians 5:22, adding the part about peace.

☐ **Make a peace painting.** Play a tape of peaceful music. While you listen, paint with watercolor paints. Paint a peaceful picture. Think about how God gives you peace.

☐ **Make a pillowcase.** Get an old sheet or other piece of cloth. Cut it into a piece 42 inches by 31 inches. Fold the long side in half so that the piece is 21 inches by 31 inches. Now ask an adult to show you how to sew up the bottom and one short side. You can color the pillowcase with cloth markers if you want. Think about peace and peaceful sleep.

☐ **Play "Stop!"** At dinner time, agree with friends or family that when anyone says, "Stop," everyone will stop. No one will move until the same person says, "Go." Watch to see how funny people look when they stop. Remember how Jesus stopped the wind and waves. *(See Tuesday's reading.)*

☐ **Take a hike** around your neighborhood or in a park. Be sure to look at the birds and flowers. Remember what Jesus said when he talked about birds and flowers. *(See Thursday's reading.)*

Beautiful! If you are a rose or a dogwood flower.

Most people go all day long without thinking about kingbirds or dogwood flowers. But God makes sure the birds and flowers are taken care of. He makes them, and he cares about them. Jesus said that if God cares about birds and flowers, he cares about you. So don't worry. God will give you what you need.

If you are worried or angry or afraid, it sometimes helps to look at what God has made. Take some time to look at the flowers and watch the birds. It may help you to remember that God knows how you feel. He is taking care of you. And he can give you the peace you need.

"Dear Father God, you take care of birds and flowers. So I know you'll take care of me. Help me remember to trust you. Give me the peace that comes from your Spirit."

FRIDAY

 Read "Where Are You Going?" page 610 in *God's Story*. Or read this part of the story:

Jesus said, "Now God is going to show his greatness in

me. I'll be here just a little longer. You'll look for me. But you can't come to the place where I'm going.

"Don't worry," said Jesus to his friends. "Trust me. Trust God. There are many rooms in my Father's house. I wouldn't say that unless it was true. I'm going there to get a place ready for you."

Then Jesus said, "I won't leave you by yourselves. My Father will send the Holy Spirit in my name. He will help you," said Jesus. "He will teach you everything. He will help you remember everything I've told you.

"I'm giving you my peace," said Jesus. "Don't worry. Don't be afraid."
John 13:31, 33; 14:1-2, 18, 26-27

Jesus told his friends that he was going away for a while. That gave them something to worry about. But then Jesus told them not to worry and not to be afraid. He said he was giving them his peace.

Jesus knew what was going to happen. And he knew his friends didn't understand. They didn't understand that he would really come back to life after he died. Jesus knew that after he died, his friends would worry. They would be afraid. They would be upset. But Jesus also knew that they didn't have to be afraid or worried or upset. Instead, they could choose to trust him. After all, he knew something they didn't. He knew he'd be alive again very soon.

Jesus knows a lot of things we don't know. When we have troubles and problems, Jesus knows what's going to happen. He knows God will make it turn out to be good for us. So we can choose. We can choose not to trust God. Then we can have worry and fear and anger. Or we can choose to trust God. Then we can have his peace. Which will you choose?

"Dear God, thank you for all the ways you take care of me. I choose to trust you. Please give me your peace."

The Fruit of God's Spirit Is Patience *(PAY-shunce)*

You can be like a good tree growing good fruit. Loving. Showing joy. Having peace. Waiting quietly. *Galatians 5:22*

MONDAY

 Read "A Time for Everything," page 262 in *God's Story*. Or read this part of the story:

There's a time for everything. . . .
A time to be born, and a time to die. . . .
A time to cry, and a time to laugh. . . .
A time to hug, and a time not to hug.
A time to hunt, and a time to give up the hunt.
A time to keep things, and a time to throw things away.
A time to tear, and a time to mend.
A time to be quiet, and a time to talk. . . .

I saw what God did. He made everything beautiful in its own time. He lets us think about things that last forever. Even then, we can't know the beginning or the end.

I know the best thing we can do. We'll be happy as long as we can. *Ecclesiastes 3:1-12*

What is patience? It's waiting quietly, waiting without fussing.

Some things can happen very fast. If you want popcorn, you can put a bag of popcorn in the microwave oven. You push a button. In four minutes, you have hot popcorn.

Some things take a little longer.

What if you're hungry, but Mom says to wait until dinner time to eat? You may have to wait longer than you want to. But it still won't be too long.

Other things take a long time. You might say, "I can't wait for Christmas to come!" But it will take a long time for Christmas to come. Fussing won't make it come any faster.

God says that his Spirit will help us grow to be patient. We will wait quietly. And we will wait without fussing.

"Dear God, it's hard to wait sometimes. Help me to wait quietly. Help me to wait without fussing."

TUESDAY

Read "Nets Full of Fish," page 522 in *God's Story.* Or read this part of the story:

Jesus asked Peter to row out on the lake. They went just a little way from the shore. Then Jesus sat down in the boat. He began to teach the people.

When Jesus finished talking, he turned to Peter. "Take the boat into the deep water now," he said. "Then put your nets out. We can catch some fish."

"We fished all night," said Peter. "It was hard work, and we didn't catch anything. But if you say so, I'll put the nets out."

The men threw out their nets. Right away, hundreds of fish swam into the nets. The nets got heavy with all the fish. The nets began to break.

James and John brought the other boat to help. . . . The men were very surprised to see all the fish. *Luke 5:3-7, 9-10*

Did you ever go fishing? People who go fishing have to be very patient. They have to wait and wait for the fish to bite on the hook. Sometimes the people leave the lake or river without catching any fish at all. That's almost what happened to

Jesus' friends. They waited and waited. They waited all night, trying to catch some fish.

Sometimes it seems like we just can't wait. Something inside us wants to fuss about how long things are taking. But that doesn't make us feel any better. God knows how to help us be patient. He has given us his Spirit to live inside us and help us. What are some things God can help you wait for?

"Dear God, thank you for giving me your Spirit to help me be patient. Please help me wait without fussing."

WEDNESDAY

Read "Working for a Wife," page 26 in *God's Story*. Or read this part of the story:

Now Laban had two daughters. Jacob loved Rachel. So he said, "Will you let Rachel marry me? If you will, I'll work seven years for you."

"That's fine," said Laban. "You may stay here and work for me."

Jacob worked for seven years

so he could marry Rachel. But it didn't seem like a long time to Jacob. That's because he loved Rachel so much. *Genesis 29:16, 18-20*

Jacob wanted to marry Rachel. And Rachel wanted to marry Jacob. But they waited seven years before they got married! Seven years is a long time! Jacob must have been very patient! How could he wait that long? He kept busy. He worked. He found lots of things to do.

When we are waiting for something, we have to choose. We can choose not to do anything but wait. Or we can find something else to do while we're waiting. If we do nothing but wait, time seems to pass very slowly. But when we find something else to do, time seems to pass faster. To Jacob, seven years seemed like only a few days.

What do you have to wait for? What can you do while you are waiting?

"Dear Father God, when I have to wait, help me find other things to do. Help me to be patient."

THURSDAY

Read "Locusts and Darkness," page 56 in *God's Story*. Or read this part of the story:

"Go back to the king," God told Moses. "I've made his heart hard. That's so I can show my wonders. Then you can tell your families what I've done. You'll know that I'm the Lord."

So Moses and Aaron went back to the king. They told him that God said these words. "How long will you let yourself be proud? Let my people go worship me. If you don't, I'll send big grasshoppers to your land. There will be so many of these locusts that they'll cover the ground.

Then God sent a wind from the east. It blew over the land all day and night. By the next

SOME THINGS YOU CAN DO THIS WEEK

☐ **Add another fruit to your mobile.** Color and cut out a paper fruit. Write *patience* on it. Hang it from your "fruit of the Spirit" mobile.

☐ **Measure your shadow.** Stand in the sunshine. Ask a friend to use a ruler to measure how long your shadow is. Wait for an hour, and measure it again. Wait still another hour, and measure it once more. People used to measure time by shadows on a sun dial. Think of different things you can do to be patient while you wait.

☐ **Play "Go Fish."** Do you have a game with pictures on cards? Maybe you have cards with animals or flowers that you can match. Give four cards to each player. Put the rest of the cards face down on the table in front of you. To start, ask the player on your left if he has a certain card that matches one of yours. If he does, he gives it to you. If he doesn't, he says, "Go fish." Then you take a card from the stack that is face down. Then it's the turn of the person on your left. Once you match four cards, you lay them down in a pile beside you. Keep going until all cards are matched. The person with the most cards matched wins. Think about how much patience it takes to fish. *(See Tuesday's reading.)*

☐ **Make snow ice.** Mix powdered drink mix, any flavor, in water. Follow the directions on the mix packet. Fill empty ice trays with the drink, and put the trays in the freezer. Wait patiently while the mix freezes. Then pop the icy drink cubes into a blender. Mix them just until they are mushy. Put the snow ice into paper cups and eat it.

morning, there were locusts all over everything.

The king quickly called Moses and Aaron. "Forgive me," he said. "I've done wrong. Pray to God. Ask him to take these locusts away."

So Moses left. He prayed to God. Then God made a strong wind blow from the west. The wind blew the locusts into the Red Sea. There was not one locust left. But the king let his heart get hard again.

Then God told Moses what to do. "Hold your hand up to the sky," said God.

Darkness came. It covered the land for three days.

The king was angry. His heart was hard. *Exodus 10:1-5, 13-14, 16-22, 27*

The king of Egypt kept changing his mind! First he said no. He wouldn't let God's people leave Egypt. Then God made the water turn into blood. So the king said yes. God's people could leave. Then he said no. They couldn't leave. So God sent frogs all over the land. So the king said yes. God's people could leave. Then he said no again. Yes. No. Yes. No. God had sent bugs and flies and boils and hail. Moses had to keep going back and forth, back and forth. Would you have gotten tired of it?

Moses must have been a very patient man. He could have said, "I give up. This king will never let God's people go. I'm going back to watching sheep." But Moses didn't give up. He kept obeying God. He kept going back to the king. At last, the king gave in. He let God's people go. God knew he would. But Moses had to trust God.

Sometimes we have a problem. We ask God to make our problem go away fast. But we have to give God time to work. God works at just the right time. His Spirit helps us to be patient.

"Dear Father God, I will keep doing the good things you tell me to do. I won't give up. I will wait for you to make everything turn out to be good in your own time."

FRIDAY

Read "Sarai Tries to Get a Son," page 12 in *God's Story*. Or read this part of the story:

Abram and Sarai did not have any children. But Sarai had a servant named Hagar. So Sarai told Abram, "Take my servant to be another wife for you. When she has a baby, it can be my baby."

Abram did what Sarai asked. He let Hagar be his wife, too. One day Hagar found out she was going to have a baby. Then Hagar began to hate Sarai.

Sarai was mean to Hagar. So Hagar ran away.

But God's angel found Hagar. The angel . . . said, " Your baby will be a boy. Name him Ishmael, because God has heard how sad you are. Ishmael will be like a wild donkey. He will fight with everyone."

Hagar went back to Sarai. She had a baby boy. Abram named him Ishmael.
Genesis 16:1-4, 6-7, 11-12, 15

Sometimes good things come slowly. God said Abram and Sarai would have a son. Many years passed. Abram and Sarai still had no children. So Sarai tried to work things out herself. But it didn't work. It was Sarai's plan and not God's plan.

Did you ever plant seeds for a garden? After you put the seeds in the dirt, it doesn't look like a garden yet. One day passes. Then two days. Where is the garden? Do you dig up the seeds, pop them open, and try to pull the plant out? No! That's not the way it works! You keep watering the dirt and waiting. When the seed is ready, it will send a green shoot up through the dirt. Slowly it will grow until at last it is full grown.

Sometimes good things come slowly. And God has sent his Spirit to help us be patient. He will help us wait without fussing.

"Dear God, it's hard to be patient. Thank you for your Spirit, who helps me wait without fussing."

WEEK 21

The Fruit of God's Spirit Is Kindness

You can be like a good tree growing good fruit. Loving. Showing joy. Having peace. Waiting quietly. Being kind. *Galatians 5:22*

MONDAY

Read "Saving Wives and Children," page 155 in *God's Story*. Or read this part of the story:

It took David and his men three days to get home. But while they were gone, some enemies had come. They had set fire to the town of Ziklag. They had taken all the women and children away. . . .

David . . . asked God, "Should we go after these enemies? Will we catch them?"

"Go after them," said God. . . .

So David and his 600 men set out. They came to a brook, and 200 men stayed there. They were

too tired to cross. But David and 400 men kept going.

David's men found a man . . . in a field. . . . "I'm from Egypt," he said. ". . . My master left me here because I got sick. We had been out to fight. We set Ziklag on fire."

"Can you take me to your master's army?" asked David. . . .

So the man led David to where the enemy army was. . . .

Then David and his men began to fight the enemy. . . . They kept on fighting until . . . David's men won. . . . David got back everything the enemy army had taken from Ziklag. He got . . . all the people, young and old. . . .

They traveled back to the brook. That's where the 200 tired men waited. . . .

Some of the men with David were mean. They said, "These men didn't go with us. They can have their wives and children back. But we won't share the other things we got."

"God gave these things to us," said David. "So you can't keep them just for yourselves. God . . . helped us win. So those who stayed behind get as much as you do. All of us will share what we got." *1 Samuel 30:1-24*

Did you ever hear anyone say, "It's not fair"? That's what David's men were telling him. They fussed about the men who didn't go to fight. The men who went with David took things from the enemies. These fighting men said that the others shouldn't get anything. But David was thinking about more than just being fair. He was thinking about being kind.

Sharing is one way to be kind. God's Spirit in us helps us to be kind to other people. Who can you share with? What are some other ways to be kind?

"Dear Father God, show me some people who need your kindness. Help me to share."

TUESDAY

Read "An Ax on the Water," page 298 in *God's Story*. Or read this part of the story:

The prophets told Elisha, "Our meeting house is too small. Let's go to the Jordan River to get logs. Then let's build a new meeting place. . . ."

"All right," said Elisha. So he went with them.

They started cutting down trees at the river. But the sharp iron top of one man's ax fell off. It fell into the river. "Oh no!" cried the man. "That's not my ax! It belongs to someone else!"

"Where did it go?" asked Elisha. The man showed Elisha where it fell into the water.

Elisha cut a stick. He threw the stick into the water. It landed where the ax fell in.

Then the heavy iron top of the ax came up. It lay there on top of the water. *2 Kings 6:1-6*

David's friend Joel liked to read. He had a book that he knew David would like. So he let David have the book for a few days. David liked the book. But when it was time to give the book back, David couldn't find it. It would have been bad enough to lose his own book. But this book wasn't even his! That made David even sadder.

David's sister Allie could see that he was sad. She told David she would help him find Joel's book. They looked and looked. At last they found it on the floor in David's closet. David was very happy. Allie was happy too, because she had been kind.

Being kind shows that God's Spirit is working in you. God's Spirit is growing you up to be like Jesus. There are many ways to be kind every day. Elisha was kind. Allie was kind. How can you be kind?

"Dear God, help me to see ways that I can be kind every day. Grow me up to be like your Son, Jesus."

WEDNESDAY

Read "The Man at Beautiful Gate," page 635 in *God's Story*. Or read this part of the story:

Peter and John went to the worship house one afternoon. . . .

Some people came in carrying a man. They were taking him to the gate called Beautiful Gate. It led to the worship house.

This man couldn't walk. So he

sat at the gate every day. People going in the gate could see him. He'd beg for money there.

The man saw Peter and John. . . . He thought they were going to give him some money.

"I don't have any silver or gold," said Peter. "But I do have something else. That's what I'll give you. In Jesus' name, get up and walk."

Then Peter reached out and took the man's right hand. Peter helped the man get up.

Right away, the man's feet got strong. He jumped up and started walking. *Acts 3:1-8*

There was once a boy who was playing in his back yard. He saw something moving in a bush. So he went to take a closer look. There in

SOME THINGS YOU CAN DO THIS WEEK

☐ **Add another fruit to your mobile.** Color and cut out a paper fruit. Write *kindness* on it. Hang it on your mobile. See if you can name all of the fruit of the Spirit on your mobile.

☐ **Bake bread-stick smiles.** Get canned, ready-made bread-stick dough. Lay one bread stick on a baking pan, and shape it to look like a smile. Break two smaller pieces off of another piece of dough. Roll them into balls and put them on the pan to make eyes. Then bake the bread. Can you do something kind to put a smile on a sad person's face?

☐ **Try a three-legged race.** You need three friends to help. Mark a start line and a finish line. Let one friend stand on your right side. Tie your right leg to his left leg. Let your other two friends do the same with each other. Now you have two teams. Race each other to the finish line. Remember the man Peter and John helped at Beautiful Gate. *(See Wednesday's reading.)*

☐ **Catch an insect.** Be careful with it. Look at it under a magnifying glass. Draw a picture of it. Then be kind to it and let it go. Think of other ways to be kind to animals.

☐ **Make nut-shell boats.** Get peanuts or walnuts in shells. Break them in half, and take the nuts out. Let the shells be boats in your bathtub or sink. Make a storm in the water. See if your boats float or sink. Remember how the people on the island were kind to Paul and his friends. *(See Friday's reading.)*

the bush was a bird. It was trapped. Somehow it had gotten its feet twisted up in some thread. The bird kept flapping its wings, trying to get free. But the thread only pulled tighter and tighter around its feet.

The boy ran to get his mother. His mother put on work gloves. She got some scissors. Holding the bird carefully in one hand, she cut the thread here and there. At last the bird's feet were free. It hopped across the yard and then flew away. It was free because the boy and his mother had been kind.

Kindness is being interested in what's good for someone else. Peter and John were kind. The boy and his mother were kind. How can you be kind?

"Dear Father God, help me to be interested in what's good for other people. Show me how to be kind."

THURSDAY

Read "Stormy Seas," page 728 in *God's Story*. Or read this part of the story:

The time came to sail to Rome to see Caesar. Paul and some others were taken out of jail. They were given to an army captain named Julius.

Some of Paul's friends went with him. They got on a ship and sailed out to sea. The next day, they landed at Sidon.

Julius was kind. He let Paul go to see his friends in Sidon.

Soon it was time to sail again.

It wasn't long before a strong wind began to blow. It was called a "northeast wind." It blew like a hurricane from the island.

The storm pushed the ship along.

But the ship hit a sand bar in the water. It got stuck there. . . .

The soldiers planned to kill the men they were guarding. They didn't want them to get away. But Julius wanted to save Paul's life. So he wouldn't let the soldiers kill anyone.
Acts 27:1-4, 14-15, 41-43

Julius was in the Roman army. He was in charge of 100 soldiers. They had to do whatever he told them to do. Julius was also in charge of some men who were going to jail. He was taking those men to Rome on a ship. Paul was one of those men. Paul had to do whatever Julius said.

But Julius was very kind to Paul. He let Paul get off the ship at one place and go to visit his friends. Julius didn't have to. But he did. He was interested in what was good for Paul. He wanted to help.

Jesus said, "Treat people the way you want them to treat you." If Julius had been in Paul's place, he would have wanted to be treated kindly. So he was treating Paul kindly.

You can be interested in what's good for other people. You can treat other people kindly. God's Spirit will help you.

"Dear Father God, thank you for giving your Spirit to help me. Help me to treat others kindly."

FRIDAY

Read "A Snake in the Fire," page 731 in *God's Story*. Or read this part of the story:

They were on an island called Malta. It was raining, and it was cold. But the people on the island were very kind. They welcomed the men from the ship.

The island people built a fire for them. Paul helped by carrying some sticks. He put the sticks on the fire.

The fire was hot. The heat made a snake crawl out of the sticks. The snake bit Paul's hand and held on.

But Paul shook the snake off. It fell into the fire. Paul was fine.

The people thought Paul would get sick. They thought he might fall down dead all of a sudden. They watched him for a long time. But nothing bad happened. *Acts 28:1-3, 5-6*

It was winter time in the big city. The nights were cold. Danny and his sister, Megan, were glad to have a warm house to stay in. But they knew that some people didn't have houses. Some people even slept outside by the buildings downtown.

So one night a week, Danny and Megan went with their mom and dad to the church building. They set up rows of cots. They laid out sheets and towels and soap. They put a pillow on each cot. And on top of each pillow, they put a small Bible.

In a little while, a van drove up. Some men who had no homes got out of the van. They came into the church building. There, Danny and Megan and their family and friends gave the men some dinner. After dinner, Danny and Megan went home. They were glad that the men had a warm place to stay too.

Danny and Megan's family didn't know the men without homes. But they were kind to the men and helped them. The island people didn't know Paul and his friends. But the island people were kind to them. How do you show kindness?

"Dear God, help me to want what's good for other people. Show me how to be kind to others."

The Fruit of God's Spirit Is Goodness

You can be like a good tree growing good fruit. Loving. Showing joy. Having peace. Waiting quietly. Being kind. Being good.

Galatians 5:22

MONDAY

Read "The Morning Star in Your Hearts," page 775 in *God's Story*. Or read this part of the story:

God gave us great promises. They're very special. So you can live as a child of God. You can get away from the rotting world. The world is rotting away because people want what's wrong.

So try your best to add goodness to your faith. Then add knowing God's ways. Then add self-control. Then add obeying God no matter what. Then add growing to be like God. Then add being kind to God's people. Then add love.

Live like this, and what you do will be important. You'll do lots of good. That's because you'll know Jesus. *2 Peter 1:4-8*

Did you ever watch how people cook soup or chili or spaghetti sauce? First they get a big pot. They might put in some onions and bell peppers. They might put in some meat and tomato sauce or water. They add a little of this and a little of that. They stir it and let it boil. It starts to smell good. *Mmmm!* When do we eat?

Peter wrote a recipe for growing to be like God. You start by believing in Jesus. Faith. Then add a little of this and a little of that. What did Peter say to add? One of the things is goodness. Goodness means doing what's right. It's not always easy to do what's right. But we can try. When God's Spirit lives in us, he helps us to become good.

"Father God, help me to add goodness to my faith. Help me grow to be more like you."

TUESDAY

 Read "On the Worship Day," page 528 in *God's Story*. Or read this part of the story:

It was a worship day. Jesus and his friends walked through some wheat fields. His friends picked some of the wheat. They ate it because they were hungry.

Some Jewish leaders saw them. They said, "You can't pick wheat on a worship day. It's against God's law."

[Jesus said,] "People were not made for the worship day.

Instead, the worship day was made for people. I am Lord of the worship day."

Another worship day came. . . . There was a man in the worship house. His right hand was small and twisted.

The leaders watched Jesus. They wanted to see what he would do. They wanted a reason to say Jesus did something wrong. . . .

Jesus looked at the man whose hand was small and twisted. . . . Then Jesus turned to the people. "Should we do good or bad on the worship day? Should we save lives or kill on the worship day?"

Nobody answered. The people were all quiet.

Then Jesus looked at the sick man. "Hold your hand out," he said.

So the man held his hand out. It reached out all the way now. It was all well.
Mark 2:23-24, 27-28; 3:1-5

In Bible times, it was all right for people to pick a few bits of grain from a field. It was all right for them

to eat it if they were hungry. But the Jewish leaders were looking for something to make a fuss about. So they said that picking a little grain and popping it in your mouth was work. And the Law said you couldn't work on a worship day.

Then they made a fuss about Jesus making a man's hand well. They were more interested in keeping their made-up law about what was work. Jesus was more

SOME THINGS YOU CAN DO THIS WEEK

☐ **Add a fruit to your mobile.** Color another paper fruit, and cut it out. Write *goodness* on it. Hang it on your mobile. Try to name all the fruit of the Spirit without looking.

☐ **Make a sundae.** Start with vanilla ice cream in a glass or bowl. Add different toppings to make it really good. Remember how Peter said we should add things to faith. *(See Monday's reading.)*

☐ **Make get-well cards** for someone who is sick, and send them. Remember how Jesus made the man's hand well. He did what was right and good no matter what day it was. *(See Tuesday's reading.)*

☐ **Make "silver-dollar pancakes."** Use baking mix (like Bisquick) to make pancake batter. Ask an adult to help you. Use a teaspoon to drop the batter onto a hot pan. Turn the pancakes over so both sides get brown. As you eat your "silver dollars," remember the servants who did a good job with the king's money. *(See Wednesday's reading.)*

☐ **Find a way to help someone** without telling the person who did it. Watch people carefully, and listen to them. See if you can find out what they need someone to do for them. Then do it when they are not looking, and don't tell them who did it. You could even leave a note signed "the Secret Servant."

interested in doing good. He was more interested in doing the right thing. And he knew the right thing was to help people whenever they needed help. Even on the worship day.

Sometimes we take a vacation from working. But we should never take a vacation from goodness and doing what's right.

"Dear God, thank you for sending your Son to show us what's good and right. Help me to do what's good and right too."

WEDNESDAY

Read "The Servants and the Money," page 594 in *God's Story.* Or read this part of the story:

Jesus and his followers were getting close to Jerusalem. . . . Jesus told them a story.

"Once there was an important man. He had to go to a land far away. He was going to have the people there make him their king. Then he would come back home. He'd be the king.

"So the man called ten servants. He gave each of them some money. 'Use this money to get more money,' he said. 'See how well you can use it until I come back.'

"Now some of the people hated this man. . . . They said, 'We don't want this man to be king.'

"But the man was made king anyway. Then he came home.

"He sent for the servants who had the money he'd given them. . . .

"The first servant came to him. He said, 'Sir, I made more money for you. You gave me one piece of money, and I got ten more.'

"'Well done!' said the king. 'You are a good servant! I see I could trust you with a little bit. Now you may be in charge of ten cities.'

"The second servant came to the king. He said, 'Sir, I made more money for you. You gave me one piece of money, and I got five more.'

"'Well done!' said the king. 'You may be in charge of five cities!'" *Luke 19:11-19*

The king told two of his servants, "Well done!" That means, "Good work!" They were good servants. Why? Because they obeyed the king. They did what he told them to do.

Did you wonder why the servants obeyed the king? Maybe they were afraid of the king. Maybe they hoped that the king would give them something special for obeying. Maybe they just really liked the king and wanted to do something good for him.

Jesus is our King. We are his servants. Some people obey him because they are afraid of what he will do if they don't obey. Some people are good because they want Jesus to give them something special. Some people are good because they love Jesus. They know he will tell them to do only what's right. And they love to do what he says.

Think of some things that your King tells you to do. Jesus loves you. He is a good king. Will you love him and be a good servant?

"Dear Father God, thank you for sending Jesus to be my King. I love Jesus. Help me to be his good servant."

THURSDAY

 Read "Right and Wrong," page 236 in *God's Story*. Or read this part of the story:

We feel happy when we remember people who do right.
But bad people's names seem to rot away.

People who do right can look forward to joy.
But a sinful person can look forward to nothing.

The right ways of good people save them.
But the bad ways of bad people trap them. Proverbs 10:7, 28; 11:6

When TV was new, lots of people liked to watch cowboy shows. They liked to watch cowboy movies. There was always a good guy and a bad guy. You could tell who the good guy was, because he wore a white hat.

It would be great if you could tell good guys from bad guys by looking at their hats. But you can't. How can you tell good guys from bad guys?

God has different plans for good

people and bad people. God wouldn't be a very good God if he let bad people get away with doing wrong. So God lets bad people get in trouble. But God saves good people.

What if you make a mistake and do wrong? Does that mean you're a bad person? No. Good people sometimes make mistakes. But they keep trying to do right. Jesus already took the blame for your sins when he died on the cross. So when you do something that's wrong, try to do what's right next time. God's Spirit will help you.

"Dear Father God, thank you for sending Jesus to die for my sins. Forgive me when I do wrong things. Help me try to do what's right. Grow the goodness of your Spirit in me."

FRIDAY

Read "What Does God Want?" page 339 in *God's Story*. Or read this part of the story:

What should I bring when I worship God?
Should I come with gifts?

No! God shows us what is good.
He wants us to be fair and to love
*   kindness.*
*   He wants us to let him be the*
*   greatest.*
*   He wants us to walk with him.*
Micah 6:6, 8

Sometimes we wonder why God gives us rules. We wonder why he wants us to be good. But God made the world and everything in it. He made it just right. When someone does wrong, it hurts something that God made. It might hurt the person who did wrong. It might hurt somebody else. It might hurt something else God made. When things and people are hurt, it brings sadness. God knows what will give us true joy. So he tells us what to do. If we obey him, we will have true joy.

How do we obey God? We choose to do good. What is good? God shows us. Micah wrote four ways to do good:

1. Be fair.
2. Love kindness.
3. Let God be the greatest.
4. Walk with God. That means you're to talk with God and listen to him. You're to read

about him and think about him as much as you can. And you're to love him. You do it because he loves you.

"Dear God, help me to be fair and to love kindness. You are the greatest! I love you, and I want to walk with you."

The Fruit of God's Spirit Is Faithfulness

You can be like a good tree growing good fruit. Loving. Showing joy. Having peace. Waiting quietly. Being kind. Being good. Keeping promises. *Galatians 5:22*

MONDAY

 Read "The Dreamer" and "At the Captain's House," pages 32 and 34 in *God's Story*. Or read this part of the two stories:

So Joseph went to Dothan. That's where he found his brothers.

"Here's the dreamer!" they said. They pulled his beautiful, long coat off. They threw him into the dry well. . . .

Now along came a line of men with camels. The brothers took Joseph out of the well. They sold him to the men. . . . Then the men and camels went on to Egypt. There they sold Joseph.

The captain of the king's guard bought him.

God took care of Joseph. He lived in the captain's house.

Now the captain's wife . . . said to Joseph, "Come and be like a husband to me!"

But Joseph wouldn't. He said, "The captain trusts me. How could I do such a thing? It would not be right. It would be a great sin against God."

Every day the captain's wife said the same thing. Every day Joseph answered the same. In fact, he tried not to be around the captain's wife.

Genesis 37:17, 19, 23-25, 28, 36; 39:2, 7-10

Joseph was far away from home. He didn't have his father with him to tell him what to do. He didn't have his brothers with him to tell him what to do. There was no one around to tell Joseph to obey God. There was no one around to tell Joseph to do what was right. But Joseph did what was right anyway. Joseph was faithful.

What does it mean to be faithful? It's being a person that people can trust. It's keeping promises. Joseph knew God. He knew God's rules. He knew how God wanted him to act. He didn't forget. He didn't turn away from God. No matter what happened, everyone could trust Joseph to do what God said was right.

Can people trust you? God's Spirit will help you to be faithful. He will help you keep your promise to obey him.

"Dear God, I want people to be able to trust me. Help me to be faithful to you."

TUESDAY

Read "Two Sons and a Grape Garden," page 599 in *God's Story*. Or read this part of the story:

Jesus went on. "Think about this. There once was a man who had two sons. The man talked to his first son. 'Go work in the grape garden today,' he said.

"His first son said no. Later, he changed his mind. He did go.

"The man talked to his other son. 'Go work in the grape garden today,' he said.

"His other son said, 'Yes, sir. I will.' But he didn't go.

"Which son did what his father wanted?" asked Jesus.

"The first one did," they said.

Matthew 21:28-31

Did you ever say you would do something, but then you didn't do it? Did you ever say you wouldn't do something, but then you did? Sometimes we forget what we said we would or would not do. Sometimes we change our minds. The first brother in Jesus' story changed his mind. Maybe the second brother forgot what he told his dad. Or maybe he changed his mind too.

To be a faithful person, we must do what we say we will do. That way, people will know they can trust us. They can count on us. No matter what happens, we will be faithful.

What do your mom and dad trust you to do? What does your teacher trust you to do? Are there other people who count on you?

"Dear Father God, help me to do what I say I will do. Help me to be a faithful person."

WEDNESDAY

Read "Two Strange Dreams," page 35 in *God's Story*. Or read this part of the story:

The waiter said, "My dream was about a vine. There were three branches on it. The vine had buds. They turned into flowers. Then grapes grew. I held the king's cup. I put grape juice into the cup. Then I gave it to the king."

"Here is what your dream means," said Joseph. "The three branches mean three days. Three days will pass. Then the king will let you out of jail. You will get to give him drinks again. You will see the king. Please tell him about me. See if you can get me out of jail, too. I did not do anything wrong. I should not be here."

Three days went by. It was the king's birthday. So he had a party. He took the waiter and the baker out of jail. He gave the waiter his old job back. But the waiter didn't tell the king about Joseph. He forgot.
Genesis 40:9-15, 20-21, 23

Joseph wanted to be free. The waiter was free now. Maybe the waiter could help Joseph get out of jail! One day passed. Nothing happened. Another day passed. Nothing happened. After a few days, Joseph knew that the waiter had forgotten him. The waiter was not faithful. How do you think Joseph felt? Joseph knew that the waiter must have forgotten him. But he also knew that God had not forgotten him. Joseph was faithful to God, and God was faithful to him.

People sometimes have a hard time remembering things. One of the most important things to remember is to pray and read your Bible every day. How can you help yourself remember? Doing these things every day will help keep you faithful to God. And God will be faithful to you.

"Dear God, help me remember to pray to you every day. Help me remember to read my Bible every day. Thank you for being faithful to me. Help me to be faithful to you."

SOME THINGS YOU CAN DO THIS WEEK

☐ **Add another fruit** to your "fruit of the Spirit" mobile. Color and cut out a fruit. Write *faithfulness* on it. Hang it with the other fruits on the mobile. Try to name all the fruit of the Spirit without looking.

☐ **Try a back-to-back stunt.** Stand with your back against a friend's back. Now both of you try to sit down without moving your backs apart. You will have to lean against each other. Try linking arms. Once you sit down, try to get back up the same way. Sometimes a person says, "You can lean on me." That means the person plans to be faithful.

☐ **Make a grape-print picture.** Dip the flat, round end of a fat crayon or marker cap into wet, purple watercolor paint. Then push it onto a piece of paper. It will make a purple circle. Keep making purple circles next to each other until you have made it look like a bunch of grapes. Remember the brothers and the grape garden. *(See Tuesday's reading.)*

☐ **Use blocks to build the city of Jericho** on a sheet on the floor. March around the sheet. To make the walls fall, hold the sides of the sheet and shake it. *(See Thursday's reading.)*

☐ **Make a wall hanging.** Space out seven index cards in a line from top to bottom along 30 inches of ribbon. Place the cards so that the long sides are at the top and bottom. Staple the top middle part of each card onto the ribbon. Print one word of what Joshua said on each card: "My family and I will serve God." Hang the ribbon and cards on a wall.

THURSDAY

 Read "Hiding on the Roof" and "Falling Walls," pages 95 and 98 in *God's Story*. Or read this part of the stories:

Joshua sent two men . . . into the city of Jericho. They went to stay at a house there. The house belonged to a woman named Rahab.

But somebody told the king of Jericho, "Some Jewish men came here tonight. . . ."

So the king sent a message to Rahab. It said, "Send me the men who came to your house. . . ."

But Rahab had let the men hide up on her roof. They were hiding under some plants. . . . Rahab went to talk to the men on her roof. "I know God has given this land to you," she said. ". . . Your God is the God in heaven and on earth.

"I've been kind to you," said Rahab. "So promise me something. Promise you'll save my life. Save my father and mother. Save my brothers and sisters." . . .

"Tie a red rope in your window," the men said. "Then bring all your family into this house. That way we can save you." . . .

Joshua told the people God's plan. . . . So they went around the city once. . . . They did the same thing for six days.

Day number seven came. They got up early. They marched around the city again. But this time, they went around seven times. Then the priests sounded a long blow on their horns.

Joshua called, "Everybody shout! God is giving you this city. But save Rahab and everyone in her house as we promised. . . ."

Then the wall of the city fell down. . . .

Joshua called the men who had stayed at Rahab's house. "Go save Rahab," he said.

So they went to Rahab's house. They brought out Rahab and her family. *Joshua 2:1-18; 6:6-23*

How do you think the two men felt, hiding under the plants on Rahab's roof? Have you ever played

"Hide-and-Seek"? Do you remember how it felt to be very still in your hiding place? The person looking for you came closer and closer. Maybe you hardly breathed, hoping he wouldn't hear you or see you.

The two men made a promise to Rahab. She watched God's people march around the city walls every day for six days. Do you think Rahab wondered if the men would keep their promise?

The two men told Joshua about their promise. Joshua helped them remember to save Rahab and her family. They were faithful.

Sometimes friends and family can help us be faithful. They can help us remember what we should do. Who helps you be faithful?

"Dear Father God, thank you for giving me friends and family who help me be faithful."

FRIDAY

 Read "The One We Will Serve," page 102 in *God's Story.* Or read this part of the story:

Joshua grew old. Then he called the leaders together.

"I'm old," he said. "You've seen everything God has done for you.

"So today, choose the one you will serve. . . . My family and I . . . will serve God."

The people said, ". . . We will serve God, too. He saved us. He did great wonders. We will obey him."

Joshua set up a big stone under an oak tree. "See this?" he said. "This stone will help you remember what you said. It heard everything God told us."
Joshua 23:1-3; 24:15-18, 24, 26-27

Why do you have a string on your finger?" asked Kaylee.

"It's to help me remember a note on my mirror," said Jenna.

"Why do you have a note on your mirror?" asked Kaylee.

"It's to help me remember the teddy bear in my closet," said Jenna.

"Why is the teddy bear in your closet?" asked Kaylee.

"I'll show you!" said Jenna. They ran to the closet. Jenna reached under the bear and pulled out a little red box. She gave the box to Kaylee. "Happy birthday!" she said.

Joshua set up a stone to help God's people remember what they said. They said, "We will serve God." Do you think they were faithful? If you read more of God's Story, you will find out. God has given you someone to help you remember to be faithful. God's Spirit will help you!

"Dear God, thank you for sending your Spirit to help me be faithful. I want to be faithful to you forever."

The Fruit of God's Spirit Is Gentleness

You can be like a good tree growing good fruit. Loving. Showing joy. Having peace. Waiting quietly. Being kind. Being good. Keeping promises. Treating people with care. *Galatians 5:22-23*

MONDAY

Read "A Silver Cup" and "Telling the Secret," pages 40 and 41 in *God's Story*. Or read this part of the second story:

The king soon heard that Joseph's brothers were in Egypt. So he told Joseph, "Bring your brothers' families here to live. You can have the best land. Take carts with you so their children and wives can ride. Bring your father, too. Don't worry about bringing anything else. You can get whatever you need when you get here."

So Joseph gave his brothers some carts. He gave them food for their trip. He gave new clothes to each of them. *Genesis 45:16-22*

The king was glad that Joseph's father and brothers were going to move to Egypt. He was glad they would bring their wives and children. But he knew it would be a hard trip over rocky roads. So he said to take carts. Then the women and children could ride. He was thinking about how to make the trip more gentle for the women and children.

What is gentleness? It's being considerate and thoughtful and kind. It's treating people in a quiet, soft way. It's having good manners. God's Spirit works in us to make us gentle. How can you show gentleness?

"Dear God, I want to be considerate and thoughtful. I want to treat people in a quiet, soft way. I want to have good manners. Help me to be gentle."

TUESDAY

Read "Lots of Babies," page 27 in *God's Story*. Or read this part of the story:

God let Leah have children. She had a baby boy. . . . Sometime later, Leah had another baby boy. . . . After that, Leah had another baby boy. . . . Later, she had another baby boy. "Praise God!" said Leah.

It was not long before Leah's servant had a baby boy. Then Leah's servant had another baby boy. Then Leah herself had another baby boy.

Sometime later, Leah had another baby boy. "This is a wonderful gift!" said Leah. "I have had six sons for Jacob!" So she named the baby Zebulun. Later, she had a baby girl. She named her baby girl Dinah.

Then God answered Rachel's prayers. She had her own baby, a baby boy. "I can feel good now," said Rachel. She named the baby Joseph and said, "May God give me another son." *Genesis 29:32-35; 30:10, 12, 17, 19-24*

Do you have a baby in your family? Or do you know someone who has a baby? Babies need to be treated gently. They can't take care of themselves. So they need other people to be thoughtful of them. They need other people to be kind to them. They need other people to treat them gently.

There are times when we do things that are not gentle. We play tag or baseball. We have pillow fights for fun. We swing and jump and climb and slide. But we can still be gentle with people's feelings, even when we are doing things that are not so gentle. We can be thoughtful and kind. And we can have good manners.

What are some games you like to play that are not so gentle? How can you treat people gently when you play those games?

"Dear God, thank you for fun games. Help me to treat people's feelings gently even when I'm playing games that are not so gentle."

WEDNESDAY

Read "Lost and Found," page 583 in *God's Story*. Or read this part of the story:

Suppose you're a shepherd. You have 100 sheep. But one of them gets lost. Wouldn't you leave the other 99 sheep out in the open? Wouldn't you look for the lost sheep until you found it?

SOME THINGS YOU CAN DO THIS WEEK

☐ **Add another fruit** to your "fruit of the Spirit" mobile. Color and cut out a fruit. Write *gentleness* on it. Hang it with the other fruits on your mobile. Try to say all the fruit of the Spirit without looking.

☐ **Play "Sheep-in-the-Pen."** Each player should have a piece of typing paper. Draw a line down the middle. One side is the palace. The other side is the sheep pen. Give each player 10 cotton balls for sheep. Take the cards numbered 5, 6, 7, 8, 9, and 10 out of a deck of cards. Mix the rest of the cards up, and place them in a stack, face down on the table. Each person draws a card. The one with the highest card starts. If a person has a number card, he can put that number of sheep in his pen. If he has a jack, he has to take one sheep out of the pen and put it in the palace. A queen takes two sheep to the palace. A king takes three sheep. A joker takes all the sheep that are in the pen. You can get sheep out of the palace and into the pen when you draw a number card. The person who gets all his sheep in the pen first wins.

☐ **Play "Hide-and-Seek."** Pretend you are a shepherd looking for his sheep. Remember to be gentle like a shepherd.

☐ **Go on a picnic.** Read Psalm 23, "My Shepherd." *(See Thursday's reading.)*

☐ **Play "Follow-the-Leader."** Be sheep following the shepherd.

Then you'd be so happy. You'd carry the sheep home on your shoulders. You'd call all your friends and neighbors. You'd say, "Be glad with me! I found my lost sheep!" *Luke 15:4-6*

The shepherd stood at the bottom of a grassy hill. He looked around carefully. His sheep were here and there all over the hill. But the shepherd saw one far away, past some bushes. So he called to his sheep dog. The sheep dog listened to the shepherd's commands. Across the hill ran the dog, past the bushes. There he found the sheep that had gone too far. The dog chased the sheep back, closer to the rest of the sheep.

The shepherd in the Bible story went after his lost sheep. When he found it, he was very gentle. He carried it back to the rest of the sheep. Jesus is like a good shepherd to us. He says we are like his sheep. Jesus is very gentle with us. His Spirit is also gentle. And when we belong to Jesus, we become gentle too! What can you do to show your gentleness?

"Dear God, thank you for letting Jesus be my shepherd. Thank you for letting me be his sheep. Help me to be gentle like Jesus is."

THURSDAY

Read "My Shepherd," page 185 in *God's Story*. Or read this part of the story:

The Lord is my shepherd.
I am like his sheep.
I won't need anything.
He takes me to green fields so I can lie down.
He brings me to quiet water.
He makes me strong again.
He leads me in the way that is right because of who he is.
Sometimes I am in danger.
I'm like a sheep in a valley full of shadows.
I may be in danger.
But I will not be afraid because you are with me.
You make me feel safe. Psalm 23:1-4

David was a shepherd. He knew how to be gentle with his sheep. But he was also brave and strong. David killed a lion and a bear with his bare hands. People can be brave and strong but gentle, too. When David wrote, "The Lord is my shepherd," he was writing about a strong, brave, gentle shepherd.

Do you know someone who is gentle? What does that person do or say that makes him or her gentle? How does that person make you feel when he or she is around? You can be gentle too. God can help you be strong. He can help you be brave. And he can help you be gentle, just like him.

"Dear God, thank you for being strong and gentle, too. Grow me up to be strong and brave and gentle."

FRIDAY

Read "A Muddy Well," page 421 in *God's Story*. Or read this part of the story:

Jeremiah told people these words from God. "If you stay in the city, you'll die. . . . But if you go out to Babylon's army, you'll live."

Some of the king's men heard what Jeremiah was saying. They put him in a well in the guards' yard. . . .

But a leader at the palace heard about it. He was from Cush. [He] got 30 men. Then he went to a room in the palace. He got some old rags and clothes. He tied ropes to them. He let them down into the well.

"Put these old rags and clothes under your arms," said the man from Cush. "That way, the ropes won't hurt your arms."

Jeremiah put the old rags under his arms. Then he put the ropes under his arms. The men pulled him up out of the well.
Jeremiah 38:1-2, 6-7, 10-13

Ropes tugged tightly around him. Men were pushing him this way and that. Then up over the side of the well he went. And down, down, down he went. All the way down to the dark, mushy, muddy bottom. Jeremiah began to sink slowly into the mud.

But a palace leader from Cush helped Jeremiah out of the well. First, he sent old rags and clothes down to make a soft padding. The leader from Cush wanted to be gentle as he pulled Jeremiah out. He didn't want Jeremiah to get hurt.

The palace leader was thoughtful and kind. He was considerate and helpful. He was gentle. How can you be thoughtful and kind? How can you be considerate and helpful? How can you be gentle?

"Dear Father God, show me how to be thoughtful and kind. Show me how to be considerate and helpful. Show me how to be gentle."

The Fruit of God's Spirit Is Self-Control

You can be like a good tree growing good fruit. Loving. Showing joy. Having peace. Waiting quietly. Being kind. Being good. Keeping promises. Treating people with care. Having control of yourself. *Galatians 5:22-23*

MONDAY

Read "Self-Control and Pride," page 240 in *God's Story*. Or read this part of the story:

If you find honey, then eat just enough.
If you have too much, you'll get sick.
Don't go to your neighbors' house too often.
They might stop liking you.

Someone who can't control himself is like a city with broken-down walls.

A fool shows all his anger.
But a wise person controls himself.
Proverbs 25:16-17, 28; 29:11

What is self-control? It's making yourself do what you know you should do. Mothers can make us do the right thing. That's mother-control. Fathers can make us do the right thing. That's father-control. Teachers can make us do the right thing. That's teacher-control. But when we make ourselves do the right thing, that's self-control.

Self-control is also keeping yourself from doing the wrong things. You may know that there is a TV show you shouldn't watch. Maybe nobody is home but you. You could watch it, and nobody would know. But God knows. And you know what's right. So you don't watch it. That's self-control.

"Dear God, help me make myself do the right thing. Help me to have self-control."

TUESDAY

Read "Visitors from Canaan" and "The Test," pages 37 and 38 in *God's Story.* Or read this part of the stories:

Joseph's brothers bowed to him. Joseph knew who they were right away. But he acted as if he didn't know them. "Where are you from?" he asked in a mean voice.

"We are from Canaan," they said. "We came to buy some food." . . .

Joseph remembered his dreams from long ago. He said, "I think you came to trick us! You came to see how you can take over this land!"

"Oh, no!" they said. "We just came to buy food. We are all brothers. We are good people. We tell the truth. . . .

Then Joseph put them all in jail.

Three days went by. Then Joseph told his brothers, "Only one of you must stay. The rest of you may go home. Take wheat with you. But bring your youngest brother back here. That way I'll know you told the truth."

The brothers began to talk to each other. "This is what we get for being mean to Joseph long ago. . . ."

They didn't know Joseph could understand every word they said. . . . But Joseph did know what they were saying. He had to turn his face away from them. He was starting to cry. In a minute, he turned around. He chose Simeon to stay in jail. And he let the others go home. *Genesis 42:6-24*

Did you ever have a secret you wanted to tell, but you couldn't? You had to use self-control. You had to make yourself keep the secret.

Joseph had to control himself. His brothers were standing there right in front of him. He hadn't seen them for many years. He even started to cry in front of them. Maybe he wanted to yell out, "I'm Joseph! I'm your brother!" But he didn't. Not yet. He kept his secret.

God's Spirit helps us have self-control. You know that you're growing up when you choose to do what's right. Nobody is making you do it. You make yourself choose right. That's self-control.

"Dear Father God, teach me what's right. Help me to choose what's right. Help me to control myself."

SOME THINGS YOU CAN DO THIS WEEK

☐ **Add a fruit to your mobile.** Color it and cut it out. Write *self-control* on it. Hang it with the other fruits. See if you can name all the fruit of the Spirit without looking.

☐ **Make a city from index cards.** Tape the short ends of index cards together to make a city wall. It can be as long as you want. Stand the wall up, and make it into a circle or square. Leave an opening to be the gate. You can make buildings by taping four index cards together and standing them up. Make towers by taping the long sides of the index cards together. Make smaller buildings by cutting the index cards in half before taping them. You may color a brick, rock, or wood design on your buildings. Draw windows and doors. Remember that "someone who can't control himself is like a city with broken-down walls." *(See Monday's reading.)*

☐ **Play "Guess My Secret."** One player thinks of a person, a place, or a thing. The other players must ask questions to see if they can guess what it is. The questions can only have yes or no for an answer. Example: "Is it red?" See if anyone can guess the answer before 20 questions have been asked. *(See Tuesday's reading.)*

☐ **Make a "Daniel dinner."** Ask an adult to help you cook your favorite fresh vegetables for dinner. *(See Wednesday's reading.)*

☐ **Give "pack-saddle" rides.** Choose two people to make the "saddle." Each person uses his or her right hand to hold the inside of his or her left arm just below the elbow. Then they face each other. With the left hand, each takes hold of the top of the other's right arm just below the elbow. This makes the saddle. The person taking the ride sits sideways on it while the other two carry him around. Remember the bit and bridle that David wrote about. *(See Thursday's reading.)*

WEDNESDAY

 Read "The King's Food," page 395 in *God's Story*. Or read this part of the story:

Nebuchadnezzar was the king of Babylon. He asked to see some of the people from Judah. He wanted to see some young men from the families of Judah's leaders. . . .

The king gave them food and wine from his table. He wanted them to study for three years. Then they could be his helpers. . . .

Daniel chose not to eat the king's food. He chose not to drink the king's wine. He wanted to keep himself right and good. . . .

"Just try it for 10 days," said Daniel. "Give us vegetables to eat. Give us water to drink. See how we look after that. Then you can choose which food is right for us."

So the man in charge did what Daniel asked.

After 10 days, Daniel and his friends looked stronger. They looked more healthy than the other young men. *Daniel 1:1-15*

What is your favorite food? God made so many wonderful tastes for us to enjoy. There are salty foods and sour foods and sweet foods. *Mmmm!* How yummy!

But God made something else. He made a special part of our brain that tells us when we are hungry. It also tells us when we have had enough to eat. If we listen to it, we will not begin eating until we feel hungry. And we will stop eating when we've had enough. That's self-control.

Lots of people have a hard time controlling their eating. It's hard to have self-control, especially around food. Do you think Daniel would have enjoyed eating the king's food? He might have wanted it. But he controlled himself. He ate only what he knew God wanted him to eat. He had a lot of self-control!

"Dear God, thank you for all the wonderful tastes you made. Help me to eat what's right and control myself."

THURSDAY

Read "Not like a Horse," page 216 in *God's Story.* Or read this part of the story:

God says, "I will teach
*   you how you should live.*
I will watch over you.
Do not be like the horse or mule.
It doesn't understand at all.
It has to be led by a bit in its mouth.
It won't move without a harness
*   and long reins."*
People who do bad things have
*   many troubles.*
But the people who trust God will
*   have God's love around them*
*   forever. Psalm 32:8-10*

The dark brown horse was beautiful. But he was wild. So before the cowboy could ride him, he had to tame him. The cowboy got in the pen with the horse. The horse galloped around the sides of the pen, trying to get away. The cowboy talked softly to the horse. He moved closer to the horse. He tossed a light blanket on the horse's back. The horse bucked the blanket off.

Day after day, the cowboy did the same thing. Soon he was able to put a saddle on the horse. Then one day, he put the bridle in the horse's mouth. On a bridle there's a bit. It's a metal bar that goes in the horse's mouth. The rest of the bridle goes around the horse's head. The rider holds the ends, called "reins." He pulls them to the right to make the horse go right. He pulls to the left to make the horse go left. He pulls back to make the horse stop. That's how he controls the horse.

King David knew about horses. He also knew about self-control. There were times when he had not controlled himself. That had gotten him into trouble. So he wrote this song to say that it was best not to be like a horse. The horse has to be controlled by somebody else. It's best to control yourself.

"Dear Father God, help me not to be like a horse that has to be controlled by its rider. Help me to control myself."

FRIDAY

Read "Judas and the Guards," page 615 in *God's Story*. Or read this part of the story:

Jesus said, "Judas! Are you going to turn against me by kissing me?"

Judas said, "Teacher!" Then he kissed Jesus. . . .

Then the guards took hold of Jesus.

Jesus' friends saw what was happening. "Lord, should we fight with our swords?" they asked.

Peter had a sword. He pulled it out. He swung it at Malchus, the high priest's servant. Peter cut off the servant's right ear.

"Put your sword back," said Jesus. . . . Then Jesus touched Malchus's ear. Malchus was well again.

Mark 14:45-46; Luke 22:47-51; John 18:10-11

Peter had a hard time controlling himself. He would often say and do things without thinking. When Judas and the guards showed up, Peter was ready to fight. So he did. And somebody got hurt. Peter lost his temper, and Malchus lost his ear!

When you feel like hitting someone but you don't, that's self-control. When you feel like yelling at someone but you don't, that's self-control. When you feel like sleeping all day but you make yourself get up, that's self-control. When you feel like eating sweets just before dinner but you wait, that's self-control.

When you have self-control, people trust you. They like to be around you. They can see that you are getting older and wiser. It's not always easy to have self-control. But it's always the right thing to do.

"Dear Father God, thank you for loving me and sending your Spirit to help me. Grow all of the fruits of your Spirit in me!"

Fun and Games

A cheerful heart can make you feel well. *Proverbs 17:22*

MONDAY

Read "Rules about Worship," page 90 in *God's Story*. Or read this part of the story:

Have a Pass Over holiday every year. This is a holiday in the spring. At this holiday, remember the time you left Egypt.

Every year have a holiday called the Holiday of Weeks. Start it seven weeks after you begin to cut your wheat. This is a holiday for the early summer.

Every year have a Horn Holiday. It will be in the fall. Play the horns to worship God.

Every year have a Day of Paying for Sins. It will be in the fall.

Every year have a Tent Holiday. It will be in the fall. It will last seven days. It's for the time when you gather in your crops. *Leviticus 23:5, 15, 24, 27, 34*

What are your favorite holidays? God gave the Jewish people lots of holidays. Most of them were times of fun. They were times when friends got together to visit. There was laughing and food and fun.

The word *holiday* is made from two other words. Can you guess what they are by looking at the word *holiday*? The two words are *holy* and *day*. When God gave people holidays, he was giving them holy days. *Holy* means special. It means something that belongs to God. So holidays were special, and they belonged to God. They were times for enjoying what God had done for his people.

Think about the holidays you have. How can you make them special days for enjoying what God has done for you?

"Dear Father God, thank you for giving us holidays. At holiday times, help me remember to enjoy what you have done."

TUESDAY

Read "Singers on the Wall," page 499 in *God's Story*. Or read this part of the story:

Now the day came to give the city wall of Jerusalem to God. It was time to say that God was in charge of it. It belonged to him. So people from the family group of Levi came to help. They led songs to give thanks to God. They played

music with cymbals, harps, and lyres.

I chose two big groups of singers to give thanks. One group went on top of the wall to the right. The next group of singers went the other way.

That day many gifts were given to God. That's because God had made the people very happy. . . . The happy sound could be heard far away. *Nehemiah 12:27, 31, 38, 43*

Our cities don't have walls around them. But long ago, there were many enemy armies. People built city walls to protect themselves. If a city's walls were broken or torn down, it was bad news! That meant the enemy could come in and take over the city. So it was very good news when the people finished building the wall around the city of Jerusalem.

When special things happen, people often want to have a special time to share their joy. Weddings. Birthdays. Finishing a year of school. There's a special word that tells what we do when we share joy at special times. *Celebrate*.

The singers on the wall celebrated something special that had happened. The wall was finished. What special times does your family celebrate? How can you enjoy God at the same time?

"Dear God, thank you for letting us celebrate special times with our friends and family. Help us to remember you at the same time."

SOME THINGS YOU CAN DO THIS WEEK

☐ **Look at old pictures** from parties and holidays you and your family have enjoyed together. Thank God for times to celebrate special things that happen.

☐ **Have a party!** Ask some friends to come over. Play games. Have something special to eat and drink. Celebrate being friends. And celebrate how good God is! *(See Friday's reading.)*

☐ **Make a special-days reminder book.** Get a colored report folder with pockets on the inside. Put 12 pieces of notebook paper in it. Write the name of a different month on each paper. Write holidays, special days, and birthdays on the page of the month they come in. Draw and color pictures on each page. Buy or make birthday cards and envelopes. Keep them in the folder pockets so they'll be ready to give when special days come.

☐ **Make celebration place mats** for each person in your family. Get two 15-inch pieces of waxed paper for each place mat. Cut small shapes out of colored construction paper. Lay them at different places on one piece of waxed paper. Chip off bits of old crayons, and let the chips drop all around on the waxed paper. Then ask an adult to help you iron the other piece of waxed paper on top of it all.

☐ **Bake celebration muffins.** Decorate them with powdered-sugar frosting. As you serve them, talk about things God has given us to enjoy.

WEDNESDAY

Read "A Bright Face," page 265 in *God's Story*. Or read this part of the story:

Wise people know the
right time to do things.
They know the right way.
There's a right time for everything.
There's a right time, even if your
troubles are hard on you.

Sometimes people who do right get treated like sinners. Sometimes people who sin get treated like people who do right. That's not good.

So I say, "Enjoy life." There's nothing better than to eat, drink, and be happy. Then you'll be happy when you work. You'll be happy all your life.
Ecclesiastes 8:5-6, 14-15

Think about a holiday or a party that you enjoyed. What do people's faces look like when they enjoy something? They smile and laugh. When God made us, he made us to be a lot like him. God has feelings like we do. He smiles and laughs too.

Have you ever watched monkeys at the zoo? Have you ever laughed at something funny a monkey did? Have you ever laughed at little kittens playing together? What other animals make you laugh? God made all of these animals for us to enjoy. God made good flavors and smells and sounds for us to enjoy too. God likes to see us enjoy his world. He likes to hear us laugh and see us smile. He laughs and smiles too. That's because we are his children and he loves us!

"Dear God, thank you for making wonderful, fun things in our world! Thank you for making us smile and laugh!"

THURSDAY

Read "A Party at Matthew's," page 525 in *God's Story*. Or read this part of the story:

"Follow me," Jesus said to Matthew.

So Matthew followed Jesus. He even gave a big dinner party for Jesus. It was at his own house. Tax workers and many other people came to his party.

Some of the Jewish leaders came to the party too.

Then the leaders said, "John's followers go without food to worship God. . . . But your followers eat and drink."

"The groom is with his friends," said Jesus. "Will his friends stop eating now? One day the groom will be gone. Then there will be days when they don't eat."
Luke 5:27-29, 33-34

Balloons were tied to chairs. Bright streamers hung around the doors. The house smelled like popcorn and cupcakes. Tessa could hardly wait until her friends came over. She was having a party, and it would be great fun.

Matthew didn't have popcorn and cupcakes at his party. He didn't have balloons or streamers. But he had lots of friends who came. Jesus came too!

What happens when friends have a party? They talk and laugh. They have a good time together. Jesus probably talked and laughed with many of the people at Matthew's party.

Jesus said that his friends should eat and have a good time. He said that he was like a groom at a wedding. His friends were his guests. He talked about a time when he would be gone and his friends wouldn't care to eat. He was talking about the time when he would die on the cross.

But now Jesus is alive again, and he still goes to parties. Since he is with you everywhere, he goes to your parties. He is with you on all your holidays. He is glad to see you enjoy your friends.

"Dear God, thank you that you are with me everywhere. Thank you for letting me enjoy good times with my friends."

FRIDAY

Read "The White Horse and Its Rider," page 820 in *God's Story*. Or read this part of the story:
Then I heard a roaring sound. It was like a great crowd of people in heaven. They shouted,

"Praise the Lord!
Let's be glad!

It's time for the Lamb's wedding.
  His bride is ready.
She is wearing clean, bright
    clothes."

The clothes stand for the right
    things God's people do. . . .

Some people will be asked to come to Jesus' wedding supper. God will bring good things to them. *Revelation 19:1, 6-9*

Have you ever been to a wedding? A wedding is a very special celebration. The bride and groom take months and months to get ready for the wedding. They choose where the wedding will be. They choose the kind of music they want to have. They choose the kind of food they want to serve. They choose their clothes. And they make lists of friends and family to ask to come to the wedding. At last the day comes. It's a day full of smiles and laughing and eating and fun.

All of God's people have been asked to come to a wedding. In fact, we will be the bride! God's people are called "the church." The church is like a bride for Jesus. Someday we will all be with him, and we'll live with him forever.

Right now, we are getting ready. We help each other choose to do what's right and good. We help each other obey Jesus no matter what happens. It's like getting ready for our wedding. It will be the best celebration ever!

"Dear Father God, thank you for planning a great party with Jesus! Help me to get ready by choosing what's right."

Friends

Being around wise people makes you wise.
Being around fools hurts you. *Proverbs 13:20*

MONDAY

Read "Friends," page 253 in *God's Story*. Or read this part of the story:

People who do right say helpful things to their friends. But sinful people lead their friends to do wrong.

A friend will love you all the time. Brothers and sisters help you through hard times.

Some people think they have many friends. But the real friend is the one who stays closer than a brother.
Proverbs 12:26; 17:17; 18:24

Robby walked slowly down the street with his hands in his pockets. He kicked a rock. He had lost the race at school. He might have done OK if his shoe hadn't come untied. It wouldn't even have been so bad to lose if everybody hadn't laughed at him when he tripped. "I guess nobody likes a loser," he said.

"I do," said a voice behind him. It was Robby's friend Marcus. "Friends are friends no matter if they win or lose."

Tall or small, fat or thin, friends are friends. Friends like you, and they stick by you no matter what.

Who are the friends that God has given you?

"Dear God, thank you for giving me friends. Help me to be a true friend and love my friends no matter what."

TUESDAY

Read "A Friend, a Spear, and a Wife" and "The Arrow," pages 140 and 143 in *God's Story*. Or read this part of the two stories:

Saul's son Jonathan became David's good friend. He loved David as much as he loved himself.

Jonathan and David made a promise to be special friends.

"I'll find out my father's plans," said Jonathan. "If he is going to hurt you, I'll let you know. Then you can get away and be safe.

The next day Jonathan went to the field. A little boy went with him. "Go find the arrows I shoot," said Jonathan.

So the boy ran. Jonathan shot an arrow into the field. The boy ran to where it landed. Jonathan called, "The arrow is far away. It is past you." Then he called, "Hurry and go fast! Don't stop!"

The boy . . . didn't know this was a message for David. . . . The boy left. . . .

Then David and Jonathan hugged each other. They both cried. . . .

"Go in peace," said Jonathan. "We've promised to be friends. God knows about our promise." *1 Samuel 18:1, 3; 20:12-13, 35-42*

Did you ever make up a secret code with a friend? A circle means A, a square means B, a triangle means C, and so on. Then you and your friend write secret notes to each other in your secret code. Nobody else can read it!

That's what David and Jonathan did. They were best friends. Their code was the arrow that Jonathan shot. That's the way Jonathan told David that King Saul was angry. David and Jonathan both knew that David had to leave. But they also knew that friends can still be friends even if they can't see each other every day.

Do you have friends you don't see every day? How can you still be friends with them?

"Dear God, thank you for friends near and far. Help me always to be a good friend to all of them."

WEDNESDAY

Read "Three Friends," page 439 in *God's Story.* Or read this part of the story:

[Satan] made Job get sores on his body. They were on the bottom of his feet. They were on the top of his head. And they were all over his body. They hurt.

Job had three friends, Eliphaz, Bildad, and Zophar. They heard what happened to Job. So they got together and went to see him.

The friends saw Job when they were still far away. But they could hardly tell that it was Job. They began to cry out loud.

SOME THINGS YOU CAN DO THIS WEEK

☐ **Make a friendship chain.** Cut a piece of construction paper into strips about one inch wide. Write the name of a friend on each strip. Make a big ring out of the first strip, and staple or tape it closed. Put the next strip of paper through the ring. Make a ring out of this strip too. Staple or tape it closed. Keep making rings. Use all of the strips of paper with your friends' names on them. When you make a new friend, add another ring to the chain.

☐ **Make a friends wreath.** Cut heart shapes from four-inch squares of paper. Use different colors. Print a friend's name on each heart. Make the hearts into a circle, with each heart overlapping the one next to it. Glue the hearts in place. Use your wreath to remind you to pray for your friends.

☐ **Make gingerbread cookies.** Buy a box of gingerbread mix. Make cookies, using the directions on the box. Paint them with frosting to look like your friends. Give each of your friends a cookie look-alike.

☐ **Play "Add-on Tag."** The first friend must stand in the center of the play area. The next friend tagged stands beside the first person and holds his hand. There must be space between them for people to run through. As friends are tagged, they join the line. To keep from being tagged, runners can go between and around the line.

☐ **Ask friends to come over** for a breakfast that you make. Think about the special breakfast Jesus made for his friends. *(See Thursday's reading.)*

They were so sad, they tore their robes. They put dust on their heads.

Then they sat down on the ground with Job. They sat there for seven days and nights. Nobody said a thing. That's because they could see how much Job was hurting.
Job 2:7, 11-13

Job was sick, and he felt terrible. Job lived long, long ago, so he didn't have the kinds of medicines we have. He didn't have a doctor like we have. But he did have friends. And his friends came to see him. They were really sorry for Job. They tried to cheer him up.

Friends care about each other. When one friend is sad, the other friend feels sad for him. When one friend is happy, the other friend feels happy for him. When one friend is sick, the other friend feels bad about it.

Did you ever visit a friend who was sick? Did a friend ever come to see you when you were sick? What are some things you can do and say to help a sick friend feel better?

"Dear Father God, help me to care about my friends. Show me what to do and say when they get sick. Help me to cheer them up."

Thursday

 Read "Going Fishing," page 629 in *God's Story.* Or read this part of the story:

"I think I'll go fishing," said Peter.

"We'll go with you," said the others.

So off they went. They got into their boat and went fishing. But that night they didn't catch anything.

"Throw your net into the water on the right side of your boat. You'll find some fish there," said Jesus.

So they threw their net over on the boat's right side. Lots of fish got caught in the net. The net got very heavy. Jesus' friends couldn't even pull it in.

"It's the Lord!" said John.

Peter . . . jumped into the water.

The other friends followed in the boat.

"Come have some breakfast," said Jesus. *John 21:3, 6-8, 12*

Jesus had many friends. Twelve of them were special friends who went with him almost everywhere. They were all different from each other. Peter was always saying and doing things without thinking first. John was a deep thinker. He thought it was amazing that Jesus loved him. James was John's brother. They were fishermen and helped on their father's fishing boat.

Thomas had lots of questions. He had a hard time believing things he couldn't see. Andrew was one of the first people to find out who Jesus was. Philip was Peter and Andrew's neighbor. He took Nathanael to meet Jesus. Nathanael was sure to tell the truth, no matter what. Matthew was good with math and money. He gathered taxes for the Romans. Simon did not like the Romans to be in charge of his country. Judas loved money and kept the money bag for Jesus and his friends. He also helped himself to some of the money. We don't know much about Thaddaeus and another James who followed Jesus.

How different all of these friends were! Jesus was a friend to all kinds of people. He wants to be your friend too.

"Dear Father God, thank you for the many kinds of friends I have. Thank you most of all for Jesus, my best friend."

FRIDAY

Read "Samson's Secret," page 119 in *God's Story*. Or read this part of the story:

Samson met a woman named Delilah. He fell in love with her.

The enemy leaders went to

Delilah. "See if you can trick Samson," they said. "Trick him into telling you what makes him so strong. Then we can catch him and tie him up. If you'll do this, we'll pay you."

So Delilah asked Samson, "What's your secret? What makes you so strong?"

Delilah begged Samson every day. At last Samson couldn't stand it anymore. So he told her his secret. "Since I've been born, I've been special to God. I'm not supposed to shave my hair off. If I do, I won't be the strongest man anymore."

Delilah let Samson fall asleep. His head was in her lap. Then a man came and shaved off Samson's braids. He was not strong anymore.

Judges 16:4-6, 16-17, 19

Samson found out that it's important to choose the right kind of friends. Samson found out the hard way.

What kind of person makes a good friend? A good friend won't make fun of what you believe. A good friend won't try to get you to do wrong things. Instead, a good friend helps you do what's right. That's because a good friend cares about you.

A good friend likes to take time to be with you. A good friend likes to work and play with you. A good friend listens to you. A good friend helps you in many different ways. A good friend knows you don't always do the right thing but likes you anyway.

It's a very special thing to have good friends. And it's a very special thing to be a good friend to someone.

"Dear Father God, thank you for giving me good friends. Help me to be a good friend to other people."

Obeying

Children, obey your mother and father. *Ephesians 6:1*

MONDAY

 Read "A Family That Obeyed," page 392 in *God's Story*. Or read this part of the story:

Jeremiah went to Recab's family. He took them to God's worship house. He took them to a side room. He set out bowls of wine. He set out cups. Then he said, "Drink some wine."

But they said, "We don't drink wine. Our father said our family should never drink wine. He told us not to build houses or plant fields. He told us we must always live in tents. We move from place to place. We are nomads. We obeyed."

These are the words God told Jeremiah to say to Recab's family. "You obeyed your father. You did everything he told you. So there will always be people in your family who serve me." *Jeremiah 35:3-8, 18-19*

Did you know that people never stop learning? People never stop learning more about how to act and talk. They never stop learning how to choose what's right.

Your mom and dad are still learning now. They learn by taking time to be with God, praying, and reading their Bibles. They learn by trusting God and watching how he helps them through their problems.

But God gave your mom and dad a very important job. They are supposed to teach you how to act and talk. They are supposed to help you learn how to choose what's right. That's why God tells children to obey their mothers and fathers. And someday it will be your turn to teach your own children how to live.

"Dear God, thank you for my mom and dad. Help me to obey them. Help me to learn how to choose what's right."

TUESDAY

Read "Ten Rules," page 66 in *God's Story*. Or read this part of the story:

God told the people, "I am the Lord your God. I took you out of Egypt. I saved you from being slaves."

Then God gave them 10 important rules.

1. Don't have any other gods.
2. Don't worship idols.
3. Treat God's name as the most important name of all. Use it for the right reasons.
4. Remember the worship day. Keep it special. God worked six days to make the earth. The next day he rested.
5. Treat your father and mother like important people and obey them. Then you'll live a long time in the land I'll give you.
6. Don't kill.
7. Have sex only with your wife or husband.
8. Don't steal.
9. Don't lie.
10. Don't want things that belong to someone else.

Exodus 20:1-17

There's a science rule that says: Everything that happens makes something else happen. When you go swimming, you push on the water with your hands. The water pushes back on you, causing you to move forward in the water.

God made science rules. And God made rules about how to live. He knows that everything we do makes something else happen.

Kindness makes more kindness. Love makes more love.

Do you know which rule comes with a promise? "Treat your father and mother like important people and obey them." God says that rule has a promise: "Then you'll live a long time."

SOME THINGS YOU CAN DO THIS WEEK

☐ **Play "Color Pick-Up."** When it's time to clean your room, get someone to time you. Let that person choose a color. Then give yourself three minutes to pick up everything that's that color. Let the person choose another color. Pick up things of that color in three minutes. Keep going until your room is clean.

☐ **Make milkshakes.** Freeze a banana. Then peel it, cut it up, and mix it in a blender. Add one cup of ice cream and three-fourths cup of milk. Mix again. Add two teaspoons of chocolate syrup. Mix again. This makes two servings. Remember how Recab's family obeyed by what they drank. (See Monday's reading.)

☐ **Make charts of play dough.** Mix one cup of flour, one cup of salt, and one-half cup of water. Add more water, a little at a time, if you need it. Pat it out to look like the stone charts on which God wrote his 10 rules. Print the rules on them with a toothpick. (See Tuesday's reading.)

☐ **Obey a recipe.** Here's one for honey cornbread. In a big bowl, mix two and one-half cups yellow cornmeal, two cups whole-wheat flour, two and one-half teaspoons baking powder, one teaspoon baking soda, and one teaspoon salt. In a small bowl, mix two and one-half cups buttermilk, one-half cup vegetable oil, two beaten eggs, and two tablespoons honey. Put the mix that's in the small bowl into the big bowl. Stir it well. Pour it all into a 9-inch by 13-inch baking pan. Bake it at 425 degrees for 22 minutes. What happens if you don't obey the recipe? (See Thursday's reading.)

"Dear God, thank you for teaching us how to live. Thank you for your rules. Help me to remember them and obey."

WEDNESDAY

Read "The Captain's Servant," page 537 in *God's Story*. Or read this part of the story:

There was once a Roman army captain who lived in Capernaum. He had a servant who was very special to him. But his servant got very sick. . . .

The captain heard that Jesus was in town. So he sent some Jewish leaders to meet with Jesus. He sent them to ask Jesus to come to his house. He wanted Jesus to make his servant well.

Jesus went with the leaders. But the captain had sent some friends to Jesus too. They met him on his way to see the captain. They gave Jesus another message.

The message said, "Lord, don't bother to come. I'm not good enough for you to come to my house. . . . Just say the word.

Then I know my servant will be well again.

"You see, I know about being in charge," the message said. . . . "I . . . tell one to come, and he comes. I tell another one to go, and he goes. I tell my servants, 'Do this' or 'Do that.' And they do what I tell them."

Jesus . . . said, "I haven't seen such great faith in the land of Israel before. . . ."

At that moment, the captain's servant got well. The friends he had sent to Jesus went back home. They saw that the captain's servant was well.
Luke 7:1-3, 6-10

The captain knew something important about obeying. He knew that when he said, "Go," his men went. When he said, "Come," his men came. They could not choose anything else. They had to do just what he said. They had to obey.

That's why the captain asked Jesus to make his servant well. He knew that Jesus was in charge of sickness. Jesus could say, "Go," and sickness would have to go.

Obeying is doing just what the

person in charge says to do. Different people may be in charge of you in different places at different times. It's their job to take care of you and others. So they may make different rules that help them take care of you. Who are some of the people who are in charge of you? How can you obey them?

"Dear Father God, thank you for the people who are in charge of me. Help me to obey them. Help me to obey you."

Thursday

Read "Abram's Travels Begin," page 9 in *God's Story*. Or read this part of the story:

God talked to a man named Abram. God said, "Leave this land. Leave these people. Leave your father's family. I will show you a new land to live in. I am going to give you a family. Your family will become a great nation. Your name will become great.

"I'll do good things for anyone who speaks well of you. I'll send trouble to anyone who says bad things about you. Good will come to everyone on earth because of your family."

Abram was 75 years old. But he did what God told him. He left for another land. His wife, Sarai, and his brother's son, Lot, went with him. They took everything they had. Then they traveled to the land of Canaan. *Genesis 12:1-5*

Molly was baking a chocolate cake with a special recipe. She mixed flour, sugar, and cocoa. She added baking soda, salt, and oil. Then she read the next thing to add: vinegar. Molly said, "Vinegar? Why would you put vinegar in a cake? Yuck!" But Molly obeyed the recipe and put vinegar in the batter.

After dinner, Molly served her cake. It was wonderful.

"What makes this cake taste so good?" asked Molly's dad.

Molly laughed. "It's vinegar!" she said.

Sometimes we don't understand why we have to obey. God told Abram to move to a new land. But God didn't tell Abram why. Abram had to trust and obey. Can you remember a time when you had to obey without knowing why? Who are the people God wants you to obey?

"Dear Father God, I don't always understand why I have to do things your way. But help me to trust you and obey anyway."

FRIDAY

Read "A Locked Jail," page 637 in *God's Story*. Or read this part of the story:

The 12 apostles did lots of wonders.

The high priest and his friends were mad. They wanted people to forget about Jesus and his friends. So they put the apostles in jail.

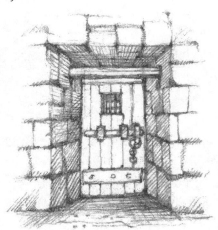

That night, an angel opened the jail doors. He brought the men out of jail. He said, "Go on. Stand in the yards of the worship house. Tell the people all about the new life they can have."

So when morning came, the apostles went to the worship house. They started teaching people again.

Then the captain of the worship-house guards took some guards with him. . . .

They took the apostles to the high priest. "We told you not to teach about Jesus," he said. . . .

"We have to obey God, not men," said Peter and the others. *Acts 5:12, 17-21, 26-29*

Soldiers guarded the jail doors. The jail doors were locked. But nobody was inside. The soldiers were guarding nothing but empty space!

Peter and his friends knew that the Jewish leaders would try to put them in jail again. But they obeyed the angel. They went back to the worship house to teach about Jesus.

The Jewish leaders sent guards to catch Peter and his friends again.

The leaders were angry that Peter and his friends had not obeyed them. "We told you not to teach about Jesus," said the high priest.

What Peter said next has become a well-known saying. He said, "We have to obey God, not men."

God told us to obey our moms and dads. He told us to obey our leaders. But what if those people tell us to do something that God has said not to do? Then we choose to obey God. He is always right.

"Dear God, help me to obey my leaders. But if they ever tell me to do wrong, help me to obey you instead."

Happy Where I Am

Do everything without fussing and fighting. *Philippians 2:14*

MONDAY

Read "Hiding Places," page 148 in *God's Story*. Or read this part of the story:

David stayed in desert hiding places. Saul kept looking for him. But God didn't let Saul catch David.

David wrote these words.

God, you are my God.
I look for you.
My soul is thirsty for you.
It's like being in a dry land
*   where there is no water.*

Your love is better than life.
So my lips will praise you.

I think of you when I go to bed at
*   night.*
You are my helper.
So I sing in the shadow of your
*   wings.*
My soul hugs you,
*   and your right hand holds me.*
1 Samuel 23:14; Psalm 63:1, 3, 6-8

David knew he was supposed to be the king. But he wasn't the king yet. Saul was still the king, and Saul was angry. David lived in the desert. He moved from place to place to hide from Saul.

David had to choose. He could fuss about having to hide from Saul.

He could say, "I'm supposed to be the king here! Why do I have to keep running? You should be running from me!" Or David could be happy where he was. David chose to be happy where he was. He chose to trust God to take care of him. And God did.

There are lots of things we could fuss about. But fussing just makes life hard on everybody. We feel a lot better when we're happy where we are.

"Dear Father God, I want to be like David. I want to be happy where I am. Help me not to fuss. Help me to trust you."

TUESDAY

 Read "Making a Fuss for Food," page 62 in *God's Story*. Or read this part of the story:

Moses led God's people. From the sea, they went into the desert. They traveled for three days. But they couldn't find any water.

At last they came to a place with water. But the water tasted bad. The people began to fuss at Moses. "What are we going to drink?" they asked.

Moses called to God. So God showed Moses a branch from a tree. Moses threw the branch into the water. The bad water turned into good, sweet water.

God's people traveled on. . . . But in the desert, they started making a fuss again. They were mad at Moses and Aaron. "We wish we had died in Egypt!" they said. "We had lots of meat there."

God said to Moses, "Tell the people they will eat meat tonight. Tomorrow morning they'll eat bread. Then they'll know that I am the Lord." *Exodus 15:22-25; 16:1-3, 11*

God's people were not happy with the way things were going. They missed the food they had eaten in Egypt. They didn't like getting thirsty in the desert. So they began fussing about it.

Sometimes we don't like what's happening. So how can we be happy where we are? We can think about everything that's good about what's happening. Some people call it "looking on the bright side." We can count all the good things and not think about the bad. Solomon wrote a wise saying about that. "People who look for what's good find what's good. People who look for what's bad find what's bad" (Proverbs 11:27).

What are some good things about where you are right now?

"Dear God, help me to always see what's good about everything that happens. Thank you."

WEDNESDAY

 Read "King Ahab and the Grape Field," page 288 in *God's Story*. Or read this part of the story:

King Ahab told Naboth, "I want your grape field. . . ."

"No," said Naboth.

King Ahab went home. He was sad and angry. He lay down on his bed. He wouldn't eat anything.

Jezebel, his wife, came in. "Why are you sad and angry?" she asked. . . .

"Naboth won't sell me his grape field," said Ahab.

Jezebel wrote some letters. . . . Here's what the letters said.

Have a big dinner party. . . . Then get two mean men. . . . Have them tell everyone that Naboth said bad things about God. . . . Then take Naboth out. Kill him by throwing rocks at him.

This is just what the leaders did.

Jezebel went to King Ahab. "You can have that grape field now," she said. "Naboth is dead." *1 Kings 21:2-6, 8-11, 15*

All that Ahab could think about was the grape field. He wanted it, and he couldn't have it. He wouldn't stop thinking about it. He started to pout. He felt sorry for himself. The more he thought about it, the sadder he got.

That's what happens when we start being unhappy with the way things are. We think about the bad things. And that makes us feel sad. Then we feel sorry for ourselves. That makes us feel sadder. We fuss about it. And that makes us feel sadder. How can we feel better again? We can start thinking about what's good. We can think about all that God has given us. Instead of wishing for what we don't have, we can be thankful for what we do have. What's good about your life right now?

"Dear Father God, help me to think about the good things and not the bad things. I thank you for all you have given me."

SOME THINGS YOU CAN DO THIS WEEK

☐ **Make a rubber-band harp.** Put rubber bands around a piece of heavy cardboard. Put a drinking straw between the cardboard and the rubber bands. Remember how David had to hide in the desert. Before that, David was happy to play his harp even though he knew he should be king. *(See Monday's reading.)*

☐ **Build stick barns.** Use clean Popsicle sticks, or get craft sticks at the store. Lay two of them side by side several inches apart. Take two more sticks. Lay one across the top and the other across the bottom of the first sticks. Glue each end to make a square. Keep gluing sticks across each other like this until you get your barn as tall as you want it. *(See Thursday's reading.)*

☐ **Draw the inside of your house** with all the rooms. You may wish your house or your room were different. But think about what's good about your house. Think about being happy where you are.

☐ **Make honey cookies.** Put two cups of buttermilk baking mix (like Bisquick) into a big bowl. Add one-fourth cup melted butter, one-fourth cup honey, one teaspoon vanilla, and one-half teaspoon cinnamon. Stir well. Add one-fourth cup of milk, and stir. Make small balls of dough, and put them on a baking pan. Press them down a little bit. Bake them at 350 degrees for 10 minutes. Remember the manna that God gave his people. They said it tasted like honey cakes. *(See Friday's reading.)*

☐ **Draw hopscotch squares** with sidewalk chalk. Make seven squares. Print one word in each square: "I can do everything with Jesus' help." Hop across the squares, saying each word as you hop across.

THURSDAY

Read "The Rich Man's Barns," page 544 in *God's Story*. Or read this part of the story:

Jesus told this story. "A rich man grew lots of crops on his farm. 'What should I do?' said the rich man. 'I don't have a place to keep all my crops.'

"Then the rich man said, 'I know! I'll take down my old barns. I will build bigger barns. Then I can store all my crops. I'll have plenty of good things stored away. They'll last for many years to come. I can take life easy. I can eat. I can drink. I can be happy.'

"But God said, 'You are foolish. You will die tonight. Then who will get the things you kept for yourself?'

"This is the way it is for some people," said Jesus. "They are people who aren't rich in giving to God. They store up things for themselves instead." *Luke 12:16-21*

Did you ever hear the story of the dog and the bone? A dog found a big bone. He was taking it back home when he crossed a bridge. He looked over the side of the bridge into the water below. There he saw his own picture looking back up at him. But he thought it was another dog with another bone. Now he wanted that other dog's bone too! So he snapped at the other dog and tried to take its bone. But when he did, his own bone fell into the water. Because he was greedy, he ended up with no bone at all.

Some people are not happy with what they have. They want more and more. That's called being greedy. That's the way the rich man was in Jesus' story. Instead of thinking about what he had, he thought about what he didn't have. If we think that way, we won't have God's peace and joy. We can have peace and joy only when we are happy with what we have.

"Dear God, help me not to be greedy. Help me to be happy with what I have. I want your peace and joy. Thank you."

FRIDAY

Read "Piles of Quail," page 77 in *God's Story*. Or read this part of the story:

Now some of the people wanted different food. "We wish we had meat to eat," they said. "We remember the fish we had in Egypt. We got it free! We ate cucumbers and melons. We had leeks and onions and garlic. But now we don't even like to eat. We don't see any food but this manna!"

Moses heard all of the people fussing at the doors of their tents. God was very angry at them.

"Tell the people to get ready," said God. "Tell them I'll give them meat. They'll eat it for a whole month. They'll eat it until it comes out their noses. They'll eat it until they hate it. It's because they turned against God. They made a fuss about having to leave Egypt."
Numbers 11:4-6, 10, 18, 20

God's people had fussed about their food once before. And God had sent them bread that they called "manna." Now they were tired of manna. They stopped being thankful for what they had. Instead they thought about what they didn't have. So they began fussing again.

Paul wrote a letter to Jesus' followers at Philippi. He wrote, "I've learned the secret of being happy all the time. I can be happy if I'm well fed. I can be happy if I'm hungry. I can be happy if I have all I need. I can be happy if I need things." Would you like to know Paul's secret? He wrote, "The secret is this. I can do everything with Jesus' help. He makes me strong" (Philippians 4:12-13).

Paul's secret was knowing that Jesus is always right there to help. So Paul didn't think about what he didn't have. He thought about what he did have: Jesus' help! If you have Jesus, you have everything you need.

"Dear Father God, now I know Paul's secret. I have that secret too. I can do everything with Jesus' help. Thank you."

Telling the Truth

Tell the truth to each other. *Ephesians 4:25*

MONDAY

Read "The Prophet Who Told the Truth," page 289 in *God's Story*. Or read this part of the story:

King Ahab called for one of his leaders. "Go get Micaiah," he said. "Bring him here."

The leader went to get Micaiah. He said, "All the other prophets are saying Ahab will win. You should say the same thing. Give a good answer."

"I can only say what God tells me to," said Micaiah. He went to see King Ahab.

"Should we fight Ramoth or not?" asked Ahab.

"Go ahead," said Micaiah.

"How many times do I have to ask?" said Ahab. . . .

So Micaiah told the truth. "I saw your army in my mind," he said. "They were . . . like sheep with no shepherd. . . . God plans terrible trouble for you, Ahab."

"Take Micaiah away," said King Ahab. "Throw him in jail. Don't feed him anything but bread and water."

Then King Ahab and King Jehoshaphat went to Ramoth to fight.

The battle lasted all day. King Ahab . . . died that evening.
1 Kings 22:9, 13-17, 23, 26-27, 29, 35

It's not always easy to tell the truth. It's not easy to tell the truth when everyone else is lying. And it's not easy to tell the truth when you know you'll get in trouble for it. Micaiah had to choose. He knew that everyone else was lying. He knew he'd get in trouble for telling the truth. What would he do?

At first Micaiah made fun of the lying prophets. He pretended to agree with them. But the king knew Micaiah didn't really agree with them. So Micaiah told him the truth. Then he got in trouble. The king sent him to jail. Micaiah knew that God hates lies. So he told the truth no matter what.

Is it ever hard for you to tell the truth? What makkes it hard?

"Dear Father God, I know you hate lies. Help me tell the truth no matter what."

TUESDAY

Read "Dipping into the River," page 303 in *God's Story*. Or read this part of the story:

Elisha sent a man out to Naaman with this message. "Go to the Jordan River. Dip down into the river seven times. Then your skin will be well."

Then Naaman went to the Jordan River. He dipped himself in the water seven times. After that, his skin was like new.

Naaman . . . told Elisha, "Now I know that God is the only God. Please let me give you a gift."

"No," said Elisha. "I won't take anything from you."

Now . . . Gehazi, Elisha's servant, began to think. He thought, "Elisha should have taken a gift. So I'll catch up with Naaman. I'll take the gift."

Gehazi ran after Naaman. . . . "Elisha . . . says to tell you that two young prophets just came. Please leave 75 pounds of silver and two sets of clothes for them."

"I'll be glad to," said Naaman. . . .

Gehazi took the silver and clothes to the house. He hid them away. . . .

"Where did you go?" asked Elisha.

"I didn't go anywhere," said Gehazi.

"I know Naaman got down from his chariot," said Elisha. "My spirit was with you when he went to meet you. This is not a time to take money. It's not a time to take clothes or fields. Now you will have Naaman's skin sickness."
2 Kings 5:10, 14-16, 20-27

Why do people tell lies? Elisha's servant lied to get things for himself. Naaman wanted to give the clothes and the silver to Elisha. Gehazi thought it wouldn't hurt if he took those things instead. So he lied to Naaman.

But there's an old saying that goes, "One lie leads to another." When people tell one lie, they often have to tell another lie. That's what happened to Gehazi. He had to lie to Elisha about what he had done. Now he had told two lies.

Lies lead to trouble. And trouble is what Gehazi got.

"Dear God, help me remember not to lie. Help me to always tell the truth. Thank you."

WEDNESDAY

 Read "Abraham Lies Again," page 15 in *God's Story*. Or read this part of the story:

Abraham moved to Gerar for a while. He told people there that his wife, Sarah, was his sister. So the king brought Sarah to his palace. He planned to make her his wife.

But God came to the king one night in a dream. God said to the king, "You are in big trouble. Sarah is already married."

"Abraham told me she was his sister," said the king. "I didn't mean to do anything wrong."

"I know," said God. "Now give Sarah back to Abraham. If you don't, you and your family will die."

Then the king called for

Abraham. "Why did you do this to me?" asked the king.

"I thought you would kill me," said Abraham. "That way, you could have Sarah to be your wife."

Then the king gave Abraham sheep and cows and servants. He gave Sarah back to Abraham too. The king said, "Live wherever you want to live in my land." *Genesis 20:1-3, 5-7, 9-11, 14-15*

Why did Abraham lie? He was afraid the king would kill him. So he lied to keep himself safe. But lies can't keep us safe. It's God who keeps us safe. Abraham's lies got him into trouble. That's the way it is with lies. Lies bring trouble.

But Jesus said, "The truth will set you free" (John 8:32). What happened when Abraham told the king the truth? The king gave Sarah back to Abraham. The king also

SOME THINGS YOU CAN DO THIS WEEK

☐ **Play "Which Is the Lie?"** Get some friends together. Take turns telling three things about yourself (like your favorite food or color or something you've done). Two of the things must be true. One thing should not be true. Everyone else tries to guess which one is not true.

☐ **Play "Whose Voice?"** Get in a circle with your family or friends. Choose a leader. All of the players but the leader should close their eyes. The leader quietly taps one person on the shoulder. That person moves to the middle of the circle very quietly. Then he tries to make his voice sound different. He says, "Tell the truth to each other." Without opening their eyes, the players guess who it is.

☐ **Make a "tell the truth" picture.** Print "Tell the Truth to Each Other" at the top of a piece of paper. Cut out magazine pictures of people talking. Glue them on the paper. Cut out sentences from newspapers, and glue them on the paper too.

☐ **Look at TV ads** and magazine ads to find lies. Many ads try to get people to believe something that's not really true.

☐ **Have a taste test** of foods that have fake flavors. Then taste the real thing. What's the difference? Try real bacon and bacon-flavored bits. Try real butter and fake butter. Try real peaches and peach-flavored diet snacks.

gave him sheep and cows and servants. And the king said Abraham could live anywhere in the land. The truth set everyone free.

Has a lie ever brought you trouble? Is there anything you need to tell the truth about?

"Dear God, I don't want to tell lies. I want to tell the truth. And I will trust you to keep me safe."

THURSDAY

Read "Jacob Tricks Isaac," page 23 in *God's Story*. Or read this part of the story:

"Who is it?" asked Isaac.

"I'm Esau," said Jacob. "... Eat some of this meat. Then you can pray for God's best for me."

"How could you get the meat so fast?" asked Isaac.

"God helped me," said Jacob.

Then Isaac said, "Let me touch you. I want to make sure you really are Esau."

Jacob moved closer to Isaac. Isaac felt his skin. "Your voice sounds like Jacob. But your hands feel like Esau. Are you really Esau?" he asked.

"Yes," said Jacob.

So Isaac prayed for God's riches to come to Jacob. . . .

It was not long until Esau came back from hunting. . . .

"Who is this?" asked Isaac.

"I'm your son Esau," said Esau. . . .

"Jacob tricked me," said Isaac. "He took the prayer I was going to pray for you."

From then on, Esau was angry with Jacob.
Genesis 27:18-24, 28-35, 41

Can you remember the very first lie that the Bible tells about? It happened when Adam and Eve still lived in the Garden. The snake wanted Eve to eat the fruit. The snake said, "You won't die. God knows that the fruit will make you wise, just like God."

But Adam and Eve did not become as wise as God. They grew older and older, too. And one day they died. The snake had lied.

Jesus said that the devil never had a bit of truth in him. "Lies are the language he speaks," said Jesus. "He is a liar, and he is the father of lies" (John 8:44).

Lies are the language of Satan's kingdom. Lies bring trouble. That's what Jacob found out. But truth is what God speaks. And God brings good to people who speak the truth. When we choose to speak the truth, we show whose side we are on.

"Dear Father God, thank you for being a wise, true God. I want to be on your side. Help me choose to tell the truth."

FRIDAY

Read "The Gold Calf," page 70 in *God's Story*. Or read this part of the story:

Now God's people . . . said, "We don't know what's happened to Moses. So make us a god. This new god can lead us."

"Bring me the gold ear rings you're wearing," said Aaron.

So the people brought their gold ear rings to Aaron. He melted the gold. He made it into

a fake god. It was an idol that looked like a calf.

Joshua was with Moses. They got closer to the camp. Then they saw the gold idol. They saw the people dancing. Moses got very angry.

Moses turned to Aaron. "Why did you lead God's people into sin?" he asked.

"Don't get angry," said Aaron. "You know how these people are ready to do wrong. They told me to make gods for them. . . . So I told them to give me their gold ear rings. They did. I threw the gold into the fire. Out came this gold idol!"

Then God made the people sick. It was because of the gold idol they made.
Exodus 32:1-4, 17, 19, 21-24, 35

Aaron's lie may sound funny to us. He said, "I threw the gold into the fire. Out came this gold idol!" Aaron was trying to keep himself out of trouble. He knew Moses would be angry if he heard the truth. But Moses knew the truth anyway.

Aaron lied because he had done something wrong, and he knew it. But his lie didn't make things better. Doing wrong is like digging a hole in the dirt and standing in it. When we lie about it, the hole gets deeper. Then we're afraid someone will find out. So the hole gets still deeper. At last there's only one way out. That's to tell the truth and say, "I'm sorry."

Is there anything you need to tell the truth about? It's not always easy, but it's the right thing to do.

"Dear Father God, when I do wrong, help me to tell the truth about it. I want to be true, like you."

Anger!

"Don't sin when you're angry." Get rid of your anger before the sun sets. *Ephesians 4:26*

MONDAY

Read "Anger, Waiting, and Selfishness," page 241 in *God's Story*. Or read this part of the story:

Wise people look up to God.
  They stay away from sin.
But fools get angry easily.
  They're not careful.

People who get angry too fast will
  get in trouble.
You might get them out of trouble.
But you'll have to do it again.

Don't make friends with people who
  get angry too fast.
You might learn to act like them.
Then you'll be trapped.
Proverbs 14:16; 19:19; 22:24-25

God made us to have feelings. One of those feelings is anger. Anger is not always bad. Sometimes we get angry at bad things that happen. Or someone hurts us or tricks us. Our anger tells us that we need to work something out with that person. We need to take care of the problem. If we think and act wisely, anger can help us find the answers to problems we have.

But sometimes we choose to do the wrong thing when we're angry. We try to hurt the person who hurt us. We might say bad things. Or we might do bad things.

So God doesn't want us to get angry too fast. He wants us to control our anger. He wants us to learn how to get rid of it.

"Dear Father God, help me not to get angry too fast. Help me to control my anger. Help me to learn how to get rid of it."

TUESDAY

 Read "Finding More Water," page 83 in *God's Story*. Or read this part of the story:

There wasn't any water in the Zin Desert. The people got together against Moses again.

Moses and Aaron went to the worship tent. . . . God told Moses, "Get your walking stick. You and Aaron call all the people together. Talk to the rock. Water will flow out of it. . . ."

[Moses] and Aaron called all the people together in front of the rock.

Moses said, "Listen! Do we have to get water from this rock for you?"

Then Moses hit the rock two times with the walking stick.

Water flowed out. The people and their sheep and cows drank.

But God had said just to talk to the rock. He told Moses and Aaron, "You did not trust me. You did not treat me like the most important one. So you won't get to lead these people into Canaan." *Numbers 20:1-2, 6-12*

God's people had been fussing again. Moses was tired of it. He got angry. So he hit the rock instead of talking to it. Moses did not obey God.

It's hard to control anger. It was hard for Moses, and it's hard for us, too. But God teaches us that it's important to control our anger. Why? Because when we don't control our anger, someone gets hurt. When anger is out of control, it starts fights. It starts hate. It leads to other kinds of sin.

How can we control our anger? First, we can ask God to help us. When we feel like we're getting angry, we can take a deep breath. We can count to 10. And we can talk it out instead of hitting it out. Do you have ideas about how to control anger?

"Dear Father God, help me to control my anger. Help me to talk it out instead of hitting it out."

WEDNESDAY

Read "The Vine," page 321 in *God's Story*. Or read this part of the story:

God didn't send trouble to Nineveh. This made Jonah upset. He got angry.

"I knew this would happen," Jonah prayed. "That's why I ran away. I know you're a loving, kind God. You're not in a hurry to get angry. You have plenty of love for everyone. You change your mind about sending trouble. So just let me die. It's better for me to die than to live."

SOME THINGS YOU CAN DO THIS WEEK

☐ **Play newspaper baseball.** Use cardboard tubes for bats and squashed pieces of newspaper for balls. Sometimes players on different teams get angry at each other. Why? What could help them not to get angry?

☐ **Play balloon ball.** Tie a string across a room or between two objects outside. Make it about waist high. Blow up a balloon and use it as a ball. Toss the balloon over the string. A friend on the other side should hit it with his or her hand and try to get it back to your side. See how long you can keep the balloon up and keep it from touching the ground. Why would someone who lost a game get angry? How can you keep from getting angry while playing a game?

☐ **Make lemonade.** First mix five cups of water with one cup of lemon juice. Try some to see how it tastes. Then mix in one cup of sugar. Try it again. Remember that anger can grow inside you. It can make your feelings and your face seem sour. *(See Friday's reading.)*

☐ **Use watercolor paints** to paint sunsets. The Bible says, "Get rid of your anger before the sun sets" (Ephesians 4:26).

☐ **Boil an egg.** Put an egg in a pan of cold water. Bring it to a boil. Then boil it for 10 minutes. What happens? Anger can make you feel like you're boiling inside. If you don't get rid of it, it can make you a hard person to live with.

"What right do you have to be angry?" asked God.

Now God made a vine grow up. It made shade for Jonah. . . .

But . . . the vine dried up. . . . The sun beat down on Jonah's head. He got tired. He was so tired that he felt like dying. "It's better for me to die than to live," he said.

"What right do you have to be angry about the plant?" asked God. . . . "You didn't make it grow. . . . But there are more than 120,000 (one hundred twenty thousand) people in Nineveh. . . . Shouldn't I care about them?" *Jonah 4:1-4, 6-11*

Sometimes our anger shows us there's a problem to work out with someone else. But sometimes it shows that there's a problem to work out inside ourselves. That's the way it was with Jonah.

Why did Jonah get angry? It was because things didn't happen the way he wanted. Nobody was treating him badly. Nobody was hurting him. Nothing was going wrong. In fact, everything was going the way God

planned. But it was not the way Jonah thought it should be. So he was angry. And it was his problem.

Jonah told the people about God. They said they were sorry. Then God forgave them. But Jonah didn't want to forgive them.

Jonah's anger came from putting himself first instead of others. Do you ever get angry because things don't go your way? How can you get rid of that wrong kind of anger?

"Dear God, I'm sorry for getting angry when things don't go my way. Help me to get rid of that kind of anger."

THURSDAY

Read "The First Children," page 6 in *God's Story*. Or read this part of the story:

One day Cain took some of his fruit. He gave it as a gift to God. Abel took some of his best sheep. He gave them as gifts to God.

God said that what Abel gave him was right. But what Cain gave him was not. Cain got mad, and he frowned.

"Why are you mad?" asked God. "Why are you frowning? Do the right thing. Then I'll like what you bring me. But what if you don't do the right thing? Then sin will wait at your door. . . ."

Now Cain asked Abel to go out to the field with him. While they were there, Cain killed Abel.

God said to Cain, "Where is Abel, your brother?"

"I don't know," said Cain. "Do I have to keep track of my brother?"

"What did you do?" asked God. "I know what happened. You're in trouble from now on. You will try to farm the land. But it won't grow food. You will have to move around from place to place." *Genesis 4:3-12*

Why was Cain angry? He wished that God liked his gifts as much as Abel's gifts. Cain was jealous of his brother. Cain did not try to talk it out. His anger led to big trouble.

Sometimes we get angry at brothers or sisters or moms or dads. When that happens, it's best to take time away from each other in different rooms. Then we can cool off. When we're no longer so angry, we can get together again and talk it out.

Some families have family meetings one night each week. Then they can talk about any problems they have. They can talk about the good things that are happening too. It's a way for everyone to help each other build a happy family. How can you help your family when you are angry?

"Dear God, help my family know when to take time to cool off. Help us talk out our problems and love each other."

FRIDAY

Read "Like a Sea Wave," page 762 in *God's Story*. Or read this part of the story:

Remember this. People should be in a hurry to listen. They shouldn't be in such a hurry to talk. They shouldn't get angry very fast. Being angry doesn't help us live the way God wants.

Don't just listen to God's

Word. Instead, do what God's Word says. *James 1:19-20, 22*

Did you ever watch a baby taste a sour pickle or a lemon? The baby makes a funny face and may shake all over.

Have you ever helped bake cookies? Did you ever smell the vanilla flavoring? Vanilla smells great. But did you ever put a little vanilla on your finger and taste it? It's very bitter.

That's the way anger works. We say it makes us sour or bitter. The Bible says, "Don't let anger grow and get you in trouble. It can hurt many people" (Hebrews 12:15). How can anger do that? Anger turns sour when it sits inside us for a long time. We are angry at someone, but we don't talk it out. We don't forgive the person. We just keep being angry. Then the way we think and talk about the person becomes mean. If we don't want anger to grow in us, we must forgive people. We must try to work out our problems with them.

Are you angry at someone? Can you work out your problems with them? How? How can you forgive them?

"Dear God, I don't want anger growing in me. I don't want to be sour or bitter. Help me to work out my problems with people. Help me to forgive and not be angry anymore."

You Can Go First

Don't do anything because you feel you're better than others.
Instead, look at other people as being better than you. *Philippians 2:3*

MONDAY

Read "Clean Feet," page 609 in
God's Story. Or read this part of the
story:

Jesus got up from the
table. He took a long cloth. He
tied it around himself like a belt.
Then he got a big bowl of water.
He started washing his friends'
feet. He dried their feet with the
long cloth.

Then he went back to his
place. "Do you understand
what I just did?" he asked.
"You call me Teacher. You call
me Lord. That's right. That's
what I am. Your Lord and
Teacher just washed your feet.

So you need to wash each
other's feet too.

"I'm showing you the way to
treat others," said Jesus.
John 13:4-5, 12-15

Jesus is God's Son. He was with
God when the world was made. He
was a great teacher. The wind
obeyed him. The sea waves obeyed
him. Sickness left when he told it to
go. Bad spirits had to obey his
command. He even brought dead
people back to life. He was the
greatest, and he could have asked
others to put him first. But he didn't.
Jesus put others first.

When Jesus washed his friends'

feet, he was showing us how to act. No matter how great we are, we should put others first. We may be rich. We may be powerful. We may be in charge. But we must still put others first.

How can you put the people in your family first? How can you put your friends and other people first?

"Dear Father God, thank you for sending Jesus to show us how to act. Help me to put my family and friends first."

TUESDAY

Read "The Neighbor," page 578 in *God's Story.* Or read this part of the story:

One day, a man who knew the Law . . . asked, "Who is my neighbor?"

Then Jesus told him a story. "There once was a man who was on a trip. . . . But robbers jumped out at him. They took his clothes. They beat him. Then they left. . . .

"Soon a priest came down the road. . . . But he . . . just passed by.

"A man who knew the Law came down the road. . . . But he . . . passed by.

"Then a man from another land came down the road. He was a Samaritan. . . . He felt sorry for the hurt man. The Samaritan went over to him and took care of his hurts. Then he put the hurt man on his own donkey. He took the man to an inn. . . .

"The next day, the Samaritan took out his money. He gave some to the person in charge of the inn. 'Take care of this man,' he said. . . .

"Which man was a neighbor?" asked Jesus.

The man who knew the Law said, "The man who was kind."

"Right," said Jesus. "Now you go and do the same thing."
Luke 10:25-37

Reed tossed a ball up in his back yard. He caught it as it came back down. Next door, Mrs. Simms walked to her mailbox. She was an older lady who lived alone.

Reed kept tossing the ball. But then he saw something awful. Mrs. Simms had fallen down by her front steps. She wasn't getting up. Reed called to his mom for help. His mom ran to help Mrs. Simms. Reed called 911 on his telephone. Then he and his mom stayed with Mrs. Simms until help came. Mrs. Simms would be all right.

Reed and his mom had many other things to do. But they were glad to put Mrs. Simms first. How have you put your neighbors and friends first?

"Dear Father God, thank you for my friends and neighbors. Show me how to put them first and help them."

WEDNESDAY

Read "Jacob in the Land of the East," page 25 in *God's Story*. Or read this part of the story:

Jacob kept going on his trip. At last he came to the land of the East. There was a well in a

SOME THINGS YOU CAN DO THIS WEEK

☐ **Play leap frog.** Line up your friends, one behind the other. The first friend gets down on his knees. The second friend jumps over the first friend's back. Then he gets down on his knees. The third friend jumps over the first two. Then he gets down on his knees. Keep going until everyone has jumped. Then the friend who was first gets to jump over everyone else. Remember to let your friends go first in games.

☐ **Practice opening doors for other people.** Watch when you and your family or friends are coming to a door. Walk ahead and open the door. Hold it open until everyone goes through.

☐ **Wash each other's feet.** Get a large bowl of water and lots of towels and wash cloths. Wash the feet of your friends or people in your family. Remember how Jesus did this. *(See Monday's reading.)*

☐ **Practice first aid.** An encyclopedia or a good first-aid book can help. Practice "stop, drop, and roll" in case you need to help someone whose clothes are on fire. Practice holding a cut place up high and pushing on it to stop bleeding. Write emergency phone numbers on a wall chart by the telephone. Remember Jesus' story of the good neighbor. *(See Tuesday's reading.)*

☐ **Make brownies.** Let someone else choose the first piece to eat.

field there. . . . But a huge stone covered the top of the well.

The shepherds would wait until all the sheep were there. Then they would take off the stone and give their sheep water.

Just then Rachel walked up. She was leading her father's sheep. She was a shepherdess.

Jacob saw Rachel. He took the stone off the well. He gave water to her sheep. Then he kissed her. He began to cry. He told Rachel that he was Rebekah's son. Rachel's father, Laban, was his uncle. Rachel ran back and told her father.

Laban came out quickly to meet Jacob. Laban hugged him and took him home.
Genesis 29:1-3, 9-13

It was hot in the daytime. It was cold at night. There were bugs and wild animals to watch for. There were rocky hills to climb. There were cold streams to cross. And there were lots of sheep to keep up with. It was a shepherd's job, and it was hard work. It's the work that Rachel did.

One day, someone new came to the well. It was Jacob. Jacob put Rachel first. What did she need? She needed to get the stone off of the opening to the well. So Jacob took the stone off. Rachel needed to water her sheep. So Jacob gave water to her sheep.

Solomon wrote, "God loves people who make others feel important" (Proverbs 3:34). When you put others first, you make them feel important. How can you put others first?

"Dear God, help me to think about what other people need. Help me to put others first."

THURSDAY

Read "Jonathan's Son," page 164 in *God's Story*. Or read this part of the story:

There was a man who had been a servant in Saul's family. . . .

"Is anybody from Saul's family still alive?" asked David. "Is there someone I can be kind to because of Jonathan?"

"There is Jonathan's son," the servant said. "He can't walk."

So David sent for Jonathan's son. His name was Mephibosheth. He came to see David. He bowed down.

"Don't be scared," said David. "I'm going to be kind to you. . . . Your father, Jonathan, was my best friend. I'll give you all the land that Saul, your grandfather, owned. I'll always let you eat at my table."

So Mephibosheth ate at David's table. He was like a part of David's family. Mephibosheth had a little boy. Saul's servant and his family helped them.
2 Samuel 9:1-3, 5-7, 11-12

Jana can't see. But Jana has a beautiful voice. She sings songs that tell people how great God is. Daniel is in a wheel chair. But Daniel has a big, beautiful smile. He helps people know that God is good. Kendall can't hear. But she has a lot of love in her heart for others.

Mephibosheth couldn't walk. But King David treated him like a king. Mephibosheth got to eat at the king's own table every day. Do you know people who can't see or hear or walk? How can you put them first? Are you a person who can't hear or walk? How can you put others first?

What would this world be like if we all obeyed God and put each other first?

"Dear God, thank you for giving all people special things they can do well. Help me to see how special other people are. Help me to put others first."

FRIDAY

Read "Sheep and Goats," page 605 in *God's Story*. Or read this part of the story:

"I'll come back," said Jesus. ". . . Then I'll put the people into different groups. . . .

"I'll put people who are my sheep into one group. They'll be on my right. . . .

"Then I'll talk to the people on my right. I'll say, 'Come! My Father has good things for you. . . .'

"I'll say, 'I was hungry, and you gave me food. I was thirsty, and you gave me a drink. I needed a place to stay, and you asked me to come in. I needed clothes, and you gave me clothes. I was sick, and you took care of me. I was in jail, and you came to see me.'

"Then I'll say, 'You did these things for other people. You did these things for people who don't seem important at all. That's when you did them for me.'

"Then I'll talk to the people on my left. I'll say, 'You never did these things for others. . . . So you left me out too.'"
Matthew 25:31-36, 40-41, 45

It was a rainy day. Libby jumped out of the school bus and ran to her house. She hung her drippy raincoat by Mom's umbrella in the hall. Then she got a snack and sat in a big, soft chair by the window. Libby could hear the wind. She could hear the soft rain. Then she heard someone tapping at the door.

Libby's mom answered the door. Libby peeked around the corner to see who it was. It was a man selling something. Mom talked a minute. She didn't buy whatever it was. But then she said to the man, "Here. Take this with you." She handed him her umbrella.

The man thanked Libby's mom. Then he walked down the street with his new umbrella over him. Libby saw it happen. But nobody else ever knew.

Jesus said that when we help others, it's as if we are helping him. We should treat others as if they are just as important as Jesus. That means we should put others first. How do you put others first?

"Dear Father God, show me what I can do to treat others as important people. Help me to put others first."

I Hope in God

God is the God of hope. Trust in him. Then he can fill you with joy and peace. Hope can flow in and out of you by the power of God's Spirit. *Romans 15:13*

MONDAY

Read "Lions," page 456 in *God's Story.* Or read this part of the story:

The other leaders tried to find something wrong with Daniel. But they couldn't.

Then the men . . . found him praying to God.

So they went back to the king. They said, "Didn't you make a law? Anybody who doesn't pray to you gets thrown to the lions."

So the king gave an order for Daniel to be brought in. Then Daniel was thrown into the lions' den.

As soon as morning came, the king . . . called to Daniel with a sad voice. "Daniel, could your God save you from the lions?"

. . . Daniel called back. "My God sent his angel. He closed the lions' mouths. They didn't hurt me. . . ."

The king was very happy. He ordered his servants to take

Daniel out of the den. They saw that he was not hurt at all. That's because he trusted God.
Daniel 6:4, 11-12, 16, 19-23

What is hope? It's more than just wishing that something would happen. It's more than just wanting something to happen. It's being sure that something will happen. When we read God's promises in the Bible, we know they will happen. That's because God always tells the truth. And he always keeps his promises. So we trust him. We have hope. We know he will do what he says. We look forward to seeing how he is going to work things out.

Daniel trusted God to take care of him. So Daniel had hope. Daniel knew that God makes everything turn out for good. He does this for people who love him. So Daniel knew that no matter how bad things seemed, God would work it out. And God did.

What do you trust God to do? Can you think of some of God's promises? What do you hope for?

"Dear God, thank you for your promises to take care of me. I trust in you. And I put my hope in you."

TUESDAY

Read "Facing the Enemy," page 291 in *God's Story*. Or read this part of the story:

One day some men came to see King Jehoshaphat. "A big army is coming this way!" they said. "They're coming to fight us!"

Jehoshaphat was surprised and afraid. He told all the people not to eat. They all came together to pray for God's help.

Then God's Spirit came on one of the men. "King Jehoshaphat! All you people! Listen!" he said. "Here's what God says. . . . You won't have to fight. Just stand there and watch. You'll see how God saves you.

"So God says not to be afraid. He says not to give up. Go out tomorrow. Face the enemy. God will be with you." . . .

Then God began to work out his plan. . . . The enemies began to fight each other. They killed each other. . . .

God's people . . . cheered for God. . . . They were very happy because God had won.
2 Chronicles 20:2-4, 14-27

Trusting God means letting him take care of your problems. You tell your worry to God, like Jehoshaphat did. God is the wisest of all. He can take care of your troubles. Sometimes God works all of it out, and we don't have to do anything. At other times, God shows us something we can do to help work it out. What did God tell Jehoshaphat to do? He said, "Don't be scared. Don't give up. Face the enemy. God will be with you."

God's people trusted God. They had hope. They marched out, praising God. And God saved them! You can trust God too. When you

SOME THINGS YOU CAN DO THIS WEEK

☐ **Make paper-sack puppets.** Draw Daniel's face on a sack. The bottom of the sack is the top of the head. Draw a king and lions on other sacks. Stick your hand inside the sack to use the puppet. Make a puppet play about Daniel in the lions' den. Tape sounds to go with it. *(See Monday's reading.)*

☐ **Make paper-plate lion masks.** Draw a lion face on a plate. Cut out the eyes. Glue on strips of paper, curling ribbon, or yarn to make a mane. Punch one hole at eye level on each side of the plate. Tie strings through the holes to make the mask. *(See Monday's reading.)*

☐ **Play "Touch the Coat."** This is like "Pin the Tail on the Donkey." Hang a coat, robe, or pair of jeans over the back of a tall chair. Stand across the room with your eyes closed. Let someone turn you around and give you a piece of masking tape. Walk across the room and stick the tape where you think the clothes are. *(See Friday's reading.)*

☐ **Play "Follow the String."** Get some treats to hide for your friends or family. Tie a long string to each treat. Then hide the treats. Let the strings hang out and cross the room. Give each friend the end of one string, and let the person follow it to find a treat. Talk about the hope everyone has that there is a treat at the end of the string. Talk about the hope that we can have in God, too. He gives us the best treat of all. We can trust in God and live with him forever! *(See Friday's reading.)*

trust God, you have hope that everything will be all right. And it will!

"Dear Father God, thank you for being a God I can trust. I trust you with my problems. I hope in you."

WEDNESDAY

Read "The Sign," page 340 in *God's Story*. Or read this part of the story:

Now the army of Aram got together with the army of Israel. They marched out to fight Jerusalem in Judah. King Ahaz and his people were afraid. They were like trees shaking in the wind.

God spoke to Isaiah. "Go see King Ahaz," he said. . . .

God said to tell Ahaz, "Be careful. Don't panic. Don't be scared. Don't give up. The kings of Aram and Israel are like fire wood that's burned up. They plan to get rid of Judah."

Then God said this.

"It won't happen.
In 65 years, there will be little left of Israel.

So stand firm in what you believe.
If you don't, you won't stand at all." 2 Kings 16:5; Isaiah 7:2-9

God wanted King Ahaz to trust him. So God sent Isaiah to tell him not to panic or give up. But then Isaiah said something else very important. Isaiah said, "Stand firm in what you believe. If you don't, you won't stand at all." God was telling Ahaz to believe in him and keep on believing. Then Ahaz could have hope.

Paul wrote a letter to the Roman people. He wrote, "God's Word from long ago is there to teach us. It helps us keep living the right way. It makes us brave. That gives us hope" (Romans 15:4). So the story of Ahaz is there to help *us* know how to live too. We can know to stand firm in what we believe. That will help us be brave. And it will give us hope.

What do you believe? What is your hope?

"Dear God, thank you for the stories of your people from long ago. Help me remember to stand firm in what I believe. I believe in you. I hope in you."

THURSDAY

Read "Faith," page 786 in *God's Story*. Or read this part of the story:

Now faith is being sure of what you hope for. It's being sure of things you don't see.

We have faith. So we understand that God made the world and all of space. He told it to happen, and it happened. He made things we see out of things we don't see.

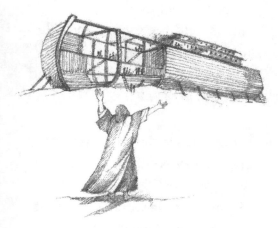

Noah had faith. God told him what was coming. So he built an ark to save his family.

Abraham had faith. . . . He didn't know where God was leading him. But he went to the Promised Land.

Isaac had faith. . . . Jacob had faith. . . . Joseph had faith. . . . Moses had faith.

God's people had faith. So they walked across dry ground at the Red Sea.
Hebrews 11:1, 3, 7-9, 20-24, 29

There was once a man who taught people in Africa about God. One day he told friends in another country about Africa. He told about the tall grass and wild animals. He also told about "bush eyes." He had to watch for wild animals hidden in the bushes or tall grass. So he said he used his bush eyes. That means he looked carefully all around him. He could see hidden dangers only if he was looking for them.

When you trust in God, it's as if you have bush eyes. You see that God is always working. You see that God will take care of you. You see that God will make everything turn out for your good. He will do it because you love him. So no matter how bad things may look to other people, you have hope. That's because you have bush eyes. They're the eyes you use to see with your heart. What can you see

God doing when you look with your "bush eyes"?

"Dear God, help me to see that you are always working. Help me to see that you will make everything turn out to be good for me. I love you. I hope in you."

FRIDAY

Read "The Sick Little Girl," page 551 in *God's Story*. Or read this part of the story:

A leader from the town's worship house . . . bowed down in front of Jesus. "My little girl is sick," he said. "She is going to die. Please come with me. Touch my little girl so she will live."

So Jesus went with Jairus. Many people followed them. . . .

A woman was in the crowd. She had been sick for 12 years. . . . This woman . . . reached out. "I just need to touch his clothes!" she thought. "Then I'll be well." So she touched Jesus' coat.

Right away, she was well. Jesus was still talking to the woman when some men came to Jairus. "Your little girl has died," they said. . . .

Jesus . . . told Jairus, "Don't be afraid. Just believe."

Jesus held the girl's hand. He said, "Little girl, get up."

Right away, the girl got up and walked! *Luke 8:41-44, 49-50, 54-55*

Two people in this story had lots of hope. Who were they? What were they hoping for?

Sometimes we wonder why God lets us have problems. But our problems let us know that we need God. We wish God would take care of all our problems right now. But sometimes we have to trust him and wait. We believe in God. We know that "there is nothing that God can't do" (Luke 1:37). So we have hope that everything will turn out for our good.

We know that God can make sick people well. But we don't see all the sick people get well. So we wonder about it. But God wants us to keep believing in him. We're to keep waiting and trusting and hoping. Why? Because we have the greatest hope of all. We will live with God forever. Then there will be no hurting, no sickness, no crying, no dying. That is our most wonderful hope! God *will* make everything turn out for our good!

"Dear God, I believe in you, and I trust you. Thank you for my most wonderful hope of living with you forever!"

You Can Do It!

Let's think about how to help each other love. Let's think about how to help each other do good. *Hebrews 10:24*

MONDAY

Read "A Look into the New Land" and "Scared of the People," pages 79 and 80 in *God's Story*. Or read this part of the stories:

So Moses chose 12 leaders. Moses told them, ". . . Find out what the land is like. Find out if the people are strong or not. . . ."

So the 12 men set out. They looked all around the land. They found a valley where grapes were growing. They cut off a branch of grapes. . . .

After 40 days the 12 men came back to Moses. . . . "It's a good land," they said. ". . . But the people who live there are strong. . . . We can't fight those people. . . . They are stronger than we are. . . ."

Joshua and Caleb were two of the 12 men who looked around Canaan. They said, "The land is very good. If God is happy with us, he will lead us there. . . .

"We'll win over those people," said Joshua and Caleb.

"Don't be scared of them. God
is with us."
Numbers 13:3, 17-31; 14:6-9

God wants us to help each other
think, *I can follow God. I can obey
God. I can do what God has given me
to do.* God doesn't ever ask us to
do things we can't do. We need
God's help to do what he asks. But
with his help, we can do anything.
And part of our job is to help other
people see that they can do things
too. A word for that is to *encourage*
others.

Moses sent 12 leaders to look at
the new land. Joshua and Caleb
came back and told God's people,
"We can do it! God will give us this
land." But 10 leaders came back and
said, "We can't." They made the
people feel helpless. They made the
people scared. Believing helps us
feel we can. Not believing makes us
feel we can't. How can you help
others think, *We can keep following
God?*

*"Dear God, thank you for helping us
do everything you ask us to do. Show
me how to help others think, I can!"*

TUESDAY

 Read "A Trip to the Cave," page
44 in *God's Story.* Or read this part
of the story:

Joseph cried when his
father died. Then he went back
to Canaan. . . . Joseph's brothers
went too.

Jacob's sons put his body in a
cave. . . . Then they all went back
to Egypt.

Now Joseph's brothers were
afraid. They said, "Joseph
might still be angry with us.
It's all because we sold him
many years ago." So they sent
Joseph a message. "Before our
father died, he told us
something. He said we should
tell you to forgive us. So we
ask you to forgive us. . . . We
will be your servants," they
said.

But Joseph was kind to them
and said, "Don't be afraid. You
meant to hurt me. But God
planned for good things to
come from it. Many lives have
been saved because of what
happened. So don't be afraid. I

will take care of you and your families." *Genesis 50:1, 7-8, 13-21*

Joseph's brothers were afraid. They had been mean to Joseph a long time ago. They had sold him to men who were going to Egypt. They had thought they would never see him again. But now Joseph was in charge of the whole land of Egypt. Joseph was even in charge of them. The brothers were afraid Joseph would try to get even with them. They were not brave now. They were scared.

Joseph could choose. He could let his brothers stay scared. They would think, *We can't live here and be safe.* Or he could help his brothers be brave. They would think, *We can live here and be safe.* Joseph forgave them. Forgiving others helps them feel better. They feel brave. They think, *I can be what God wants me to be.* We can encourage others by forgiving them.

"Dear Father God, help me to forgive people who have hurt me. I want to help other people feel brave."

WEDNESDAY

 Read "In the Grain Fields," page 112 in *God's Story*. Or read this part of the story:

Ruth went to the fields. She started picking up grain that was left over. She was working in Boaz's fields. . . .

Boaz came back from town. He . . . talked to the man in charge of the workers. "Who is that young woman over there?" he asked.

"That's the woman who came back with Naomi," he said. "She . . . asked us if she could gather grain that was left over. . . ."

Boaz went over to talk to Ruth. "You can stay right here in my field," he said. "Don't go anywhere else. Follow along after my servant girls. I told my workers not to bother you. If you get thirsty, drink from our water jars."

Ruth bowed down. "You've made me feel much better. You've been kind to me."
Ruth 2:3-10, 13

Ethan helped his mom at a special store. They sold clothes that didn't cost much to people who didn't have much money. They gave people food, too. Sometimes an old man came to the store. He didn't have money to buy the things he needed. Ethan and his mom helped the man find work he could do. He could empty the trash. He could sweep the floor. He could clean the parking lot. Then they gave him clothes or food. The man always felt better when he worked for what they gave him.

Naomi and Ruth didn't have money to buy what they needed. So Ruth worked in the field, picking up grain that was left over. Boaz was kind to share his grain with her. Boaz encouraged Ruth. He helped her think, *I can get the food we need.* Sharing and being kind to others is a way to encourage them.

SOME THINGS YOU CAN DO THIS WEEK

☐ **Take a wheelbarrow walk.** Get down on your hands and knees. Ask a friend to hold up your legs at the ankles. Walk forward on your hands while your friend holds your legs. Then trade places. Let your friend be the wheelbarrow. Think of how to help each other think, *I can do this!*

☐ **Play "I Spy."** Take turns with friends asking each other to guess something you see. Give clues. Remember the spies. *(See Monday's reading.)*

☐ **Tear a piece of plain paper** into a few pieces. Choose one piece for yourself. Look at it, and think of something it looks like. Glue it onto a piece of colored paper. Then use crayons and markers to draw around it. Make a picture of the thing you think it looked like. Do this with friends and help them think, *I can do this!*

☐ **Get different kinds of dry cereal.** Try to get kinds that are made with different grains. Taste each one. Can you tell the difference between the way corn and wheat taste? Can you tell that rice and oats taste different? Ruth gathered a grain called "barley." *(See Wednesday's reading.)*

☐ **Make name pictures** for people in your family. Try to find out what each person's name means. Then print each person's name on a paper plate. Under the name, print what it means. Hang the plates by putting ribbons through two holes at the top of each plate.

It helps them be brave. It helps them think, *I can.*

"Dear Father God, thank you for people who encourage me. Help me to encourage other people."

THURSDAY

Read "The Lamb of God," page 514 in *God's Story.* Or read this part of the story:

Andrew and his friend . . . followed Jesus. . . . At the end of the day . . . Andrew went to get his brother. "We met the Promised One!" Andrew said. Then he took his brother to meet Jesus too.

Jesus took a good look at Andrew's brother. He said, "Your name is Simon. But I'm going to call you Peter, the rock."

Jesus wanted to go to Galilee the next day. He saw Philip and said, "Come with me."

. . . Philip went to find Nathanael. . . . Nathanael went with Philip.

Jesus saw Nathanael coming. "Here is a man who tells the truth," said Jesus. "There are no lies in him!"

"How could you know me?" asked Nathanael.

"I saw you before," said Jesus. "You were under the fig tree. . . ."

"Teacher!" said Nathanael. "You are God's Son! You are the King of God's people!"
John 1:40-49

What if you had lived when Jesus was here on earth? What do you think Jesus would have said about you? Jesus told Simon, "I'm going to call you Peter, the rock." What would Jesus have called you? If you don't know what your name means, ask your mom and dad. They may be able to find a name book that tells about your name.

Jesus told Peter, "I'm going to call you Peter, the rock." That helped Peter feel stronger and braver. Jesus said about Nathanael, "There are no lies in him." That helped Nathanael feel stronger and braver. Jesus let Peter and Nathanael know that he liked them. He let them think, *I can be Jesus' friend!*

When we say good things to others, we help them feel brave. It's one way we can encourage them.

"Dear Father God, thank you for knowing my name. Thank you for letting me know I can be Jesus' friend. Help me to let others know that they can be Jesus' friends too."

FRIDAY

Read "Being Trained to Do What's Right," page 234 in *God's Story*. Or read this part of the story:

Listen when someone shows you what's right. That shows you how to live. People who don't listen lead others to do wrong.

Teach your children the right way to live. Then they will live that way when they grow older.

Make sure that your children get into trouble when they do wrong. It may save them from bigger trouble later on.
Proverbs 10:17; 22:6; 23:13-14

Sometimes we need people to help us think, *I can. I can do what's right.* And sometimes the way they help us is by teaching us what's right and what's wrong. God wants us to be brave about doing what's right and scared about doing what's wrong. God wants to encourage us to do what's right. He wants to discourage us from doing what's wrong.

Who are the people who teach you what's wrong and what's right? How do they help you think, *I can do what's right?*

When you choose what's right, that helps other people choose what's right. They see you doing the right thing. So they think, *I can do the right thing too.* Doing right encourages other people. Who watches you and learns to do what's right?

"Dear God, thank you for the people who teach me what's right and what's wrong. Help me to do what's right. Then I can help others know that they can do right too."

Saying No to Wrong

God won't let a sin come to your mind unless he knows you can say no to it. . . . God gives you a way to say no. *1 Corinthians 10:13-14*

MONDAY

Read "Hiding in My Heart," page 208 in *God's Story*. Or read this part of the story:

Good things come to
people who do what's right.
They keep God's rules. They obey
him.
They look for God with all their
hearts.
They don't do wrong.
You have told us your rules, God.
We should obey all of them.

I have hidden your word in my
heart so I won't sin against
you.
I'm glad to follow your rules.

I will not forget your word.
Psalm 119:1-4, 11, 14, 16

The air was dry. The bright, hot summer sun beat down. There were only two good places to be. One was indoors with cold air blowing. The other was at the pool, where most of the children were. They dipped and dived into the cold water. On a wall beside the life guard was a big sign. "Walk, don't run." "No diving from side." "No glass bottles." And there were other rules. They were there to keep people safe.

God gave us rules too. They help keep us from sinning. The Bible tells us how to live the way God wants. But God's words need to be in our hearts, too. How can we get God's words into our hearts? We can learn to say some of them without looking. Then God's words are with us all the time. And having his words in our hearts helps to keep us from sinning. What are some of God's words that you have in your heart?

"Dear Father God, help me to learn more of your words. I want to hide your words in my heart so I won't sin."

TUESDAY

 Read "Trying to Make Jesus Do Wrong," page 513 in *God's Story*. Or read this part of the story:

Satan tried to make Jesus do wrong. "Are you really God's Son?" he asked. "Then why don't you turn the rocks into bread?"

Here's what Jesus told Satan: "God's Word says that people don't live just by eating bread. They live by believing every word God says."

Then Satan took Jesus to Jerusalem. They stood on the tallest part of the worship house. "If you really are God's Son, jump off," said Satan. "God's Word says that his angels will keep you safe. . . ."

But Jesus gave this answer to Satan: "God's Word also says not to test the Lord your God."

Then Satan . . . showed Jesus the riches of all the world's kingdoms. "I'll give all this to you," Satan said. "Just bow down and worship me."

"Get away from me, Satan!" said Jesus. "God's Word says to worship only the Lord your God. Serve only him." *Matthew 4:1, 3-10*

Satan tried to get Jesus to do what was wrong. But Jesus had God's words in his heart. So Jesus answered Satan by saying God's words. He told Satan why he wouldn't sin. That's the way Jesus said no.

Satan would like us to do wrong too. But we can say no. In fact, we can fight sin the same way Jesus did. We can learn Bible verses that help us say why we choose God's way.

The Bible tells us that God's Word is like his Spirit's sword. So we can use it to fight Satan. We can say, "No. I won't be afraid. God's Word says, 'I trust in God. I will not be afraid'" (Psalm 56:4). What things do you need to say no to? How can God's Word help you?

"Dear Father God, thank you for giving me your Word to fight sin. Help me to stay away from sin."

WEDNESDAY

 Read "A Way to Say No," page 683 in *God's Story*. Or read this part of the story:

I want you to know something. God's people who lived in Moses' time followed God's cloud. But God wasn't happy with most of them. Most of them died in the desert.

This happened to teach us that we shouldn't want to sin. That's what they did.

The only sins that come to your mind are sins everyone has problems with. God won't let a sin come to your mind unless he

knows you can say no to it. Let's say a sin comes to your mind. Then God gives you a way to say no. That way, you can win over sin.

You may eat. You may drink. But whatever you do, do it to show how great God is.
1 Corinthians 10:1, 5-6, 13, 31

Long ago, when the world was new, Cain got angry at Abel. But God said something important to Cain. God said, "What if you don't do the right thing? Then sin will wait at your door. Sin wants to catch you. But you must not let it get to you" (Genesis 4:7).

Sin is all around us in our world. Sometimes it's easier to sin than to do what's right. Sin wants to catch us, just like it caught Cain. But God doesn't want us to let sin get to us. So God helps us. He won't let a sin come to our minds unless he knows we are strong enough to say no. He always gives us a way to say no. Sometimes we just have to look for the way and ask him to help.

What do you need the most help saying no to?

"Dear God, I don't want to sin. But sometimes I do sin. Forgive me, and help me to say no to sin."

Thursday

Read "In Saul's Camp at Night," page 153 in *God's Story*. Or read this part of the story:

Saul was in the middle of the camp. His men were sleeping all around him.

"Who will go with me into the camp?" asked David.

"I will," said one of David's men.

So that night, David and the other man went quietly into Saul's camp. They went up to

Some Things You Can Do This Week

☐ **Draw a maze** for everyone in your family. Give them the mazes, and see if they can find the way out. Remember how God helps us find a way out of the sins that come to our minds.

☐ **Play "Hide the Word."** Ask one person to hide a small Bible while you close your eyes. Then look for the Bible. Let the other person tell you if you are near (hot) or far (cold) from the Bible while you look. Think about hiding God's Word in your heart. *(See Monday's reading.)*

☐ **Look at ads** in magazines and on TV. Sometimes ads put sinful ideas into our minds. Sometimes they make us want to sin. See if you can find ads like this with your family. Talk about what's wrong with them.

☐ **Make sugar cookies.** Mix one stick of softened butter and three-fourths cup of sugar. Beat in one egg, one-half teaspoon of vanilla, and a few drops of food coloring. Mix two and one-half cups of flour, one teaspoon baking powder, and one-fourth teaspoon salt. Add this to the butter mix. Roll dough out. Cut with a heart-shaped cookie cutter. Before baking the cookies, choose a letter from alphabet-shaped cereal to press onto the middle of each heart. Put a *G* for God, *J* for Jesus, *B* for Bible, *HS* for God's Holy Spirit. Bake at 375 degrees for 8 minutes. Think about hiding God's Word in your heart. *(See Monday's reading.)*

☐ **Cut out a sword from cardboard.** Color the handle. Put foil around the blade to make it silver. Remember that the sword of the Spirit is God's Word. *(See Tuesday's reading.)*

Saul. He was sleeping. His spear was sticking into the ground by his head. . . .

"This is the day!" said the man with David. "God is giving your enemy to you. I can kill him with one blow. Let me pin him to the ground!"

"No," said David. "He is the one God chose to be king."

David took Saul's spear and jug of water. Then the two men left.

David yelled to Abner. . . . "You didn't guard your king. Just look! Where is the king's spear? Where is the jug of water that was by his head?"

Saul knew David's voice. He said, "Is that you, David?"

"Yes, my king," said David. . . . "You're hunting me like you'd hunt birds in the mountains. . . ."

"I have sinned," said Saul. . . . "I won't try to hurt you anymore. . . ."

"Here's your spear," said David. . . . "God gave you to me today. But I wouldn't kill the one God chose as king. . . ."
1 Samuel 26:5-9, 12, 14-17, 20-23

David hadn't done anything wrong. But King Saul was trying to kill him. David had to leave home and hide in caves. Now he had his chance. He could kill King Saul. He could stop running. He could be the king. But David would not kill Saul.

Even one of David's men tried to get David to let him kill King Saul. But David wouldn't let him do it. David knew it would be wrong. The sin came to his mind. But David said no to it.

Sometimes our friends try to get us to sin. That makes it much harder to say no. We don't want to hurt our friends' feelings. Or we're afraid that if we say no, they'll stop being our friends. But God will help us say no to sin, even if we have to say no to our friends.

Did a friend ever try to get you to do something wrong? What will you say if a friend asks you to do wrong?

*"Dear Father God, I want to be like
David. Help me say no to sin, even if
my friends ask me to do wrong."*

FRIDAY

 Read "Jesus' Brothers and Sisters,"
page 780 in *God's Story*. Or read
this part of the story:

Now people have
human bodies. So Jesus became
human too. That way, when he
died, he could get rid of Satan.

Jesus . . . wasn't helping
angels when he died. He was
helping people. So he had to be
human.

Jesus had to become human
like us. That's so he could
understand us. Now he can tell
God what it's like to be human.

It hurt Jesus to have sins come
to his mind. He had to say no to
sin. Sins come to our minds too.
But Jesus knows what that's
like, so he can help us.
Hebrews 2:14, 16-18

Because we are human, our human
bodies want to sin sometimes. Sin
looks good to us. And even though
we know we shouldn't, we
sometimes sin.

Did you ever think about how
much Jesus was like you? He was
like you while he lived on earth.
When a sin came to his mind, he
said no.

Jesus' human body wanted to
sin sometimes. Sin probably
looked good to him sometimes
too. But Jesus always said no. He
always chose to do what was right.
He never sinned. But he
understands what it's like for us to
want to sin.

What if I don't know what things
are wrong? Paul wrote, "Do
everything in Jesus' name giving
thanks to God" (Colossians 3:17).
I might wonder if it would be a sin
to do something. I can ask, "Can I
do it in Jesus' name? Can I give
thanks to God while I'm doing it?"
That's one way of choosing when
to say no.

*"Dear Father God, thank you for
sending Jesus. Thank you that he
knows what it's like to be human. Help
me to know what's right and wrong.
And help me to say no to sin."*

Feeling Good about Myself

My help comes from God. He made heaven and earth. *Psalm 121:2*

MONDAY

Read "Fire!" and "The Snake,"
pages 49 and 50 in *God's Story*. Or
read this part of the stories:

Moses . . . came to
Horeb Mountain. . . . God came
to Moses there. He showed
himself as fire that was burning
on a bush.

"I've seen how unhappy my
people are," said God. "I've
heard them crying in Egypt.
I'm sending you to the king.
You'll bring my people out of
Egypt."

"But who am I?" asked Moses.
"I'm not strong enough to go to
the king. How can I bring the
Jews out of Egypt?"

"I'll be with you," said
God.

Then Moses said, "I've never
been good at talking to
people. . . . I'm too slow."

"Who gave people their
mouths?" asked God. "Who
makes people able to hear or
see? Don't I do that? So go. I'll
help you talk. I'll teach you what
to say."

"Please, God," said Moses.
"Send somebody else."

Then God became angry at
Moses. "How about Aaron, your

brother? He can talk well. He is already on his way here. He will be glad to see you. You'll talk to him and tell him what to say. I'll help both of you."
Exodus 3:1-2, 7, 10-12; 4:10-15

God chose Moses to do something important. But Moses didn't feel very good about himself. Moses said, "I'm not strong. I'm not good at talking. Send somebody else." That's when God got angry. God already knew that Moses couldn't do it. But God wasn't worried. Moses couldn't do it, but God could do anything. All Moses had to do was trust and obey. As long as Moses trusted God and obeyed, he could do anything God asked.

You are just as important to God as Moses was. God loves you just as much as he loved Moses. And if God says you can do something, you can. Jesus told Paul, "My power shows up best when you're weak" (2 Corinthians 12:9).

What do you need God to help you do?

"Dear Father God, I am not strong, but you are. Thank you for being strong in me. Help me to always trust and obey you."

TUESDAY

 Read "I'm like a Child," page 380 in *God's Story.* Or read this part of the story:

These are Jeremiah's words.

God spoke to me. "I knew you before I made you inside your mother. I chose you before you were born," said God. "I chose you to be a prophet. I chose you to tell my words to the nations."

"Lord God," I said. "I'm not good at talking to people. I'm like a child."

"Don't say that you're like a child," said God. "You have to go where I tell you to go. You have to say what I tell you to say. Don't be afraid of people. I'm with you. I will take care of you."

Then God touched my mouth with his hand. He said, "I've put

my words in your mouth. Tell my people what I say. . . .

"I have made you like a fort," said God. . . . "You'll stand against kings, leaders, priests, and people. They'll fight you. But they won't win, because I'm with you. I'll save you."
Jeremiah 1:1, 4-9, 17-19

Moses wasn't the only one who didn't feel good about himself. Jeremiah felt like that too. God chose Jeremiah to do something important. But Jeremiah said, "I'm not good at talking to people. I'm like a child." That sounds a little like what Moses said.

But God told Jeremiah not to say that. God said, "I'm with you. I will save you." That was the important thing. Paul wrote, "I'm glad to brag that I'm weak. . . . I may not be strong by myself. But I'm very strong in Jesus" (2 Corinthians 12:9-10).

You are just as important to God as Jeremiah was. God loves you just as much as he loved Jeremiah. How does God help you to be strong?

"Dear Father God, I am weak. But I know you are strong. Thank you for loving me and for choosing me. I can be strong with you."

WEDNESDAY

Read "On Top of the Water," page 557 in *God's Story*. Or read this part of the story:

Out on the lake, a strong wind was blowing. The water was getting wavy.

From the hill, Jesus saw his friends in their boat. They were rowing hard. They were trying to go one way. But the wind was blowing them the other way.

About three o'clock in the morning, Jesus went out to them. He walked right on top of the water.

Jesus' friends . . . got scared when they saw him. They yelled! They thought he was a ghost.

"It's just me," said Jesus. "Don't be afraid."

"If it's really you, tell me to come to you," said Peter. "Let me walk on the water too."

"Come on," said Jesus.

So Peter got out of the boat. He stepped onto the water. He began to walk to Jesus. Then he saw the waves. He got scared, and he started going down into the water.

"Lord! Save me!" Peter cried.

Right away, Jesus reached out to Peter. He lifted Peter up. "Your faith is so small!" said Jesus. "Why didn't you believe?" *Matthew 14:24-31*

What do you think it was like that night with Jesus' friends in the boat? They were all strong men, pulling hard on the oars. But the boat just wouldn't move against the wind and waves.

Then Jesus' friends thought they saw a ghost! Now they were really scared! Peter was glad when he heard Jesus' voice. Peter was ready to jump out and go to Jesus. And

SOME THINGS YOU CAN DO THIS WEEK

☐ **Blow up five balloons.** Print one word on each balloon: "My help comes from God" (Psalm 121:2). Ask someone to pop one balloon by sitting on it. Then say the verse. Say the missing word when you come to it. Pop another balloon, and say the verse. Keep going until all the balloons are popped.

☐ **Play "Electricity."** Ask friends to sit in a circle with you and hold hands. Choose one person to be "it" in the middle. When "it" is not looking at you, squeeze one hand that you're holding. That person squeezes the next person's hand, and so on around the circle. But try to squeeze hands when "it" is not looking, because his job is to see someone squeezing hands. That's where the "electricity" is. If "it" finds it, he trades places with that person. Think about power and weakness.

☐ **Make a stormy soap-flake sea.** Mix a little water with some powdered soap for washing clothes. Use an electric mixer. Add water a little at a time while you're mixing. Keep adding it until you can make fluffy peaks, like waves. Add blue food coloring. Put some on a paper plate, and make a stormy lake. Cut out a paper boat for it. (See Wednesday's reading.)

when Jesus told him to come, he did. He didn't feel bad about himself until he stopped looking at Jesus. He saw how big the waves were. He must have thought, *I can't walk on water!* And he was right. But as long as Peter kept trusting Jesus, he could do anything Jesus said.

We are like that too. As long as we trust God and his Son, Jesus, we can do anything God asks us to do. That's because it's God's power at work, not ours. What does God's power help you to do?

"Dear God, help me remember to keep trusting you. I am weak by myself. But with you, I'm strong!"

THURSDAY

Read "God Chooses Gideon," page 107 in *God's Story*. Or read this part of the story:

One day God's angel came and sat under an oak tree. That's where Gideon was. . . .

"God is with you, strong fighter," said the angel.

"Go," said God. For the angel was really God. "You are strong. Save your people from the people of Midian. I'm sending you."

"How can I save them?" asked Gideon. "My family is not strong. And everyone in my family is more important than I am."

"I'll be with you," said God. "You'll win over the people of Midian."

Now the enemy armies got together. They camped in a valley. But God's Spirit came upon Gideon. Gideon blew a horn. Fighters from God's people came to help him.
Judges 6:11-12, 14-16, 33-35

It was a day like any other day. Gideon was a common young man doing everyday work. Then God's angel showed up and said God had chosen Gideon. But Gideon didn't think he was good enough. "My family is not strong," he said. "And everyone in my family is more important than I am."

But God already knew that. That's why God chose Gideon. If Gideon had been strong or important, people might have said, "Gideon is great! Look what Gideon did!" But since Gideon wasn't strong or important, people could say, "God is great! Look what God did!"

You don't have to be strong or important or smart to do great things for God. All you have to do is trust God and obey him. Then God can show how great he is!

"Dear God, thank you for choosing me even though I may not be strong or important or smart. I will trust and obey you and let others see how great you are!"

FRIDAY

 Read "Where Is the Thinker?" page 675 in *God's Story*. Or read this part of the story:

Some people don't follow God. What do they think? They think the news about the Cross is foolish. But we are being saved. So to us the Cross is power.

Where is the wise person? Where is the thinker? God made the world's wise thinking look foolish. All of people's wise thinking did not show them God.

God saved people who believed what they were taught about him. The things they were taught seemed foolish. But that's the way God wanted to do it.

Think about what you were like when God chose you. Not many of you were wise. Not many of you were strong. Not many of you were from rich, important families.

God chose things that look foolish to the world. That way, wise people don't seem so important. God chose things that look weak to the world. He chose things the world doesn't like. That way, what the world thinks is important looks like nothing.
1 Corinthians 1:18, 20-21, 26-28

Have you ever looked at a leaf and then it jumped? It looked like a leaf, but it was an insect called a "leaf hopper." Or have you stood by a tree and seen part of the bark fly away? It looked like bark, but it was really a little moth.

God must have had fun making animals that look like the place where they rest. God likes to do things that make us wonder. God likes to surprise people who think they're smart. So he chooses people who don't seem important to the world. He gives them the important jobs in his kingdom.

You may feel small and not very important. But to God, you are still very important. That's because he can use you. He won't do it to show how great you are but to show how great he is.

What does God want you to do? How can you be smart enough and strong enough?

"Dear Father God, I'm not smart, strong, or important. But you are. I will trust you to make me what you want me to be."

Important People

Show people that they're important. Love God's people. Treat God as the most important one. Say good things about the king.

1 Peter 2:17

MONDAY

Read "A Chance to Kill the King," page 150 in *God's Story*. Or read this part of the story:

Saul and his men passed some sheep pens. Then they came to a cave. Saul had to go to the bathroom. So he went inside the cave. It was the same cave where David and his men were hiding. They were at the back of the cave. . . .

David quietly cut off a piece of Saul's robe. But then David felt bad about it. He said, "I shouldn't have done that to Saul. He is the king God chose." So David wouldn't let his men hurt Saul.

"You're a better person than I am," said Saul. "You were good to me. But I've been mean to you. I hope God will pay you back with good things. I know you'll be king. Now promise that you won't kill my family."

So David promised.

1 Samuel 24:3-7, 17, 19-22

How do you think David and his men felt to see King Saul coming? Maybe they were surprised. Maybe they were afraid. Maybe they felt glad. Saul had walked right into a trap. Now they could get rid of their enemy!

But David wouldn't kill Saul. Why? Because Saul was the king. Saul wasn't a very good king. But a king is an important person. So David treated him like an important person. David honored King Saul and treated him with respect.

God wants us to treat our leaders as important people. Who are your leaders? How do you honor and respect them?

"Dear Father God, help me to treat my leaders as important people. Help me to honor and respect them."

TUESDAY

 Read "Rules for Treating People Right," page 93 in *God's Story*. Or read this part of the story:

When you gather crops, leave some in the field for the poor people. Leave it for people who come from other lands.

Stand up when an old person is with you. Be kind to old people.

Be kind to women whose husbands have died. Be kind to children whose mother and father have died.

Someone from another land may choose to live with you. He should follow the same laws your people follow. Treat him like one of your own people. Love him as you love yourself.

Don't say bad things about people who can't hear. Don't put something in the way of someone who can't see.

. . . Don't try to get back at someone who has done you wrong. Love your neighbor as you love yourself. *Exodus 22:22; Leviticus 19:9-10, 14, 18, 32-33*

Do you know any older people, like a great-grandmother or a great-grandfather? God tells us to treat older people as important people. They have worked hard for many years. They have grown wise in many ways. God wants us to honor them and show them respect.

How can we help older people

feel important? We can talk to them. We can listen to them. We can give them our chairs. We can hold the door open for them. We can stand up when they walk into a room. That's a sign of honor and respect.

God tells us how to treat other people right. People from other lands. People who can't see or hear. Women whose husbands have died. How do you show these people that they are important? How do you show older people that they are important?

"Dear Father God, people are important. Help me treat them with honor and respect. Thank you for these people."

SOME THINGS YOU CAN DO THIS WEEK

☐ **Play "Bow-Down Tag."** Play this like you play tag, but when you tag someone, that person has to bow down. Think about how people would show that a king or queen is important. *(See Monday's reading.)*

☐ **Visit an older adult.** Ask that person to tell you about a time when he or she was a child. Practice listening and speaking kindly to that person. *(See Tuesday's reading.)*

☐ **Play "I'm Going to Jerusalem."** Get together with family or friends. Begin the game by saying, "I'm going to Jerusalem, and I'm taking a _____." Name something that starts with the letter A. The next person says, "I'm going to Jerusalem, and I'm taking a [what you said] and a _____." He names something that starts with the letter B. Keep going around the circle and down the alphabet. Remember Jesus' trip to Jerusalem. *(See Wednesday's reading.)*

☐ **Make VIP name tags.** VIP means "Very Important Person." Make a tag for someone you want to honor. Write VIP on it. Then print the person's name on it and give it to your VIP.

☐ **Make a VIP place mat.** With a permanent marker, print VIP on a piece of waxed paper that's 15 inches long. Put some bits of old crayon all around on top of the waxed paper. You can even sharpen the crayons over the waxed paper with a pencil sharpener. Crayon pieces will fall off. Then place another piece of waxed paper on top of the first piece. It should be the same size. The crayon pieces should be between the two pieces of waxed paper. Let an adult help you iron this so that both pieces of waxed paper stick together to make a place mat.

WEDNESDAY

Read "In the Big City," page 510 in *God's Story*. Or read this part of the story:

Once a year, Joseph and Mary went to Jerusalem. They went for the Pass Over holiday. When Jesus was 12 years old, he went too.

After the special holiday for God, Joseph and Mary began the trip home. But Jesus stayed in Jerusalem.

Joseph and Mary . . . thought he was with their friends or their family. So they traveled for a whole day without him.

Then Joseph and Mary began to look for Jesus. . . . But they couldn't find him. So they went back to Jerusalem. . . . At last they found Jesus. He was in the worship house, sitting with the teachers.

Mary said, "Son, why have you done this to us? We've been worried. We've been looking for you."

"Why did you have to look for me?" Jesus asked. "Didn't you know I would be in my Father's house?"

Jesus went back to Nazareth with Joseph and Mary. Jesus obeyed them, and he grew. He grew taller. He grew wiser. He grew as a friend to God. He grew as a friend to people, too. *Luke 2:41-46, 48-49, 51-52*

Jesus is God's Son. But God sent him to be born to a human mother. God sent him to live in a human family. He had brothers and sisters. And he treated them as important people. After Mary and Joseph found Jesus in Jerusalem, he went home with them. And Jesus obeyed them.

God wants us to treat our moms and dads as important people. God wants us to honor and respect them. How can we do that? We can obey them. We can speak kindly to them. We can help them. Can you think of other ways to treat your mom and dad as important people? How can you show the other people in your family that they are important too?

"Dear Father God, thank you for my family. Thank you for my mom and dad. Help me to treat them as important people."

THURSDAY

Read "Felix and His Wife," page 724 in *God's Story*. Or read this part of the story:

Governor Felix held his hand out toward Paul. That showed it was Paul's turn.

Paul said, "You've judged this nation for many years. So I'm glad to speak to you. I worship God. I'm a follower of Jesus."

Felix ordered the guard to watch Paul. But Felix said to let Paul have some freedom. . . .

A few days passed. Then Felix asked Paul to come see him again. Felix's wife, Drusilla, was with him. She was Jewish. She and Felix listened to Paul.

Paul talked to them about believing in Jesus. . . . He talked about how God would judge people someday.

Felix felt afraid. "That's enough!" he said. "Leave for now. I'll ask you to come again another time."

Felix hoped Paul would pay him money to be set free. So he often called Paul to come talk with him. *Acts 24:10, 14, 23-26*

Paul had been trapped by the Jewish leaders. They said he had done things that were against the law. So he was in jail until someone could say who was right. Paul had to tell his story again and again to different people. Felix himself heard Paul's story many times. Felix hoped that Paul would pay him to get free.

Felix was a Roman. He was in charge. So how did Paul treat Felix? Paul treated him as an important person. Paul waited for his turn to talk. Paul spoke kindly.

Who are some of the people in charge of you? How do you show them that they are important people?

"Dear God, thank you for the people you have put in charge of me. Help me to show them that they are important people. Help me to speak kindly to them."

FRIDAY

Read "A Night in the Barn" and "A Deal at the City Gate," pages 113 and 115 in *God's Story*. Or read this part of the stories:

So that night Ruth went to the barn. . . . Late in the night, Boaz woke up. He turned over. He saw someone lying by his feet. It was a woman. "Who are you?" he asked.

"I'm Ruth," she answered. "You are from my husband's family. Would you take care of me?"

"God will bring good things to you," said Boaz. . . . "But . . . another man from your husband's family . . . gets to marry you first if he wants. . . . In the morning, I'll ask him. . . ."

Ruth stayed in the barn until early morning. That same morning Boaz went to the city gate. He sat down. Soon the other man in Naomi's family came by.

"Hello, friend!" called Boaz. ". . . Naomi . . . is selling land that once belonged to our family. . . . Ruth . . . comes with the land," said Boaz. . . .

"Then I can't buy the land,"

said the man. "You buy it yourself."

So Boaz married Ruth. Later, God gave them a baby boy. *Ruth 3:6-14; 4:1-6, 13*

The story of Ruth starts with sadness. But it shows how God makes everything turn out to be good for people who love him.

At first, Naomi's husband died and Ruth's husband died. But Ruth treated Naomi as a very important person. And Naomi treated Ruth as a very important person. They honored and respected each other. They honored and respected God, too.

Then Boaz treated Ruth and Naomi with respect. He spoke and acted kindly to them. He treated them as important people. And when Boaz went to the city gate, he treated the city leaders with respect. He spoke kindly to them. He followed the laws.

So the story of Ruth is about people treating each other as important people. And God treated them as important people. He chose Ruth to be the great-grandmother of King David. Many years later, Jesus was born into that family.

Who are the people you need to respect? How can you show that they are important people?

"Dear Father God, thank you for people who treat me as an important person. Help me to treat others as important people too."

A Cheerful Look

Looking happy gives people joy. *Proverbs 15:30*

MONDAY

Read "Happy and Sad," page 254 in *God's Story*. Or read this part of the story:

Each person has sad times.
And each person has happy times
*   that nobody else quite*
*   understands.*

When you're happy, your face
*   shows it.*
But a sad heart makes your spirit
*   feel unhappy.*

People who do wrong are trapped by
*   their own sin.*
But people who do right can sing
*   and be happy.*
Proverbs 14:10; 15:13; 29:6

Do you know this song?

If you're happy and you know it, clap
*   your hands.*
If you're happy and you know it, clap
*   your hands.*
If you're happy and you know it, then
*   your face will surely show it.*
If you're happy and you know it, clap
*   your hands.*

It's true that when you're happy, your face shows it. And what happens when you are around someone whose face is cheerful? It's easy for you to start feeling and looking cheerful yourself!

Look around. Think of all the wonderful things God has given you.

Thankful hearts make smiling faces. What do you have to smile about?

"Dear God, thank you for all the wonderful things you've given me. Help my face to show the happy feelings I have."

TUESDAY

Read "Laughing and Joy," page 471 in *God's Story*. Or read this part of the story:

> *Enemies had taken us away.*
> *But God brought us back to Jerusalem.*
> *It was like a dream.*
> *We were full of laughing and joy.*
> *God has done great things for us.*
> *We are full of joy.*

> *People may go out crying, holding seeds to plant.*
> *But they will come back with happy songs.*
> *They will bring the crops they have gathered.* Psalm 126:1-3, 5-6

When do you hear lots of laughing and joy? King Solomon wrote, "A happy heart can make you feel well"

(Proverbs 17:22). Some people say it this way: "Laughter is good medicine." After a big laugh, you feel all peaceful and happy inside. Laughing *is* good medicine.

Why do we laugh? Sometimes we laugh because we see or hear something funny. Sometimes we laugh when we hear good news. We can hardly believe it. Our smiles get bigger and bigger, and soon we're laughing. We laugh when we're amazed at the wonderful things God does for us. That's why God's people laughed when they went back to Jerusalem. God had brought them home!

What makes you laugh?

"Dear Father God, thank you for smiles and laughter!"

WEDNESDAY

Read "Riches," page 264 in *God's Story*. Or read this part of the story:

> *People are born with no clothes.*
> *They leave the world that way too.*
> *They don't take anything from their work with them.*

They can't carry anything in their hands. . . .

Then I saw that it's good to get riches and health from God. He lets us enjoy them. He wants us to be happy with the days he gives us. They're a gift from God. So we hardly think about our days. That's because God keeps us glad.
Ecclesiastes 5:15-20

Try something. First frown. How does this make you feel? How does this make you look? Now smile. How does that make you feel? How does that make you look? Your face has lots of muscles in it. But it takes more muscles to frown than to smile. So it's much easier to smile.

King Solomon says that God wants us to be happy with the days he gives us. He gives us good gifts and wants us to enjoy them. Think of all the different gifts God gives us. He didn't have to make foods with many different tastes. God could have made every food taste the same. But he didn't. He wanted us to enjoy tastes. It's the same with colors and sounds and smells. They are all here for us to enjoy. Now that's something to smile about!

"Dear Father God, thank you for giving us such a wonderful world to enjoy. Thank you for keeping us glad."

THURSDAY

Read "Abraham's Visitors" and "Two Sons," pages 13 and 16 in *God's Story*. Or read this part of the story:

Abraham looked up and saw three men. So he got up and went to meet them. One of them was really God.

Abraham rushed into the tent. "Hurry, Sarah," he said. "Bake some bread."

Abraham brought out milk and meat and bread.

Then God said, "Sarah will have a baby boy. It will happen next year about this time."

Sarah was in the tent, near the door. She was listening. She laughed to herself when she heard what God said. That's because she and Abraham were very old.

God kept his promise to Sarah. She and Abraham had a son, even though they were old. The baby came just when God said it would. Abraham named the baby Isaac. Abraham was 100 years old when Isaac was born.

"God has let me laugh," said Sarah. "Anyone who hears about this will laugh and be happy too. Who would have thought Abraham and I would have a child? But I had a baby boy for old Abraham!"
Genesis 18:2, 6, 8, 10-12; 21:1-3, 5-7

Sarah laughed when she heard that God was going to give a baby to her and Abraham. They were too old to have children. So it sounded like a joke to her. Now it was a year later.

SOME THINGS YOU CAN DO THIS WEEK

☐ **Take some pictures of your family.** Think of some funny things you can say or do to make everyone smile.

☐ **Play "Guess Who."** One person thinks of a person that everyone knows about. It could be a real person or a pretend person. The other players take turns asking questions to try to guess who this person is. The questions must have only yes or no answers. But the leader answers by smiling for "yes" or frowning for "no." Players try to guess who the secret person is in 15 questions or less.

☐ **Make a favorite family snack** without telling the people who like it the most. Watch their faces when you serve the snack to them.

☐ **Make smiling mini pizzas.** Put pizza sauce on half of a plain English muffin. Put sliced olives, pepperoni, cheese, and other toppings on the sauce to make a face with a smile. Heat it and eat it!

☐ **Make funny faces.** Cut lots of eyes out of magazine pictures. Cut out lots of noses. Cut out lots of smiling mouths. Put eyes in one stack, noses in another, and smiles in another. Now choose a set of eyes and glue them onto a piece of paper. Choose a nose and glue it on. Choose a smile and glue it on. Now draw hair and a body.

Sarah laughed again. This time, she laughed because she was amazed and happy. She even named the baby Isaac, which means "he laughs." Sarah knew her friends would be amazed and laugh with her.

Let's say you have two friends. One smiles all the time. One frowns all the time. Which friend would you want to be around? Why?

There's an old saying: "The most important thing you wear is your smile." That just means it's not your clothes that make people enjoy you. It's your smile. When you smile, people feel that everything's all right. When you frown, people feel that something is wrong. What kind of friend do you want to be?

"Dear Father God, help me to wear a smile. Help me to be the kind of friend that people enjoy being with."

Friday

 Read "Seventy-Two Men," page 577 in *God's Story*. Or read this part of the story:

Jesus chose 72 helpers. He put them in pairs. He sent them ahead of him two by two.

Sometime later, the 72 helpers came back to Jesus. They were full of joy. They said, "Lord! Even the bad spirits left in your name."

"I saw Satan fall from heaven like a flash of lightning," said Jesus. "I've given you power . . . greater than the power of Satan, the enemy. Nothing will hurt you.

"But don't be glad just because the spirits follow your orders. Be glad because your names are written in heaven," said Jesus.

Then Jesus was full of joy. He said, "I praise you, Father. You're the Lord of heaven and earth. You hid your truth from people who thought they were wise. You showed this to people who look foolish to the world. Yes, Father, this is what you enjoy." *Luke 10:1, 17-21*

What do you think Jesus looked like? Long ago, painters made lots of pictures of what they thought Jesus looked like. In most of those pictures, Jesus looks sad.

Jesus did look sad sometimes. But

much of the time, he was happy and smiling. Jesus even laughed. When his 72 helpers came back, they were full of joy. Then Jesus was full of joy too.

Jesus would meet people who were sad, and he would leave them smiling and laughing. He met people who were sad because they were sick. He healed them and left them smiling and praising God.

What about God the Father? Does God smile and laugh? The Bible says, "God is happy with people who love him. He is happy with people who trust in his love. He is happy when they know that his love never ends" (Psalm 147:11). So God is happy with you. He smiles when he sees you.

"Dear Father God, thank you for loving me so much. Thank you for smiling and laughing and enjoying me. I enjoy you, too. I think you are wonderful!"

Even a Child

Even children show what they're like by how they act. You can tell they are good if what they do is right. *Proverbs 20:11*

MONDAY

Read "The Princess and the Basket," page 47 in *God's Story*. Or read this part of the story:

One Jewish mother hid her baby boy. The baby's sister stayed a little way off. She watched to see what would happen.

The princess went down to the Nile River that day. . . . The princess saw the basket among the water plants. . . .

When the princess opened the basket, she saw the baby. . . .

Then the baby's sister spoke to the princess. "Shall I go find a

Jewish woman? She could take care of the baby for you."

"Yes," said the princess. So the baby's sister went and got the baby's mother.

The princess told her, "Take care of this baby for me. I'll pay you for it."

So the baby's mother took him home. She took care of him for the princess. He grew from a baby to a young boy. Then one day his mother took him to the princess.

The boy became the son of the princess. She called him Moses.
Exodus 2:2, 4-10

Some people think that adults do most of the important things in this world. But God has always given children important jobs too. Miriam had a very important job. She watched her baby brother. And she had to do some quick thinking when the princess found him. What good idea did she have?

Miriam's idea was very important. Baby Moses' own mother got to take care of him. She got to teach him important things about God before he went to live with the princess. Moses grew up to be a great leader of God's people. And Miriam helped to make it happen.

Think about what Miriam did. What was she like? When people see what you do, what can they learn about you?

"Dear God, thank you for giving important jobs to children. Help me to do quick, wise thinking when I need to. Show me how to help like Miriam did."

TUESDAY

Read "Jehu Tricks the Idols' Prophets" and "Tricking the Queen," pages 310 and 311 in *God's Story*. Or read this part of the stories:

Ahaziah's sister found out that Athaliah was killing every prince. So she hid Ahaziah's baby, Prince Joash, in a bedroom. Then she moved him to the worship house. Her husband was a priest. She hid the little prince for six years. All that time, Athaliah ruled as queen. . . .

The next year the priest said, "Prince Joash will become the king.". . . Then the priest brought Joash out and put a crown on his head. . . . King Joash was only seven years old.

Joash was a good king. He did what was right. The priest was his teacher.
2 Kings 11:2-4, 12, 21; 12:2

How old are you? Do you have any friends who are seven years old? Can you think what it might have been like to be Joash? He had been hiding from the mean queen all his life. Now he was the king. He was a good king.

Joash was very young. Do you know what made him a good king? The priest was a good teacher. The priest loved God, and he taught Joash how to love God. As long as Joash followed God's ways, he was a good king.

Who teaches you? How can you learn to follow God's ways?

"Dear Father God, thank you for my teachers. Thank you for the people who teach me to follow your ways. Help me to learn more about you."

WEDNESDAY

Read "Finding a Book," page 386 in *God's Story*. Or read this part of the story:

Now Josiah . . . sent some men to God's worship house to fix it. "Go to the priest," he said. "Tell him to get the money the people have given. Use it to pay workers to fix the worship house. . . ."

So the priest got the money. He gave it to men who worked on the worship house. The men did good work. They kept at it.

While all of this was going on, the priest found something. It was the book of laws God gave Moses. The priest went to one of the king's helpers. "I found the Law Book in the worship house!" said the priest.

The king's helper took the Law Book to King Josiah. . . . The king heard the words of the Law Book. Then he called the leaders together. He led them to the worship house. All the other people went too. There Josiah read all the words of the Law Book.

The king stood by a tall post. He promised to . . . obey God with all his heart. He asked all the people to promise the same thing. The people did.
2 Kings 22:3-5, 8, 10; 23:1-3

Do you have any friends who are eight years old? That's how old Josiah was when he became the king. He was a good king. How could people tell that he was a good king? The Bible says, "He did what was right. He followed God with all his heart and soul and might" (2 Kings 22:2).

Josiah showed that God was important to him. He sent men to fix the worship house. When they found God's Law Book, he read it to the people. Then he promised to obey God.

Do you want to show that God is important to you, too? You can read

Some things you can do this week

☐ **Make a paper-bag basket.** Open a small lunch bag. Cut it down so it is about four inches tall. Cut a strip of paper about 12 inches long. Staple it onto the sack for a handle. Line it with tissue paper or foil. Fill it with cookies, candies, or flowers, and give it as a gift. Think about the basket boat that Moses' mother made. *(See Monday's reading.)*

☐ **Clean out a closet or box or drawer.** See if you find any "treasures" that you had forgotten about. Remember the Law Book that the men found as they fixed the worship house. *(See Wednesday's reading.)*

☐ **Play "Into the Well."** Inside a large box, on the bottom, mark a big X from corner to corner. Now you have four parts marked off. Write "1" in one part, "2" in the next, "3" in another, and "4" in the last. Make a bean bag. Put dried beans or rice into an old clean sock. Tie a knot in the sock just above the beans or rice to keep them in. Mark a place across the room or yard to stand. Toss the bean bag into the box. See where it lands, and give yourself that number of points. Remember the young men in the well. *(See Thursday's reading.)*

☐ **Make hot-chocolate mix.** In a big bowl, mix an eight-quart box of powdered milk, two cups of powdered coffee creamer, eight ounces of instant chocolate-drink mix, and one-half cup of powdered sugar. Put the mix into jars, and give them as gifts. For hot chocolate, put one-third cup of mix into a coffee cup. Add hot water to make one cup. Think about the boys who helped their mother fill jars with oil. *(See Friday's reading.)*

what God says in the Bible. You can listen to what it says. And you can promise to obey God with all your heart, soul, and might.

"Dear God, you are important to me. I will obey you. I will follow you with all my heart and soul and might."

THURSDAY

Read "Absalom Takes Over" and "Who Has the Best Idea?" pages 174 and 177 in *God's Story*. Or read this part of the stories:

David went up Olive Mountain. . . . David's friend Hushai met him there. . . . David said, "Go back to the city. Tell Absalom you'll serve him. . . .

"The priests with the ark box are in the city too," said David. "Tell them the news you hear at the palace. Then they will send their sons to tell me what's going on."

So David's friend Hushai went back to Jerusalem.

"Call Hushai," said Absalom. . . .

"Your father has done lots of fighting. . . . So here's what I say," said Hushai. "Gather all the fighting men together. . . . We'll fight David wherever we find him. . . ."

Then Hushai went to the two priests. He told them what he told Absalom. He said to send a message to David right away. He said to tell David, "Don't stay at the river crossing tonight. Cross over. If you don't, they'll catch you."

Now the priests' two sons were staying close by. . . . But a young man saw the priests' sons. . . . So the priests' sons left in a hurry. They went to another town. A man there had a well in his yard. They climbed into the well to hide.

Then the two sons came out of the well. They took their message to King David. "Cross the river right away," they said. *2 Samuel 15:30-37; 17:5-18, 21*

Two young men were part of King David's secret plan. Their job was very important. They had to be brave because there was danger all around. They had to be wise so they wouldn't get caught. They had to keep the message a secret so King David would be safe. They had to hurry so King David could get away in time.

King David could trust these young men. He could count on them to do their job.

When we do our jobs well, people see that they can trust us, too. They can count on us to do a good job.

What jobs do you have to do? Can people trust you to do your jobs well? Can people count on you?

"Dear God, help me to do my jobs well so people can trust me. Help me to be brave and wise."

FRIDAY

Read "Oil to Sell," page 296 in *God's Story*. Or read this part of the story:

One day a prophet died. His wife went to Elisha, crying. "My husband is dead," she said. "You know how much he loved God. But he owed some money. The man he owed it to wants to take my two boys. . . ."

"What's in your house?" asked Elisha.

"Nothing," she said. "There is just a little oil."

"Go to your neighbors," said Elisha. "Ask . . . for lots of jars. Then go into your house with your sons. Close your door. Fill each jar with oil."

So the woman left. She did what Elisha said. After their door was closed, her boys brought the jars to her. She put oil from her jar into the other jars. At last all the jars were full. . . .

The woman went to tell Elisha that they were finished.

"Now go and sell the jars of oil," said Elisha. "Pay the man the money your husband owed him." *2 Kings 4:1-7*

It takes a lot of work to keep a family going. There's food to cook. There are dishes to wash. There are floors to sweep. There are clothes to wash. Everyone in the family uses the house and gets things dirty. So everyone in the family helps to clean it up. That way, everyone has a part, and nobody has to work too hard.

Elisha told the woman how to get money. She did what he said. What were her sons like? How can you tell? This is how. You can see what they did. They helped their mom. They chose to do what was right and good.

How do the people in your family help each other? What jobs do you do around your house? Is there something you could do to help more?

"Dear Father God, thank you for making families so everyone can help each other. Show me how to do a great job of helping my family."

Someone Greater

I am what I am because of God's kind love. *I Corinthians 15:10*

MONDAY

Read "The Tower," page 8 in *God's Story*. Or read this part of the story:

After some time, there were many people in the world. Everyone spoke the same language.

"Let's make some bricks," said the people. ". . . Let's build a city and a tower. We will build the tower as high as the sky. Then everyone will know who we are. . . ."

But God . . . said, "These people speak the same language. So they can plan together to do many things like this. Let's mix up their language. . . ."

So God gave them different languages. Then the people stopped building. They did not stay together. They went here and there around the earth.

Everyone called the city Babel. *Genesis 11:1, 3-9*

Right now there are people all over the world who are practicing. They will try to be the fastest runners in the world. Or the best swimmers, or the highest jumpers. Or the most beautiful people.

Some people are like the people who built the tower. They try to be the best so that everyone will know who they are. They want to be the greatest.

Other people try to do their best because they are working to please God. It's their way of showing how great God is. They want God to be the greatest.

There is nothing wrong with being the best at what you do. You just need to let people know that God helped you do it. It's God who was and is and always will be the greatest.

"Dear God, you are the greatest. Help me do my best so I can show how great you are."

TUESDAY

Read "Looking Up to God," page 232 in *God's Story*. Or read this part of the story:

Looking up to God brings life.
It keeps people from the traps of death.

Looking up to God teaches people to be wise.
Knowing you're not so important comes before being important.

Good things come to people who always look up to God.
But some people won't let themselves care about God.
They are headed for trouble.
Proverbs 14:27; 15:33; 28:14

King Solomon wrote, "People get tested when others say good things about them" (Proverbs 27:21). Sometimes people are praised for who they are or what they've done. Then they might think they're better than others. That's being *proud*. Or they might know that God helped them do what they did. That's being *humble*. So people are tested when they are praised. It's a test to see if they are *proud* or *humble*.

Has anyone ever praised you? Did someone tell you that you did a good job? It's all right to be praised, as long as you don't start thinking you're the best. It's God who is the best. He made you who you are. So you look up to God. You *respect* him because he is the greatest.

"Dear Father God, when people praise me, I still know you are the best. I thank you for helping me do so many things."

WEDNESDAY

Read "People Who Wanted to Worship Paul," page 654 in *God's Story*. Or read this part of the story:

A man in Lystra could not walk. He had been that way since he was born. Paul talked, and this man listened.

Then Paul looked right at the man. Paul knew that the man believed he could get well. So

Paul said, "Stand up on your feet!"

The man jumped up. He started walking!

The crowd saw this. They shouted, "The gods are here! They are in human bodies!" They called Barnabas "Zeus." They called Paul "Hermes." That's because Paul did most of the talking. . . .

The priest of Zeus brought . . .

SOME THINGS YOU CAN DO THIS WEEK

☐ **Build a tower from paper cups or blocks.** If you use paper cups, turn them upside down. Line them up. Put more cups on top of them. Rest each cup in the second row on the rims of two cups under it. See how high you can build your tower. After it's built, you can "bowl" it down by rolling a ball at it. Think about the story of the tower called Babel. *(See Monday's reading.)*

☐ **Make sprout pitas.** Put some of your favorite fresh vegetables into pocket pita bread. Put some alfalfa sprouts in it too. Think about the king who ate grass. *(See Thursday's reading.)*

☐ **Draw a crown.** Print on it: "God is the greatest." Glue colored dry cereal on the crown to look like beautiful stones. Or use old buttons. You can also color the crown with markers or crayons. If you want to wear the crown, cut it out. Staple or tape a strip of paper to one side. The paper should be two inches wide. Place the crown on your head. Let someone staple or tape the end of the strip to the other side of the crown. Think about King Herod, and remember that it's God who is the greatest. *(See Friday's reading.)*

☐ **Make a paper-plate wreath.** Cut a large circle out of the center of a paper plate. Cut leaves out of green paper, and glue them around the edge of the plate. Think of the people who wanted to worship Paul and Barnabas. They brought wreaths to them. *(See Wednesday's reading.)*

circles of green leaves. The people wanted to offer worship gifts to Paul and Barnabas.

Paul and Barnabas heard about this. They ran out to the crowd. "What are you doing?" they asked. "We are just people like you. We're telling you good news. Don't worship things that aren't good for anything. Worship the living God."
Acts 14:8-15

When Paul lived, the Greek people worshiped many fake gods. The people made up stories about them. Zeus was their chief god. They said he had a wife who ruled over women. Hermes was the fake god who took messages for the other gods.

Paul and Barnabas were teaching people who believed in those fake gods. The people heard Paul's wise words. They saw Paul talk to a man who could not walk. All of a sudden the man was well! So they thought Paul was Hermes. And they said Barnabas must be Zeus. The people began to worship them.

Paul and Barnabas could have kept quiet. They could have let themselves be treated like the most important people in the world. But they knew that wouldn't be right. They didn't make the man well. God did. And God was much greater than they could ever be.

So what can we say when people call us great? We can say, "It is God who is really great. He has made me what I am."

"Dear Father God, I want to do the best I can at whatever I do. But help me remember that you are the one who is great. You help me do everything well."

THURSDAY

 Read "The King Who Lived with Wild Animals," page 434 in *God's Story*. Or read this part of the story:

I, Nebuchadnezzar, was home in my palace. I felt good about having plenty of everything. I felt rich. One night . . . I had a dream that scared me very badly. . . . But no one could tell me its meaning.

At last, Daniel came. So I told him my dream.

"My king," said Daniel. . . .

"You will . . . live with wild animals. You'll eat grass like a cow. . . . Seven years will pass. Then you'll . . . be king again. You'll say that God is the greatest king.

A year later, I was walking on my palace roof. I said, "This is the great Babylon that I built. I built it by my strong power. It shows how great I am!"

I had hardly stopped talking when . . . I was sent away from my people. I ate grass like a cow. . . . My hair grew out like eagle feathers. My nails grew out like bird claws.

After seven years, I, Nebuchadnezzar, looked up to heaven. My right mind came back to me. Then I praised the Most High God who lives forever. I treated him as the most important one. I spoke about his greatness. . . .

Then . . . I went back to being the king again.
Daniel 4:4-8, 25-26, 29-36

Jamie and his friends used boards to build a small ramp in his back yard. They rode their bikes down Jamie's driveway. Then they jumped the bikes off the ramp. Jamie called his mom to watch. "Look, Mom! The greatest show on earth!" He zoomed down the driveway and over the ramp. But his bike's front wheel turned too far. Jamie made a crash landing but didn't hurt himself. Mom said later that he hurt only his pride.

Did you ever do something like Jamie did? You were doing a job well. But then you wanted someone to see how well you did it. That's when you messed up! King Solomon wrote, "Thinking you're the best comes before you get into trouble" (Proverbs 16:18). *Pride* is thinking you're better than others. Being *humble* is knowing that there is always someone better. And it's God who is the greatest of all.

"Dear God, I will not brag about how good I am. Instead, I will tell people how great you are. And when I do a good job, I will thank you for helping me."

FRIDAY

Read "Peace As Wide As a River," page 365 in *God's Story*. Or read this part of the story:

"See? I took out the sin in you.
I tested you with hard times.
I did this because of who I am.
  How could I let people say bad
    things about me?
  I will not let anyone else be called
    the greatest.

"I'm the Lord, your God.
  I teach you what's best for you.
  I show you the way you should
    go.
I wish you had listened to my rules.
  Then peace as wide as a river
    would be yours."
Isaiah 48:10-11, 17-18

Isaiah wrote something very important that God said: "I will not let anyone else be called the greatest." Many years later, people said that King Herod looked like a god. It made him feel proud. He didn't stop anyone from praising him. But then Herod died. God showed everyone that Herod was not the greatest (Acts 12:21-23).

Isaiah knew about God's greatness. He wrote, "If we've done anything good, it's because of what you've done for us" (Isaiah 26:12). And he wrote, "We want everyone to know who you are. That's what our hearts really want" (Isaiah 26:8).

It's not important to be the greatest. It's not important for everyone to know who we are. But it *is* important for everyone to know who God is. So sometimes God helps us do something great. Sometimes he lets us be leaders. Then it's our job to let people know, "I am what I am because of God's kind love" (1 Corinthians 15:10).

"Dear God, I want everyone to know who you are. I will tell people about your kind love. If you make me into a leader, I will tell people how great you are."

Out of My Mouth

Saying the right things makes everyone happy. A word said at the right time is good. *Proverbs 15:23*

MONDAY

Read "A Small Fire in a Big Forest," page 764 in *God's Story*. Or read this part of the story:

Your mouth is a small part of your body. But it talks big! A small fire can burn down a whole forest. Your mouth is like a fire.

Think of all the parts of your body. Your mouth can bring the most pain. It can make you sin. . . .

People can train all kinds of animals. . . . But nobody can train a mouth. It doesn't rest. It can be full of hurtful things to say.

Good words and bad words come from the same mouth. It shouldn't be this way. *James 3:5-8, 10*

Long ago, the state of Texas belonged to Mexico. But the people of Texas wanted to be free. They turned a small, brown church building into a fort called the Alamo. The Mexican army came to fight them there. The Mexican army won. Almost everyone in the Alamo died in the fight. Only two women, one baby, and one boy lived to tell the story. But the people from Texas didn't give up. They would yell, "Remember the Alamo!" When they said those words, everyone would get angry. They were ready to fight!

Can you think of words someone said that started a fight? Can you think of words someone said that stopped a fight? Our words are very powerful. Words can start a war. And words can make peace. That's why God wants us to be careful about what we say. What's something good you could say right now?

"Dear Father God, I can see that my words are very powerful. Help me to say things that bring peace."

TUESDAY

Read "The Words We Say," page 244 in *God's Story*. Or read this part of the story:

People who please God think about what they're going to say.
But sinful people rush to say bad things.

Kind words are like honey.
They are sweet to the soul.
They keep our bodies well.

A sinful person starts fights.
A person who talks about others turns friends into enemies.
Proverbs 15:28; 16:24, 28

There is an old story about two frogs. It hadn't rained in a long time, and they were looking for water. At last they came to a deep well. "Let's jump right in!" said the first frog. "There is lots of water. No one else is here. It can be all ours." But the second frog said, "Wait! We can jump in. But if the well dries up, we won't have a way out!"

The lesson to that story is to look before you leap, then think about what you see! And God says that we should think before we speak.

It's easy to say something we don't really mean. And we can't take words back. Once we say them, it's too late. We can say we're sorry about the bad words. But we can't erase what we said.

"Dear Father God, I want to say the right things. Help me remember to think before I speak."

WEDNESDAY

Read "An Angel and a Donkey" and "From These Mountains of Rock," pages 85 and 87 in *God's Story.* Or read this part of the stories:

God's people traveled to Moab. The king of Moab sent a letter to a man named Balaam. It said, "Some people have come from Egypt. . . . Come and pray for bad things to happen to them. . . ."

The king's men took the letter to Balaam. "Don't go with these men," said God. "You'd better not pray for bad things for these people. These people are to get good things."

SOME THINGS YOU CAN DO THIS WEEK

☐ **Play "Solomon's Cat."** Sit in a circle with family or friends. Start the game by saying, "Solomon's cat is a(n) _____ cat, and its name is _____." Fill in the blanks with words that start with *a*. The next person says the same sentence, filling in different words that start with *a*. Have everyone say the sentence with *a* words. Then start over again, using words that start with *b*. See how far you can get in the alphabet before someone can't think of a word. Remember what Solomon said about our words. *(See this week's Bible verse and the readings for Tuesday and Friday.)*

☐ **Play "Pass the Bow."** Sit in a circle. Pass a gift-wrap bow around. Play music from a tape. When you stop the music, stop passing the bow. Then have everyone say something nice about the person holding the bow. Start the music, and go around again. Talk about what it means to *bless* people. *(See Wednesday's reading.)*

☐ **Make a "talking heart."** Cut a large heart out of paper. Fold the heart down the middle from top to bottom. Half way down, cut into the heart at the fold for about one inch. Open the heart a little. From the back, push in the paper with your finger just above and just under the cut. Then fold the heart back the same way you had it. These parts around the cut will fold the other way. Now open the heart and gently move the sides back and forth. The cut place becomes a mouth that moves. Draw eyes on the heart. Think about where Jesus said words come from. *(See Thursday's reading.)*

The next morning Balaam got up. He put a saddle on his donkey. He started out with the men to go see the king of Moab.

But God was angry with Balaam. God's angel stood in the road to stop him. . . . The road got narrow. . . . There was a wall on each side of the road. . . . The donkey saw the angel. So she moved very close to one of the walls. Balaam's foot was pushed against the wall. . . .

Balaam was very angry. He beat his donkey with his walking stick.

Then God made the donkey able to talk. She said, "What did I do? Why did you beat me?"

Then God made Balaam able to see the angel. "Go with the men," said the angel. "But say only what God tells you to say."

Balaam went back to the king of Moab. He told the king what God said. . . . "God . . . tells me to pray for good things for his people. I can't change that." *Numbers 22:1, 4-7, 12, 21-25, 28, 31, 35; 23:17-20*

God's words are the most powerful words of all. The Bible says, "God's Word is alive. It's doing its work. It is sharper than a sword with two edges" (Hebrews 4:12). God used his words to make the world. All he had to do was say, "Let's have some light." And there was light! His words are powerful!

But God made our words powerful too. Our words can *curse* and ask for bad things to happen to people. Or our words can *bless* and ask for good things to happen to people. We must choose which kind of words we will speak. Balaam chose good words. He said, "I can say only what God tells me to say." What are some good things you can say to your friends and family?

"Dear God, your words are very powerful! But I see that my words are powerful too. Help me to choose words that you want me to say. Help me to bless people with my words."

THURSDAY

Read "A Pack of Snakes," page 540 in *God's Story*. Or read this part of the story:

Then some people brought in a man controlled by

bad spirits. . . . Jesus made the man well.

The Jewish leaders heard about this. They said, "Jesus gets power from the prince of the bad spirits. That's how he sends spirits away."

"You're just a pack of snakes!" said Jesus. "You're full of sin. So how can you say anything good?

"The mouth says what comes from the heart. Good things come from good hearts," said Jesus. "Sin comes from sinful hearts. Someday God will judge the world. People will have to tell why they said words without thinking. You'll be made clean from sin because of your words. Or you'll be dirty with sin because of your words." *Matthew 12:22, 24, 34-37*

Have you ever tasted different kinds of honey? Some honey is called clover honey. The bees that make this honey make it from the juice of clover flowers. Other bees make honey from flowers of orange trees. Some honey comes from alfalfa plants and goldenrod and asters. People who eat different kinds of honey can taste the different flowers. When they taste honey, they can tell what kind of flower it came from.

Words are a little like honey. When you hear words, you can tell what kind of heart they came from. Jesus said, "Good things come from good hearts. Sin comes from sinful hearts" (Matthew 12:35). Solomon wrote, "Kind words are like honey. They are sweet to the soul" (Proverbs 16:24).

What kind of words do people hear when you talk?

"Dear Father God, I want my words to be like sweet honey. Make my heart good so my words will be good too."

FRIDAY

Read "Come, My Children," page 146 in *God's Story*. Or read this part of the story:

Come, my children, and listen to me.
I will teach you to love God.
If you want to love life, then don't say bad things.

If you want to have many good
days, don't lie.
Turn away from sin. Do good.
Look for the way of peace.

People who do right cry to God, and
he hears.
He saves them from all their
troubles.
God is near people who have broken
hearts.
God saves people who are sad.
Psalm 34:11-14, 17-18

Your words are not all that's important about what you say. The *way* you talk is important too. Pretend you are talking to a pet dog. Speak very kindly and say, "Come here." Now say the same words, but say them in a firm way. Next, say the same words, but say them in an angry way. You can also try saying "I love you" in a nice, kind way. Now say it in an angry way. Does it sound like you really love someone?

The way your voice sounds when you talk is called the "tone" of your voice. Your tone of voice can sound kind or rude. It can sound silly or scared or upset. Your words may be fine. But if you say them in an angry way, you might start a fight. Remember what Solomon wrote: "Some people are too loud early in the morning. They may say good things, but it sounds bad to their neighbors" (Proverbs 27:14).

We can choose how we want to talk. We can choose our words. And we can choose our tone of voice. How do you want to talk?

"Dear God, thank you for the people
who speak kindly to me. Help me to
speak kindly to others, too. Help me to
use a kind tone of voice."

Listen!

People should be in a hurry to listen. They shouldn't be in such a hurry to talk. *James 1:19*

MONDAY

Read "The Shepherd's Voice," page 576 in *God's Story*. Or read this part of the story:

"The sheep listen for the shepherd's voice," said Jesus. "He calls his sheep by their names. He leads them out. All of them come out. Then he walks on in front of them.

"The sheep follow the shepherd," said Jesus. "They know his voice. They'll never follow a stranger. In fact, they run from strangers. They don't know the stranger's voice.

"I am the Good Shepherd,"

said Jesus. "The Good Shepherd will die to save his sheep.

"I know my people. They are my sheep. My sheep know me, just like the Father knows me." *John 10:3-5, 11, 14-15*

Alex had a little white cat named Sugar. Sugar loved to chase the light from a flashlight. The flashlight made a tapping sound when Alex shook it. Sugar knew that sound. All Alex had to do was shake the flashlight. Then Sugar would come running. That's because she knew that Alex would turn on the light and play with her.

Sheep know their shepherd's voice. They come when he calls. Jesus said he is the Good Shepherd. We are his sheep. That means we know his voice. How do you get to know someone's voice? You listen to that person a lot. So how can we know Jesus' voice? We read his words in the Bible. When we pray, we talk and we listen. We hear Jesus' quiet message deep inside us. It's as if his voice is helping us know where to go and what to do.

"Dear Father God, thank you for sending your Son, Jesus, to be our good shepherd. Help me to know and hear his voice."

TUESDAY

Read "All This Work," page 579 in *God's Story.* Or read this part of the story:

Jesus and his followers came to a town called Bethany.

A woman named Martha lived there. She said Jesus was welcome to stay at her house. So Jesus did.

Martha had a sister named Mary. She sat down at Jesus' feet. She listened to what he said.

But Martha . . . thought about all the things she had to do. . . . "Lord," she said. "My sister left me to do all the work by myself. Don't you care? Tell Mary to help me."

"Martha, Martha," said Jesus. "You're upset. You're worried about so many things. There is only one thing that's important right now. That's what Mary chose to do. She is taking time to be with me. I won't take that away from her." *Luke 10:38-42*

Has someone ever come to eat dinner at your house? Maybe it was your grandmother. Or maybe friends came from another city. What did you do to get ready for their visit?

Think about what it would have been like to be Mary and Martha. What do you think they did to get ready for Jesus' visit? Maybe they cleaned house. Maybe they cooked special food. All of that was important until Jesus got there. Then the most important thing to do was to take time to be with Jesus. And that's what Mary did. She sat and listened to what Jesus said.

What keeps you busy every day? Do you take time every day to be with Jesus? Do you listen to him by reading his words in the Bible? Do you take time to talk with him by praying? Jesus said that being with him is the most important thing.

"Dear Father God, sometimes I get very busy. But help me remember to take time to be with Jesus every day."

WEDNESDAY

Read "A Voice at Night," page 124 in *God's Story*. Or read this part of the story:

God called to Samuel. "I'm right here," said Samuel.

SOME THINGS YOU CAN DO THIS WEEK

☐ **Use a tape recorder** and tape different sounds around your house. Play them back for your friends or family. See if they can guess the sounds. Think about how God wants us to listen.

☐ **Make a graham-cracker house.** Use the crackers to be the sides and roof of the house. Make them stick together with canned cake frosting. Paint the house with frosting. Then add candy windows and a door. You may want a marshmallow chimney. Think about all the things Mary and Martha may have done to get ready for Jesus' visit. (See Tuesday's reading.)

☐ **Make moon rolls.** Get a can of crescent-roll dough from the cold food case at your food store. Roll the dough up like it says on the can. Bend it into a crescent-moon shape. Think about how Samuel listened to God at night. (See Wednesday's reading.)

☐ **See what rain does to dirt.** Put sand or dirt in one end of a long box or cake pan. Put large rocks at the other end. Fill a watering can with water. Let the water run slowly out of the watering can onto the sand or dirt. What happens? Let it run over the rocks. What happens? When sand and dirt wash away, we say the land *erodes*. Think about the wise builder's house. (See Thursday's reading.)

He ran over to Eli. . . .

"I didn't call you," said Eli. "Go back to bed."

So Samuel went back to bed. God called again. "Samuel!"

Samuel got up again. He went to Eli. . . .

"I didn't call you, son," said Eli. "Go back to bed." . . .

God called Samuel again.

Samuel got up and went to Eli. . . . Then Eli knew that God was calling Samuel. . . . Eli told Samuel to say these words if God called again. "I'm your servant. I'm listening, God."

So Samuel went back to bed.

Then God . . . called, "Samuel! Samuel!"

"I'm your servant," said Samuel. "And I'm listening."

"I'm getting ready to do something," said God. . . . "I will do what I told Eli I'd do. I said I'd judge his family. . . ."

In the morning . . . Eli called for Samuel. "What did God tell you?" he asked. . . .

Samuel told Eli everything God had said.

"He is God," said Eli. "Let him do what he thinks is good." *1 Samuel 3:4-18*

Kerry liked to go to her grandmother's house during the summer. She slept in a room upstairs. And she left the window open all night. She liked to lie in bed and listen to the night sounds outside. The bugs buzzed a sleepy song. The frogs sang a deep tune at the pond down the road. The wind whispered softly. It was Kerry's special song at night.

What kinds of sounds do you think Samuel heard at night? How do you think he felt when he knew God was talking to him? God must have had a very kind voice because Samuel thought it was Eli. But then he found out it was God. And he said, "I'm listening."

How can you hear God's messages for you? This is one way. You might read something in your Bible that sounds very important to you. Then you can do what Samuel did. You can say, "I'm listening." And you can think about what you read. When is the best time for you to read your Bible each day?

"Dear Father God, thank you for talking to me. I will try to take time to listen to you every day."

THURSDAY

Read "Listen and Learn," page 230 in *God's Story*. Or read this part of the story:

> *These sayings will teach people the wise way to think.*
> *They'll help you do what's right and fair.*
> *They'll make fools become wise.*
> *They'll help young people know and choose what's good.*
> *So if you're wise, listen and learn even more.*
>
> *Treat God as the most important one.*
> *That gets you started to know what's right.*
> *The person who hates what's wise is a fool.* Proverbs 1:2-5, 7

Bryn and Cole jumped off the long rock wall. They ran across the sandy beach to the lake. They played in the water. Then they built a sand city. It had sand roads and sand houses. But that night, it rained. The next morning, Bryn and Cole jumped off the long rock wall. It was still there. But the sand city was gone. The rain had washed it away. Did you ever build a sand castle? What happened to it?

Jesus said that if we listen but don't obey, it's like building houses on sand. If we don't obey, we're not living the right way. We're not following God. So when trouble comes, we can't handle it. It's like the sand city that washed away.

But if we listen and obey, it's like standing on a rock wall. When trouble comes, we will be all right. That's because we're following God, and he is right there to help us. The rock wall doesn't wash away.

So it's good to listen. It's even better to listen and learn and obey. Are you listening to God and obeying him?

"Dear God, I want to be like the wise builder. Help me to listen and learn. Help me to obey and follow you."

FRIDAY

Read "The Secret Plan," page 722 in *God's Story*. Or read this part of the story:

Paul looked right at the leaders. He . . . knew that these

leaders often fussed with each other. They fussed about what they believed. . . .

The fussing was getting out of control. The captain was afraid that Paul would be torn to pieces. So he told the guards to take Paul back to the army building. . . .

The next day, the Jews got together. . . . "Ask the captain to bring Paul to you," they said to the leaders. . . . "We'll kill him before he gets here."

Now, Paul had a sister, and she had a son. Her son heard about the Jews' plan. He told Paul about it.

Paul called one of the guards. . . . The guard took the young man to the captain. . . . "What do you want to tell me?" the captain asked.

"The Jews will ask you to bring Paul to their leaders tomorrow. But don't do it," he said. "More than 40 men will be waiting to kill Paul.". . .

The captain called two guards. "Get 200 soldiers ready," he said. "Also get 70 soldiers who ride horses. And get 200 soldiers with spears. . . . Give Paul a horse. Take him safely to Governor Felix.". . .

The guards followed the captain's orders. *Acts 23:1-31*

Sometimes we are so busy talking that we don't listen. But listening can be very important. When we listen, we can learn.

A wise old owl sat in an oak.
The more he heard, the less he spoke;
The less he spoke, the more he heard.
Why aren't we all like that wise old bird?
(an old Mother Goose rhyme)

Paul had a sister, and her son was listening. He heard something very important. But he didn't just listen. He also did something. He told Paul what he heard. Paul listened. Then he sent the boy to see the captain. The captain listened. He called the guards and told them what to do. The guards listened. And they obeyed. Paul's life was saved because everybody listened to someone else.

Who are the people that God wants you to listen to?

"Dear God, help me to be wise and listen to other people. Most of all, help me to listen to your words."

Harvest Time

A farmer will get the kind of plant he planted. It's the same with you. *Galatians 6:7*

MONDAY

Read "Big Letters," page 662 in *God's Story.* Or read this part of the story:

Don't believe a lie. You can't make fun of God. A farmer will get the kind of plant he planted. It's the same with you. The person who sins will get trouble. But let's say the person lives to please God's Spirit. Then he will get life from the Spirit. It will be life that lasts forever.

Don't get tired of doing good things. Someday we'll get paid back for doing good. But we must not give up. Let's do good whenever we can. Most of all, let's do good to God's people.

See the big letters I'm making as I write to you? I'm writing with my own hand! I pray that Jesus' kind love will be in your spirit. Yes! Amen!
Galatians 6:7-11, 18

One spring, Peter helped his grandfather plant a garden. They planted corn and beans and carrots. They took care of the garden all summer long. At last, the time came for the harvest. That's when the crops are gathered in. Peter and his grandfather picked their vegetables. Guess what had grown from the seeds they planted. Squash? Apples? No! They got what they planted!

The things people do and say are like seeds they plant. If they do and say bad things, will good things come from the bad? Of course not. Bad things grow from bad seeds. So trouble grows from the bad things people do and say. But good things grow from good seeds. And good things grow from the good things people do and say. What kind of life do you want to have? What will you need to do to get it?

"Dear Father God, I want to grow good things in my life. So help me to do and say good things now."

TUESDAY

Read "Birds' Food and Flowers' Clothes," page 534 in *God's Story*. Or read this part of the story:

"Don't blame people for what they do," said Jesus. "Then you won't be blamed for what you do. Forgive people. Then you will be forgiven.

"Give, and good things will come to you in return," said Jesus. "You will get plenty. God will shake it up. Then he will push it down to make room for more. God will give you so much! It will run over and flow out onto your lap. God will be fair to you. He will give to you the same way you give to others." *Luke 6:37-38*

Nobody was ever good enough for Mrs. Penny. If you went to see her, she would talk about other people. She'd tell about wrong things they had done. Or she'd make fun of them. After you left, you wondered what she said to other people about you!

It really didn't hurt other people for Mrs. Penny to talk about them. It hurt Mrs. Penny. Why? She worried about what other people said about her. Mrs. Penny made fun of other people. So she thought they made fun of her.

Jesus said, "Don't blame people. Then *you* won't be blamed. Forgive people. Then *you* will be forgiven." Here is another way to say Jesus' words: "In the same way you judge others, you will be judged." In other words, you get what you plant.

"Dear Father God, I don't want people to say bad things about me. So help me not to say bad things about other people."

WEDNESDAY

 Read "Keep On Running," page 789 in *God's Story*. Or read this part of the story: We've all had human fathers. We looked up to them when they trained us. God is the Father of our spirits. So it's even more important to let him train us.

Our fathers trained us for a while. They did it in the way they thought was good. But God trains us so we can be sinless like he is.

When you're being trained, it may not seem fun. It might be hard. Later, we see the good it does. People who have been trained know and do what's right. They have peace.

Hebrews 12:9-11

SOME THINGS YOU CAN DO THIS WEEK

☐ **Have a pumpkin-seed snack.** Get an adult to help you gather the seeds out of a pumpkin. Wash the pumpkin seeds and toast them in the oven. Salt them, and have a snack! You may want to use some of the seeds to make a heart shape. Remember that you grow what you plant in your heart.

☐ **Match fruits and seeds.** Ask an adult to cut seeds out of different fruits. Wash them off, and mix them up. Now see if you can match the seeds to the fruits they came from. Think about growing what you plant in your heart.

☐ **Make food prints.** Get a bell pepper, an apple, a small squash, a carrot, and a piece of corn on the cob. Cut the foods in half across the middle. Pour a little tempera paint onto a paper plate. Dip the foods into the paint. Then press them onto a piece of paper to make prints. Think about growing what you plant.

☐ **Play "What's Missing?"** Set different fruits and vegetables on a tray. Ask the people in your family to look at the tray carefully. Then ask them to close their eyes. Take one thing off the tray. Ask them to open their eyes and guess what's missing. Do it again.

Did you ever get in trouble for doing something wrong? Did you find that something good happened when you did what was right? We are all being trained to live the right way. When we get in trouble for doing wrong, that's part of learning. That's part of being trained. God knows that when we do what's right, good things will happen. And God wants the best for us.

Parents and teachers train us. But they are still learning too. So who trains them? God does. If they choose to sin, they get in trouble. So all people, young and old, are being trained to do right. We may not like it or see the good it does right away. But someday we'll see it.

It's like the farmer who plants seeds. It's hard work to plant the seeds and water the garden. It's hard work to pull the weeds. But if he doesn't give up, it's great to eat what grows in his field!

Name some people who train you. How can you help them?

"Dear Father God, thank you for the people who train me. Help me to make their job easy by choosing to do what's right."

THURSDAY

 Read "Bad Weeds in a Good Field," page 324 in *God's Story*. Or read this part of the story:

God said to his people, "I told you to plant what's right.
Then you'd grow a crop of my love that never ends.
I wanted you to know that it's time to look for me.
I wanted you to keep looking until I'd bring what's good and right.
But you planted sin.
You are like bad weeds in a good field.
You trusted your own power. . . .
But the battle will come against your people.
All your forts will be torn down. It's all because of your sin."
Hosea 10:12-15

Harvest is a time of joy for farmers. They have worked very hard, plowing, planting, watering, and weeding. At last they get to gather their crops and enjoy the food they grew. They get to sell some of it and make some money.

Every year, God's people had holidays at harvest time. They had a Holiday of Weeks in the early summer. That's when they gathered in the first new wheat. In the fall, they had a Tent Holiday. That's when they gathered in the rest of their crops. But what if the farmers didn't take care of their fields? Then weeds would come up and grow over the good plants. There would not be much food to gather.

Bad habits are like weeds. What are some bad habits that boys and girls your age might have?

If you let your bad habits stay with you, they grow and grow. They keep good habits from growing. Just like a farmer pulls weeds, you have to get rid of bad habits. Then your birthday can become a joyful holiday every year. You can see how your life keeps growing better when you choose to do what's right.

What are some bad habits you need to get rid of?

"Dear God, I want to be like a good garden. Help me to get rid of bad habits. Help me to grow good habits instead."

FRIDAY

Read "The Big Gift," page 699 in *God's Story*. Or read this part of the story:

You're ready to help. I've been bragging about it to the people in Macedonia. I told them you've been ready to give for a year. They know you want to give, so most of them are giving too.

Remember this. If you plant a little, you will grow a little. If you plant a lot, you will grow a lot. People should give because they want to, not because they have to. God loves people who are happy to give.

God will make you rich in every way. Then you can give a lot any time. Your big giving will bring thanks to God.

And we thank God for his Son. He is the best gift!
2 Corinthians 9:2, 6-7, 11, 15

Kay Lynn chose four flower seeds. She put them in a pot and covered them carefully with dirt. Then she saw her little brother dump a whole pack of seeds into his flower pot.

"Wow!" said Kay Lynn. "You're going to grow lots of flowers!"

 Kay Lynn was right. When the flowers grew and bloomed, her pot had four beautiful flowers. But her little brother's pot had lots of flowers growing up and out and over the sides.

James wrote, "People who make peace are like farmers. They plant peace. Then they pick a crop of doing what's right" (James 3:18). Paul wrote, "If you plant a little, you will grow a little. If you plant a lot, you will grow a lot" (2 Corinthians 9:6). What kind of person do you want to grow to be? Kind? Joyful? Thankful? Then plant a lot of kindness, joy, and thanks.

"Dear God, when I grow up, I want to be a _____ person. Help me to plant that by choosing to do what's right while I'm young."

I Will Not Be Afraid

God is with me. I will not be afraid. *Psalm 118:6*

MONDAY

Read "The Giant," page 138 in *God's Story.* Or read this part of the story:

A winning fighter was in the enemy camp. His name was Goliath. He was more than nine feet tall! . . .

One day Goliath stood up. He shouted at God's people. "Choose a man to come out and fight me. . . ."

God's people ran from Goliath. They were very scared. . . .

"Nobody should be scared of Goliath," said David. "I'll go fight him. . . . I've killed lions and bears. This man Goliath will be just like them. He has come against God's army. God . . . saved me from the lion and the bear. He will save me from Goliath.". . .

David . . . went to a brook. He took five smooth stones from the water. He put them into his shepherd's bag. Then David . . . walked toward Goliath. . . .

David got a stone from his bag. He swung his sling around. The stone flew out. It went right into the front of Goliath's head. Goliath fell down with his face to the ground.

1 Samuel 17:4-49

Get a ruler, and find out how tall you are. Then measure nine feet up the wall or across the floor. That's how tall Goliath was. Stand or lie down next to the nine-foot place you measured. Think about how David might have felt when he saw the giant.

Do you know why David wasn't afraid? He knew God. He remembered how God had helped him before. God had helped him kill a lion and a bear. David also knew that God is much stronger than a giant. Most important of all, he knew that God was with him. So Goliath had lost before he ever got up that morning.

Can you be brave like David? Of course you can! How can you do it? Get to know God. Remember how God helped David. You are just as important to God as David was. Remember: God is with you. You don't have to be afraid.

"Dear Father God, make me brave like David was. Thank you for being with me. Help me not to be afraid."

TUESDAY

Read "A Night Fight," page 109 in *God's Story*. Or read this part of the story:

God told Gideon, "You have too many men. I don't want them to say they saved themselves. . . ."

Gideon told his men to go home if they were scared. So 22,000 (twenty-two thousand) of them went home.

"You still have too many men," said God. . . . "Watch them drink. . . ."

Gideon watched. Three hundred men lapped water out of their hands. The others got on their knees.

God said, "Take the 300 men who lapped water. . . ."

That night God told Gideon, "Go down into the camp. . . ."

Gideon . . . heard a man talking to his friend. "I dreamed about bread," said the man. "A big round loaf rolled into our camp. It hit our tent so hard, the tent fell down."

"That dream is about Gideon!" said the other man. "God is going to let Gideon win!"

Gideon . . . went back. . . . He called to everyone, ". . . God is going to let us win!". . . He gave each man a horn. He gave each man a jar. In each jar was a stick with fire burning on it. . . . They went down into the valley. . . .

Gideon blew his horn. He broke his jar. The other men blew their horns. They broke their jars. They shouted, "A sword for God and for Gideon!" Then they just stayed where they were.

SOME THINGS YOU CAN DO THIS WEEK

☐ **Try a "trust fall."** Ask a strong adult to stand behind you. Hold your arms straight down at your sides. Keep your knees straight. Lean backward, and fall back into the adult's arms. Is it easy or hard? Think about how you show that you trust God.

☐ **Make giant cookies.** Get a roll of sugar-cookie dough, and roll it out onto a pizza pan. Cover it with colored sugar or chocolate chips or other candies. Heat the oven the way the package tells you to, and bake the dough. Think about Goliath. *(See Monday's reading.)*

☐ **Make a target out of cardboard.** Set it up in your yard. Take turns with friends throwing a softball at the target. Remember how David threw a rock at Goliath. *(See Monday's reading.)*

☐ **Make static electricity "lightning."** Blow up a balloon. Go into a dark room or turn lights off. Rub a wool sweater against the balloon. Then touch the balloon. Watch the "lightning." Think about how Gideon's men must have looked in the night. They were holding sticks with fire burning on them. *(See Tuesday's reading.)*

☐ **Draw in the dark.** Ask friends or people in your family to do this with you. Go into a dark room or close your eyes or turn off the lights at night. Each person should draw a picture of a king on a piece of paper. Then turn on the lights, and see what your kings look like. Remember how King Saul hid. *(See Thursday's reading.)*

But the enemy army didn't stay. They were afraid, so they shouted and ran.
Judges 7:2-21

Kline loved to play soccer. Kids from different schools were on his team. They tried hard to win every game. One week some kids had their spring break. When Kline went to the game that week, there were only six people on his team. The other team had ten people. Six against ten. It didn't look very good for Kline's team. So the other team let some of their players play on Kline's team. And they played a game just for fun.

How do you think Kline felt, standing there with his six players against ten? Do you think Gideon felt the same way? Then Gideon heard the dream in the enemy camp. And he knew that God was with him. He didn't have to be afraid.

What makes you afraid? How can you be brave like Gideon?

"Dear God, even if other people are not brave, help me to be brave. Thank you for being with me. I trust you."

WEDNESDAY

Read "What Elisha Saw," page 302 in *God's Story*. Or read this part of the story:

Every time Aram's army moved, Elisha . . . would tell King Joram.

The king of Aram got very angry. He talked to his officers about it. "Which of you is telling King Joram where we are?"

"None of us," said one officer. "It's Elisha who is telling where we are. . . ."

"Then go find Elisha," said the king of Aram. "I'm going to catch him."

So his men . . . rode out with horses and chariots. They . . . got in a circle around the city.

Elisha's helper, Gehazi, . . . saw the horses and chariots. . . .

"Don't be scared," said Elisha. "Our army is bigger than theirs."

Then Elisha prayed. He said, "God, let Gehazi see."

So God let Gehazi see . . . another army all over the hills. It was an army of horses and chariots of fire.

The army of Aram began to come toward the city.

Elisha prayed to God. He said, "God, please make them so they can't see." So God took away their sight. . . . Then Elisha led them all the way to Samaria. . . . God made them see again.

After that, the army of Aram stopped fighting Israel.
2 Kings 6:10-20, 23

What do you do when you first wake up in the morning? Do you rub your eyes? Do you hold your arms out wide and yawn? Do you look out the window to see what kind of day it's going to be? Does it take awhile before you really feel awake? Maybe Elisha's servant did those same things. But when he looked out the window, what he saw made him wake up fast!

Do you know why Elisha wasn't afraid? He knew that God was still in control. God is always in control. Nothing is more powerful than God. Elisha's servant was thinking about armies of people that he could see. Elisha was thinking about God's armies, which most people couldn't see. Elisha's servant learned that

even when we can't see them, God's armies are there to help God's people.

You are just as important to God as Elisha was. How can you remember not to be afraid?

"Dear Father God, thank you for being near me even when I can't see it. You are always with me. I will not be afraid."

THURSDAY

Read "Long Live Our King!" page 131 in *God's Story*. Or read this part of the story:

Samuel . . . put some oil on Saul's head. . . . He said, "God has made you king of his people."

Saul left Samuel. And God changed Saul's heart. . . . God's Spirit came upon him. He had power.

Now Samuel called God's people together. He told them that God said, ". . . You have asked for a king to rule you. So now you must come and stand in front of me."

But no one could find Saul.

They asked God, "Is Saul here yet?"

"Yes," said God. "Saul is hiding behind the boxes and bags."

The people ran over to the bags. They pulled Saul out. He stood up. He was tall. His head and shoulders were above everyone else.

"See this man?" said Samuel. "God chose him to be your king. There's no one else like him."

"Long live our king!" the people shouted.

1 Samuel 10:1, 9-10, 17-19, 21-24

Why was King Saul hiding when it was time for him to be the king? Maybe he was afraid to be the king. Sometimes we are afraid we'll make a mistake. Or we're afraid that people will look at us or laugh at us. Do you think that's how Saul felt?

Are there things you are afraid to do? Maybe you're afraid you might make a mistake. But everybody makes mistakes sometimes.

Thomas Edison made the first electric light. He tried lots of things that didn't work before he found what did work. When he wanted to make a battery, he tried 10,000 (ten thousand) things that didn't work. A friend asked him if he felt bad about failing so many times. "I haven't failed," he said. "I've just found 10,000 ways that won't work."

God tells us in his Word, "I'm the Lord. I'm your God. I hold your right hand. I tell you not to be scared. I will help you myself" (Isaiah 41:13-14).

"Dear God, help me not to be afraid of making mistakes. Thank you for holding my hand and helping me."

FRIDAY

Read "Trying to Scare Nehemiah," page 494 in *God's Story*. Or read this part of the story:

Sanballat and Tobiah . . . sent me a message. "Come meet with us in one of the towns."

But they were planning to hurt me. So I sent a message back to them. "I'm very busy. I can't come. . . .

They sent me the same message four times. . . . Then Sanballat sent his helper to see me. He had a letter in his hand. It said, "We hear that you're . . . going to fight against the king. . . . We hear that people are going to make you their king. . . . "

I sent this message back. . . . "The things you say are not happening here. You're just making them up."

They were trying to scare us. They thought we would be too scared to work. Then the work wouldn't get finished.

But I prayed, "Make my hands stronger."

One day I went to see a man at his home. He said, "Let's go meet in God's worship house. Let's close the doors behind us. Men are coming to try to kill you. . . ."

Tobiah and Sanballat had paid him to scare me. . . .

Soon the wall was finished. Our enemies . . . saw that God had helped us do this work.
Nehemiah 6:2-16

The wall around Jerusalem had been broken down for a long time. Now Nehemiah was leading the people to build the wall back up.

The enemies didn't like that. So they tried to scare Nehemiah and make him stop building the wall. But Nehemiah wouldn't let them scare him. He knew he was doing what was right, so God would help him.

But what if you're scared because you did something wrong? After Adam and Eve ate the fruit, they hid. Adam said, "I hid because I was scared." If you are scared because you did something wrong, there is only one thing to do. Tell God about the wrong thing you did. Say you're sorry. That's the right thing to do.

John wrote, "If you love, you don't have to be afraid. Love pushes fear away" (1 John 4:18). The greatest love is God's love for you. He loves you so much, he is always with you. And you don't have to be afraid.

"Dear Father God, thank you for loving me. Thank you for being with me. Thank you that I don't have to be afraid."

Sin Fools People

Help each other want to do what's right every day. Don't let sin's lies make your hearts hard so you don't care about God. *Hebrews 3:13*

MONDAY

Read "The Snake's Trick," page 5 in *God's Story*. Or read this part of the story:

Now the snake . . . talked to the woman. "Did God say not to eat fruit from the trees?"

"No," she said. "We may eat fruit. Just not from the tree in the middle of the Garden. God said we can't even touch that tree. We'll die if we do."

"You won't die," said the snake. "God knows that the fruit will make you wise. Just like God. You will know good and bad."

The woman . . . ate some. Adam was with her. So she gave some to Adam, too. And he ate it.

Right away they saw they had no clothes on. All of a sudden, they felt bad. So they made clothes out of fig leaves.

Then they heard . . . God walking in the Garden. . . . "Did you eat the fruit I said not to eat?". . .

God told the woman,

"You will have children. But there will be pain. . . ."

God told Adam, . . . "You'll eat the plants that grow in the field. But you'll have to work hard to get anything to grow. . . ."

God sent Adam and Eve out of the Garden.
Genesis 3:1-23

Lee Ann's mom took fresh peaches from the food sack. Lee Ann chose a big yellow one. She washed it off and took a big bite. Yuck! It was mushy. And it didn't taste good. Lee Ann threw it away. "It's hard to tell if fruit is good just by looking," said her mom. "See if another one is better."

Sin is kind of like a mushy peach. It may look good. But after you do it, you see that it wasn't so great. In fact, that good-looking sin brings lots of trouble.

That's what happened to Adam and Eve. The snake said they would be like God, knowing good and bad. It sounded great. They had known only good things before. But after they ate the fruit, they wished they had never wanted to know bad. So

when you see a sin that looks good, watch out! Sin fools people.

"Dear God, help me to remember that sin fools people. Help me to stay away from sin."

TUESDAY

 Read "Lot Chooses His Land," page 10 in *God's Story*. Or read this part of the story:

Lot was the son of Abram's brother. . . . There wasn't enough land for both Abram's animals and Lot's animals.

Abram told Lot, "Let's not fuss and fight. Let's not allow our servants to fuss and fight. . . . You might want the land to the left of us. Then I'll live in the land to our right. . . . Or choose the land to the right of us. Then I'll live in the land to our left."

So Lot looked around. He saw all the land around the Jordan River. It was good land. It had plenty of water. It was like a garden. So that's where Lot chose to live. He set up his tents near the city of Sodom. But people in that city were sinful. They did many sinful things.

Abram went to live in Canaan. . . . He set up his tents there. And he built an altar to God. *Genesis 13:5-6, 8-13, 18*

There were green trees. There was green grass. There was a big river, where Lot and his family could get water. The land looked very good. So that's where Lot chose to live. But the people who lived there sinned in terrible ways. It was so bad that God got rid of the whole city. You can read about it in the stories after "Lot Chooses His Land."

The beautiful, green valley by a river fooled Lot. He thought it would be a good place to live. But it only brought Lot trouble. Sin is like that. Sin can look very beautiful and good on the outside. People think, *It won't hurt to do this wrong thing just once.* Or they think, *No one will ever find out.* But sin fools people. It always brings trouble.

"Dear Father God, sometimes sin looks good to me. Help me remember that sin fools people. Help me stay away from sin."

WEDNESDAY

Read "Eating and Drinking Too Much," page 242 in *God's Story.* Or read this part of the story:

Because of wine, people make fun of others.
Because of beer, people start fights.
People who sin because of wine and beer are not wise.

Don't get together with people who drink too much wine.
Don't get together with people who eat too much food.
These people become poor.
They get sleepy and lazy.
In the end, they have no good clothes. Proverbs 20:1; 23:20-21

Let's say you could go anywhere you wanted to go to eat. Where would you go, and what would you eat?

Most people like to eat. But did you ever eat too much? After you were full, the food still looked good. So you ate it. You ate so much that you really didn't feel good anymore. Maybe your stomach hurt. All that food only brought you trouble.

That's the way sin is. It looks good. But after we do something sinful, it brings us trouble. Even if you liked sin the first time, it takes more of it to make you feel good the next time. It's a trick and a trap. That's the way Satan works. So look out! Sin fools people.

"Dear God, help me remember that sin is sin no matter how good it looks. Help me stay away from the tricks and traps of sin."

SOME THINGS YOU CAN DO THIS WEEK

☐ **Make a trick snack.** Give each of your friends a piece of *baking* chocolate (not sweet chocolate) for a treat. It looks good, but it tastes bitter. Then give your friends a good treat and talk about how sin fools us.

☐ **Play "Hot Potato."** Sit in a circle with your friends. Choose someone to start and stop some music on a tape player. When the music begins, pass a potato around the circle. When the music stops, the person holding the potato has to leave the circle. Try to pass the potato quickly so you won't be caught holding it. Think about sin as a "hot potato." You don't want to be near it.

☐ **Play "Jail Bird."** Play this like you would play tag. But when you tag someone, you have to put the person in "jail." "Jail" can be a corner of the yard. The players who have not been tagged try to touch someone in jail. Then that person gets out. Think about how sin is like a jail.

☐ **Make coin rubbings.** Lay some coins on a table. Put a piece of paper over them. Rub over the paper with the side of a crayon to make the coin's picture on the paper. Gather as many pennies as you can find. Try to collect pennies from different years. Then think of something helpful to do with your pennies. Remember not to love money. *(See Thursday's reading.)*

THURSDAY

Read "Loving Money," page 753 in *God's Story*. Or read this part of the story:

Here's what is best. It's being good and being happy with what you have. We didn't bring anything into the world with us. We can't take anything out of the world with us. We should be happy to have food and clothes.

People who want to get rich have problems. It's like getting into a trap. They get pulled into doing wrong things. They begin wanting foolish things. They want things that end up hurting them.

Loving money brings all kinds of trouble. Some people wanted money so badly, they stopped believing Jesus. Then they had lots of problems that made them sad. . . .

Run away from all these sinful things. Go for what's right. Go for what's godly. Go for believing. Go for love. Try to keep your faith even in hard times. Try to be kind.
1Timothy 6:6-11

Do you know the story of King Midas? He wished that everything he touched would turn to gold. When his wish came true, he was very happy. He would be the richest king in the world! But at breakfast, his pancakes turned to gold, and he went hungry. In his garden, the rose he touched turned to gold. He couldn't smell his roses. And when his little daughter ran to hug him, she turned to gold. Then the king wished that everything was back the way it had been. He didn't want to be rich anymore. He saw that it was better to be poor and enjoy his food, his flowers, and his little girl.

There is nothing wrong with money. God lets some people have lots of money so they can give to people who need it. But it's the *love* of money that is sin's trap. Loving money brings trouble. It's sin. And sin fools people.

"Dear Father God, thank you for the money you give my family. Help us not to love money but to use it to help people."

FRIDAY

Read "Like Mean Animals," page 776 in *God's Story*. Or read this part of the story:

Some prophets were fake prophets. They lied. There will be teachers who lie too. . . . They will even say Jesus is not the Lord. . . . Lots of people will follow these lies. . . .

Long ago in Noah's time, people turned away from God. God didn't save the world then. But he did save Noah and his family. That's because Noah did what was right.

God burned the city of Sodom because of its sin. . . . But he saved Lot.

So God knows how to save godly people from trouble. But he remembers sinful people. He will judge them someday. Even now, they're paying for their sins. . . .

The teachers who lie don't understand what they're talking about. They're like mean animals. They just do what they feel like doing. They'll get paid back for the bad things they do. . . . These teachers lead others into their sin. They lead those who aren't strong in their faith. *2 Peter 2:1-7, 9-14*

There's a saying that goes, "Wise people learn from their mistakes. But wiser people learn from other people's mistakes." Look around and watch people. Listen to other people talk. Think about what they say. You can learn about bad things that happened because of somebody's sin. People were fooled. What they thought would be good turned out to be bad.

Moses knew that sin was a trap. Moses "grew up in the palace. But he wouldn't let himself be in the king's family. He . . . could have enjoyed sin for a little while. But he knew it was better to be treated badly for God. It was better than all the riches of Egypt" (Hebrews 11:24-26).

It may look easier to sin than to do what's right. It may look more fun, too. But remember: Sin fools people. In the end, people who sin have trouble. But God makes everything turn out to be good for people who do right.

"Dear Father God, help me remember that sin fools people. Help me choose to do what's right."

I Can Serve!

Share with God's people who need things. *Romans 12:13*

MONDAY

Read "Adam's Helper," page 4 in *God's Story*. Or read this part of the story:

God put Adam in the Garden of Eden. Adam could work there and take care of the Garden.

Then God said, "It's not good for Adam to be alone. I'll make a helper for him."

Now God had made all the animals. So he showed them to Adam. He wanted to see what Adam would call them. . . .

But God didn't find any animal that was able to help Adam. So God made Adam go to sleep. Adam slept very deeply. Then God took one rib from Adam. He made a woman from it.

God showed the woman to Adam. Adam said, "I will call her 'woman' because she came from a man." *Genesis 2:15, 18-23*

When you go out to eat, you sit at a table and someone comes to *serve* you. Or you may go to a counter where you *serve* yourself. What does *serve* mean? It means to help. It means to give people something they need.

When God made Eve, he made her to be a helper for Adam. But

Adam also helped Eve in many ways. When Adam and Eve had children, they helped too. Happy families play together. They work together too. Families need each other. That's the way God planned it to be.

How do the people in your family serve you? How can you serve the people in your family?

"Dear God, thank you for my family. Help me to serve them. Help us to work together and be a happy family."

Tuesday

Read "Water from a Rock," page 64 in *God's Story*. Or read this part of the story:

Then an enemy army came out to fight against God's people. Moses called for Joshua. Moses told him, "Choose some men. Take them out to fight. I'll stand on the hill tomorrow. I'll hold the walking stick that God has used before."

So Joshua took some men out to fight. Moses and Aaron and Hur went up the hill. They watched from the top. When Moses held his hands up, God's

people would win. When he put his hands down, the enemy would win.

Moses' hands got tired. So Aaron and Hur pulled a big rock over to Moses. Moses sat on it. Then Aaron stood on one side of Moses. Hur stood on the other side. They held Moses' hands up until the sun set. So Joshua and his men won the fight.
Exodus 17:8-13

Here are some pretend story people. See if you can name a friend of each one.

Winnie the Pooh _____

Batman _____

Mickey _____

Tom Sawyer _____

Barbie _____

Now here are some real people from the Bible. See if you can name a friend of each one.

David _____

Samson _____

Daniel _____

Moses _____

Ruth _____

How did these friends help and serve each other? How can you help and serve your friends?

"Dear Father God, thank you for my friends. Show me how to serve my friends better."

WEDNESDAY

Read "Jethro's Good Idea," page 64 in *God's Story*. Or read this part of the story:

The father of Moses' wife was named Jethro. Now Jethro brought Moses' sons and his wife to him in the desert.

The next day Moses went to work. He was a judge. He would listen to people who did not agree with each other. He would tell them who was right and who was wrong. From morning until evening he judged people.

Jethro watched Moses. Then he said, "What are you doing? Why are you the only judge for all these people? It takes you all day. . . .

"You're going to get too tired. It's too much work. You can't do all this by yourself. Let me give you an idea. Teach the people how to live. But choose some

men to help you. These should be men who follow God. They should be men you can trust. They can be the judges of the easy problems. They can bring the hard problems to you. That way you'll be able to do this hard job. And the people will be taken care of."

So Moses did what Jethro said. He chose some leaders. They were judges for the people. They took care of the easy problems. But they took the hard problems to Moses.
Exodus 18:1, 5, 13-26

Mrs. West carried a big box to the door of the church building. Right away, a man opened the door for her. A boy said, "Let me carry that box for you." A lady said, "May I help you find the room you're looking for?" Everybody helped. Everybody served. It didn't matter who came. When someone walked into the church building, the people there were ready to help.

Moses needed help for his hard job. The men he got were leaders. But they served Moses by helping him.

Jesus told his followers the secret

of being great in God's kingdom. He said that if you want to be great, you must serve other people.

How can you serve other people?

"Dear Father God, thank you for the people who help and serve me. Show me how to help and serve other people."

Thursday

Read "Friends and Helpers," page 529 in *God's Story*. Or read this part of the story:

Jesus went up on a mountain to pray. He spent all night there, praying to God.

In the morning, Jesus called

Some Things You Can Do This Week

☐ **Make a paper-plate basket.** Cut one paper plate in half. Lay one-half of it on the table. Turn the other half upside down, and lay it on top of the first one. Use a hole punch to punch holes through both plates on the curved sides. Make the holes about an inch apart. Cut a piece of string, yarn, or ribbon. Make it 36 inches long. Start at one side of the straight edge. Put the yarn in one hole and out the other all the way around. When you're back to the straight edge, tie the two ends of the yarn together. That makes the handle of the basket. Think about Paul's friends helping him in the big basket. *(See Friday's reading.)*

☐ **Draw around your feet.** Take your shoes off. Stand on a piece of paper and draw around your feet. Now make the footprints look like people by drawing faces inside them. Draw around your toes to make funny hair. One time Jesus washed his friends' feet to serve them. How can people serve each other now?

☐ **Make fruit turnovers.** Get a can of crescent-roll dough. Put a canned peach or apple slice on top of each triangle of dough. Put a little butter, sugar, and cinnamon on top of that. Fold the dough over to cover the fruit. Press the edges of the dough together. Follow the directions on the can to bake the turnovers. Now serve them to your family or to some friends.

☐ **Make a caterpillar.** Sit on the floor facing a friend. Both of you should bend your knees and put your feet on the floor. The legs of one will be between the legs of the other. Sit on each other's feet, and hold each other's arms above the elbow. To move across the room, one of you lifts up and scoots. Then the other lifts up and scoots. Flatten your knees as your friend sits down. Have your friend bend his or her knees as you sit down. You can race other friends this way. Friends can serve each other by helping each other have fun!

his friends. He picked 12 of them to be his special friends and helpers.

Jesus took these men to a big, flat place. A large crowd of his followers stood there. People had come from all over the place. They were there to listen to Jesus.

Some people had come to be made well. People bothered by bad spirits were set free.

Everyone tried to touch Jesus. Power was coming from him. He was making everyone well. *Luke 6:12-13, 17-19*

Over hills and through valleys. In the hot sun and in the cold wind. Sailing on the quiet lake or walking through the noisy city. Jesus' 12 special friends followed him in all of these places. Crowds of other people followed him too. And Jesus served them.

How did Jesus serve people? He listened to all of them, even the poorest people. He shared food with them. He made them well. He taught them about God.

How can we serve other people? We can listen to them. We can

share food with them. We can pray for them to get well. We can teach them about God. We can be like Jesus.

How will you serve somebody today?

"Dear God, Jesus showed me how to serve people. Help me to become more like Jesus every day. Help me to serve people too."

FRIDAY

 Read "In Danger," page 700 in *God's Story.* Or read this part of the story:

Think about what others brag about. I will also dare to brag. Are they Jewish? So am I. Are they God's people? So am I. Are they from Abraham's family? So am I. Do they serve Jesus? I serve Jesus even more. . . .

I've been in danger from rivers. I've been in danger from robbers. I've been in danger from my own people and from people who aren't Jewish. I've been in danger in the city and in the country. I've been in danger at sea. And I've been in danger from people who were not true believers.

I've worked hard. Lots of times I've gone without sleep. I've been hungry and thirsty. I've often had no food. I've been cold. There were times when I didn't have enough clothes.

Every day I worry about Jesus' followers. When others aren't strong, I don't feel strong. When others sin, I get upset.

In Damascus, the man in charge wanted to catch me. So he set guards up all around the city. But my friends put me in a basket. Then they let the basket down out of a window in the wall. So I got away.

2 Corinthians 11:21-33

Not long ago, two men went to a country far away to teach people about Jesus. They stayed in a little town, where they made many friends and taught them. But the town was in danger. That's because there was lots of fighting in that country. One day, the man in charge of the town came to the two men. He told them they must leave right away. The fighting was coming closer and closer.

But there was a problem. The roads were closed. The only way out was over the mountains. So the man in charge got a jeep. Then he and his son took the two teachers over the bumpy land. They went up and over the mountains to get the teachers to a safe place. They served their friends by taking them away from danger.

That's what Paul's friends did for him. They saved his life by letting him down over the wall in a basket. It was a very special way that they could serve their friend.

Most of the time, our friends are not in danger. But there are many ways that we can serve them. What's one way that you serve your friends?

"Dear Father God, thank you for friends who help and serve me. Show me ways to help and serve them, too."

Giving Thanks

We should thank God. We should worship him and tell how great he is. *Hebrews 12:28*

MONDAY

Read "Ten Men and One Thank-You," page 577 in *God's Story*. Or read this part of the story:

Jesus headed toward Jerusalem. As he came near a town, he saw ten men.

These men had a very bad skin sickness. So they stood a little way off. They called out loudly, "Jesus! Master! Feel sorry for us!"

"Go to the priests," Jesus called. "Let them look at your skin."

So the men started out to see the priests. While they were walking, they looked at their skin. Their skin was well!

One of the men ran back to Jesus. He cheered loudly for God. He bowed down at Jesus' feet. He thanked Jesus. . . .

"Weren't there ten men who got well?" asked Jesus. "Where are the nine other men?"

Then Jesus said, "You can get up and go. You're well because you believed in me." *Luke 17:11-17, 19*

When people are thankful, it means they are glad for something that happened. They know they did not make it happen. So they thank the one who did make it happen.

Thanking God tells him we know he made something good happen. It lets him know we're glad. And it shows we think he is wonderful for being so good to us.

Have you ever done something for a person who didn't thank you? That's what happened when Jesus made 10 men well. Only one came back to thank him.

God does many, many things for people every day. He gives people many, many things every day. But some people never thank him. Sometimes even we forget to thank him.

What do you want to thank God for right now?

"Dear God, you are wonderful. You give us so many wonderful things. I want to thank you for all of them. Thank you!"

TUESDAY

Read "Solomon Bows and Prays," page 226 in *God's Story*. Or read this part of the story:

King Solomon called all the leaders of God's people to come. It was time to bring the Ark to the worship house.

The priests carried the ark box. They . . . put it in the Most Holy Place. It . . . had the two stone charts in it. . . .

Solomon talked to God. . . . "I built this great worship house for you, God. It's a place where you can live forever.". . .

Solomon bowed down. He held his hands out toward heaven. "There is no God like you," he said. "You promised to love people who follow you. You've kept your promise."

Solomon got up. He talked to the people in a loud voice. "Praise God! He promised he would give us rest. He has kept his promise. I pray that God will be with us. I pray that he will give us what we need each day. . . . Love him with your whole heart. Live the way he says to live. Obey his rules."

. . . The people . . . worshiped God for seven days. They thanked him. "God is good," they said. "His love lasts forever."

They offered gifts on the altar. The priests blew their horns.

For the next seven days they had a special holiday for God.

After that, the people went home happy. They all were glad about the good things God had done. *1 Kings 8:1-23, 54-61, 65-66; 2 Chronicles 7:3-4, 6*

King David had wanted to build a worship house. But God wouldn't let him. There had been too much fighting in David's kingdom.

In Solomon's kingdom there was

SOME THINGS YOU CAN DO THIS WEEK

☐ **Play "Ann, Thankful for Apples."** Sit in a circle with friends. The first person says his or her name. Then that person says something to be thankful for. It should start with the same letter as the name. For example, "I'm Ann (Andrew), and I'm thankful for apples." The next person names something else starting with the same letter. Keep going around the circle until no one can think of anything more that starts with that letter. Then another person says his or her name. And everyone thinks of more things to be thankful for. These things start with the first letter of that person's name. Keep playing until all of the players have given their names.

☐ **Choose and eat a snack food** that you are very thankful for. Be sure to thank God for it.

☐ **Make praying hands pictures.** Put your hand on a piece of paper. Keep all your fingers together. Draw around your hand. It will look like praying hands. Color the hands and the rest of the paper. Then put a little bit of baby oil on a cotton ball. Put the paper on newspaper to keep the table clean. Rub the baby oil onto the paper to make it look like a stained glass window. Put the picture in your bedroom window. And remember to pray every day, thanking God for his gifts.

☐ **Make figures out of play dough or clay.** Use them to tell one of this week's Bible stories.

☐ **Write a thank-you card** to your mom and dad. Thank them for the things they have done for you.

peace. So God let Solomon build the worship house. Now, at last, it was finished. All the people were glad. They had a special holiday time for thanking and praising God.

We should thank God every day for what he gives us. But we also have special times to thank God. We have holidays when we take time to remember how good God has been to us.

What are some things that you are thankful for this year?

"Dear Father God, I thank you for _____. I praise you for giving me so many great things."

WEDNESDAY

 Read "A Figure in a Dream," page 396 in *God's Story*. Or read this part of the story:

Now King Nebuchadnezzar began to have dreams. He . . . couldn't sleep.

So the king called all his magic men. He said, "I had a dream. It troubles me. . . . So just tell me my dream. . . ."

"Nobody in the world can do that!" said the men. . . .

This made the king very angry. He ordered all the wise men to be killed. Daniel and his friends were wise men. . . .

Daniel . . . told his three friends . . . to pray to God about this. . . .

That night God showed Daniel a picture of the king's dream. God told Daniel what it meant. Then Daniel praised God. . . .

"I thank you, God. I praise you.
You made me wise and strong.
You showed me what we asked for.
You showed us the king's
dream."

Daniel went to the captain of the guard. He said, ". . . Take me to see the king. I'll tell him about his dream."

Then the king bowed to Daniel. . . . He said, "I'm sure your God is the God of gods. . . . I know that's true, because you were able to tell my dream!"

The king . . . put Daniel in charge of . . . all the wise men.
Daniel 2:1-3, 9-24, 46-48

Do you remember a funny dream you've had? Dreams can be strange or scary or wonderful or funny. It's a good idea to pray about your dreams before you go to sleep. Ask God to be in charge of your dreams.

King Nebuchadnezzar had a strange dream. Daniel knew that only God could tell him the meaning of the dream. He and his friends prayed about it. Then God told Daniel the dream and its meaning. But Daniel didn't go to see the king right away. The first thing he did was praise and thank God.

God gives us many things before we even ask for them. Look around you, and you'll see some of those things. But sometimes we ask for something special from God. That's what Daniel did. So just like Daniel, we should remember to thank God right away when he answers us.

Can you remember a prayer that God answered for you?

"Dear God, thank you for giving me so many wonderful things. Thank you for hearing and answering my prayers."

THURSDAY

 Read "His Sheep," page 205 in *God's Story*. Or read the story here:

Let all the earth shout to God with joy.
Worship God and be glad.
Come to him with songs of joy.
Know that the Lord is God.
He made us. We are his people.
We are like sheep from his field.

Go through God's gates giving thanks.
Go into his palace with praise.
Give thanks to him.
Cheer for his name, because God is good.
His love lasts forever.
He always keeps his promises.
Psalm 100

When people made fake gods to worship, they made up stories about the fake gods. Their fake gods were angry gods. They made bad things happen unless you could make them happy. People were scared of them. People did sinful things just to try to make these fake gods happy.

But our God, the one true God, is not an angry God. He doesn't get angry very fast. He is full of love. He is like a kind shepherd. We are like his sheep. God loves us and takes care of us. He is a good God.

So when we talk to God, we start by thanking him. It's like going through his gate to visit him. The first thing we say is, "Thank you!" We praise him for all the wonderful things he has done. He is good. And his love lasts forever!

"Dear Father God, thank you for being a good God. Thank you for being a caring, loving God. Thank you for loving me."

FRIDAY

Read "Love That Lasts Forever," page 469 in *God's Story*. Or read this part of the story:

Give thanks to God. He is good.
His love lasts forever.
Let the people that God saved say so.
He saved people from many lands.

Some people went here and there in the desert.
They could not find a city to stay in.
They were hungry and thirsty.
Then they called to God, and he saved them.
He led them on a road that did not turn.
He led them to a city where they could stay.
So let them thank God for his love that lasts forever.
Let them thank him for the wonderful things he does.
Psalm 107:1-8

After many years in the enemy's land, God's people came back home. Then they could see that God never forgot them. He never left them. All the time, he had his plan to make everything turn out for their good. So God's people sang about how God kept his promises. And they thanked God over and over again for his love that lasts forever.

It has been a long time since God's people first sang those songs about his love. The world has changed a lot. But God's love has not changed at all. He still loves his people. He still takes care of his people. He never forgets us or leaves us. He still has his plans to make everything turn out for our good. So we can sing about how God keeps his promises. And we can thank God over and over again for his love that lasts forever!

Look around you. Name things that God has given you because he loves you.

"Dear God, thank you for keeping your promises. Thank you for making everything turn out for our good. Thank you for your love that lasts forever!"

A Cheerful Giver

People should give because they want to, not because they have to. God loves people who are happy to give. *2 Corinthians 9:7*

MONDAY

Read "Bread for Everyone," page 556 in *God's Story*. Or read this part of the story:

"Come to a quiet place with me," said Jesus. "Let's get some rest."

They got into a boat. They sailed across Lake Galilee. . . .

People saw them leave. They knew it was Jesus and his friends. So they . . . ran to the place where Jesus would be landing. . . .

When Jesus and his friends landed, there were the people. . . . Jesus felt sorry for them. . . . So he started teaching them. He told them about God's kingdom. He made the sick people well.

It got later and later. . . . "We . . . need lots of food," said Philip. . . .

"Look at this little boy," said Andrew. "He brought his own supper. He has five rolls and two small fish. But that won't feed many people."

Jesus took the five rolls and the two fish. He looked up to heaven. He thanked God. . . .

Jesus' friends began to give the rolls to the people. . . . They gave fish to the people too. . . . All of the people got to eat as much as they wanted.

After supper, Jesus' friends cleaned up the leftovers. They filled up 12 baskets. About 5,000 men had eaten there. Women and children had eaten there too. *Mark 6:31-35; John 6:7-9; Matthew 14:18-21*

Do you ever go on picnics? Where do you go? Sometimes a whole group of people from one church will go on a picnic together. Everyone brings food to share. At Jesus' picnic, there were 5,000 men, plus women and children. But only one boy brought food!

If Jesus' picnic had been today, what do you think the boy would have had in his lunch? Maybe it would have been pizza. It might have been peanut butter and jelly sandwiches. Or maybe it would have been hot dogs and potato chips. Could Jesus have made those lunches feed 5,000 people? Yes! But just like in Bible times, Jesus would have made it happen when one boy chose to give.

If you give a little, God will make it into a lot.

"Dear Father God, help me remember that if I give the little bit I can, you'll make it do a lot of good."

TUESDAY

 Read "Peter Travels," page 646 in *God's Story.* Or read this part of the story:

A woman named Dorcas lived in Joppa. She did good things. She helped poor people. But she got sick and died. Her body was put in an upstairs room.

Jesus' followers in Joppa . . . sent two men to see Peter. "Please come right away!" they said.

So Peter went with them to the place where Dorcas was. They took him upstairs. Women were standing around. They showed Peter the clothes Dorcas had made.

Peter told them to leave the room. Then he got down and prayed. He looked at the woman. "Dorcas, get up," he said.

Dorcas opened her eyes. When she saw Peter, she sat up.

Peter held her hand and helped her stand up. Then he called her friends in. He gave Dorcas back to them. She was alive again! *Acts 9:36-41*

Have you ever seen anybody make a sweater out of a big ball of yarn? When your grandmother and great-grandmother were growing up, lots of people made their own clothes. Lots of people made sweaters out of yarn. Sometimes they would give the clothes as gifts to other people.

Dorcas made clothes. The clothes must have been very special to the women Dorcas knew. The women showed the clothes to Peter.

Giving a gift is a very special thing to do. It means you thought about that person. And you chose something just for him or her. It's even more special if you make the gift yourself! What can you make to give someone?

"Dear God, show me what I can make that will be a special gift. Help me to be a cheerful giver."

WEDNESDAY

Read "Looking for a Wife," page 18 in *God's Story*. Or read this part of the story:

One day Abraham called his best servant to him. Abraham said, ". . . Promise you'll find a wife for Isaac. . . . Go back to the land I came from. . . ."

So the servant promised. . . . And he left on his trip.

After many days, the servant stopped at a well. . . . The servant prayed. ". . . The women are coming to get water here. I'll speak to one of the girls. . . . Show me the one you choose, God. Have her give me a drink. Have her say that she will give my camels water too. . . ."

Rebekah came to the well. . . . The servant quickly went over to her. . . .

"Have a drink," said Rebekah. She took her jar down from her shoulder. She gave him a drink.

Then she said, "I'll give your camels some water too.". . .

"Is there room at your house for us?" he asked. "Could we spend the night?"

"Yes," said Rebekah. . . .

The servant told Rebekah's family about his promise to Abraham.

The next morning the servant said, "We must go."

Rebekah and her maids got on their camels. They rode off with the servant.

One evening Isaac was out in a field. . . . He looked up and saw camels coming his way. So he went to meet them. . . . The servant told Isaac what had happened. Isaac married Rebekah. He loved her.

Genesis 24:2-38, 54, 61-67

Some people have a hard time giving. They are afraid that if they give too much, they won't have anything left. Other people are happy to give much more than they have to. They enjoy giving. Rebekah

SOME THINGS YOU CAN DO THIS WEEK

☐ **Eat a dinner of fish and bread** like the boy shared at Jesus' picnic. *(See Monday's reading.)*

☐ **Give some clothes away.** Gather some sacks or boxes of clothes from your house and from your neighbors. Take the clothes to a place where someone can give them to needy people.

☐ **Play "Musical Gift."** Put several layers of gift wrap on a box that has a special treat in it. Sit in a circle with your family or friends. Ask someone to start and stop music on a tape. When the music starts, pass the gift around. When the music stops, the person holding the gift gets to unwrap one layer of paper. Start the music again, and go around the circle again. The person to take the last layer of paper off gets to keep the gift. (You may want to have smaller treats for everyone else.) Think about Bible people who were happy to give.

☐ **Play "Squares."** On a piece of paper, make rows of dots about a half-inch apart. The first person connects two dots that are side by side. The second person connects two dots. The goal is to try to be the one to draw the last line to make a square. That person gives the square to the other person. Print the first letter of his name in the square. When all the dots are connected, the person with the most squares wins.

☐ **Make a bean-soup mix.** Get different kinds of dried beans. Mix them together, and put them in jars. Give them as gifts.

was like that. The servant asked her for a drink, and she gave him one. But she didn't stop there. She gave water to all his camels, too. Then she told him that he could stay at her family's house.

God wants us to give much more than we have to. Do you know why? Because God gives much more than he has to. God knows how much fun it is to give. And he does it all the time. He doesn't want us to miss out on the fun of giving!

What is the most fun gift you have ever given?

"Dear Father God, thank you for giving more than you have to. Help me to do that too. Thank you for making giving fun!"

THURSDAY

Read "Gifts," page 184 in *God's Story.* Or read this part of the story:

David talked to the leaders of God's people. He said, "I am giving lots of gold and silver for God's house. Now, who else will give to God today?"

Then the leaders gave gifts for the worship house. They gave a lot of gold and silver. They gave tons of metal and iron. They gave beautiful, shiny stones.

David praised God. He said,

"We praise you, God. . . .
You own everything in heaven and
*   earth.*
You are ruler over everything.
Riches and greatness come from
*   you."*

Then David told everyone, "Praise your God." So everyone bowed down before God and King David.

The next day they offered many gifts on the altar.
1 Chronicles 29:1-8, 10-12, 20-21

People can give many different kinds of things. King David and his people gave silver and gold. They gave beautiful, shiny stones. They gave metal and iron. Long ago, those were some of the gifts that cost the most.

Most of us don't have silver and gold now. We don't have beautiful, shiny stones or metal and iron.

What can we give today? We can give money. We can give clothes for needy people. We can gather cans of food to give to people who need food. We can write cards and notes to people who are sick or sad. We can give flowers to people even if there is no special reason.

But some of the best gifts are things we can't put in a box. We can give a smile. A smile is a little gift that means a lot. We can also give our time. We can take time to help people. We can take time to listen to people. Sometimes that's the best gift we can give.

What kinds of gifts can you give?

"Dear God, show me what I can give to help you and to help other people. I want to be a cheerful giver."

FRIDAY

 Read "The Most Money," page 602 in *God's Story.* Or read the story here:

Jesus sat down at the worship house. He was across from the place where people gave money. He was watching people put money into the offering box.

Lots of rich people came by. They threw in lots of money. Then a poor woman walked up. Her husband had died. She dropped in two small pennies.

"Look!" said Jesus to his friends. "This woman put the most money into the offering box. It's more than what the rich people put in! The other people gave only part of their riches. This poor woman gave all the money she had." *Mark 12:41-44*

Jesus saw what was happening at the money box. He saw that it was like a riddle.

The man gave a lot of money.
The woman gave only a little.
But the woman gave more than the man.
Now tell me how that could be.

The woman wasn't afraid to give her last bit of money. Maybe she already knew God's promises about giving. Jesus had taught about it before. "Give, and good things will come to you in return. . . . You will get plenty. God will shake it up. Then he will push it down to make room for more. God will give you so much! It will run over and flow out onto your lap. God will be fair to you. He will give to you the same way you give to others" (Luke 6:38).

Jesus also said, "It is better to give than to get" (Acts 20:35). So give and enjoy!

"Dear God, thank you for giving to me. Help me to give just for the fun of it!"

Is It What It Looks Like?

God said, ". . . People only see what others look like. I see what's in their hearts." *I Samuel 16:7*

MONDAY

Read "No More Wheat" and "Dinner at Joseph's House," page 39 in *God's Story*. Or read this part of the stories:

Jacob called his sons. "Go back to Egypt," he said. "Buy some more food for us."

"We can't do that," said Judah. "The man told us we must bring our youngest brother next time. . . ."

"Why did you tell him about Benjamin?" asked Jacob.

"He asked us about our family," they said. . . .

"Send Benjamin with me," said Judah. "We must go right away. If we don't, our families will die of hunger. I promise I will bring him back safely to you. . . ."

"All right," said Jacob. "Then take some of the best gifts we have. Give them to this man."

Joseph's brothers went quickly to Egypt. They went to see Joseph.

Joseph . . . called his chief servant. "These men will eat with me at noon today," he said. . . .

The servant led the brothers to Joseph's house.

When Joseph got there, his

brothers gave him their gifts. They bowed to him.

Joseph ate by himself. The brothers ate together in a group. . . . Joseph's brothers . . . were seated in the order of how old they were. . . . They all looked at each other. They were surprised.

Genesis 43:2-11, 15-17, 26, 32-33

Egypt was a land of pyramids and palm trees. Many people lived by the long, wide Nile River. Paintings on walls in Egypt tell about the people's way of life. We can see what their kings and leaders looked like. So we know that Joseph's face was shaved. He may have had a long narrow beard right under his chin. His eyelids may have been painted. And he may have worn a big head covering like the king's. He looked like a ruler from Egypt. And that's who his brothers thought he was.

God likes to surprise us. He takes things that look one way to our eyes. And he uses them to show us something different. You may hear someone say, "There is more to this than meets the eye." That's true with God. Things aren't always what they seem to be. The night seems dark. But God can see right through it. It looks like you're alone. But God is with you. Can you think of anything else that's not the way it seems?

"Dear God, thank you for being with me even when it looks like I'm alone. Thank you for being a God who is greater than what I can see."

TUESDAY

Read "The River Stops Flowing," page 96 in *God's Story*. Or read this part of the story:

Joshua told the people, "Get ready. Tomorrow God will do some wonderful things."

Then Joshua told the priests to get the ark box. . . .

God told Joshua, ". . . I'll be with you as I was with Moses. Tell the priests to take the ark box to the river. Tell them to stand in the river."

So Joshua told the people, "The priests will step into the river with God's ark box. Then the river water will stop flowing. It will stand up in a pile."

Now the river was very deep at this time. But the priests stepped into the river. Then the water stopped flowing. It piled up at a town far away.

The priests stood in the middle of the river. It was dry there now. The people crossed the river, walking on dry ground.

God's people traveled to some flat land. They camped there.

Fourteen days passed. Then it was time to have the Pass Over holiday. So God's people had their holiday. The next day they ate food grown in the Promised Land. After that, God did not send any more manna to eat. *Joshua 3:5-9, 13, 15-17; 4:19; 5:10-12*

It was a time of year when the river was full. Sometimes it flowed over its sides. So it was deeper than at other times of the year. It looked like people needed a boat to get

SOME THINGS YOU CAN DO THIS WEEK

☐**Find out if you are short waisted or long waisted.** Put your hands on your shoulders and your elbows at your waist. If your waist is below your elbows, you are long waisted. If your waist is above your elbows, you are short waisted. If your elbows are at your waist, you are in between. Remember that you can't tell by looking at the outside what a person is like on the inside. *(See Monday's reading.)*

☐**Bake a cake for Jesus' birthday.** Toss coconut in yellow food coloring, and use it to make hay on top. Stand animal crackers around in the hay as if they are the animals at the stable. *(See Thursday's reading.)*

☐**Paint a tree picture by blowing.** Put a small spoonful of brown watercolor paint on a piece of paper. Blow through a drinking straw at the paint. It will move out in streams that look like branches. You can control where the branches go by where you blow and how hard you blow. Think about Zacchaeus. *(See Friday's reading.)*

☐**Play "Who Gave?"** One person, a "getter," sits with his back to the others. The others choose a "giver." The "giver" walks up and sets a small gift box on the floor behind the first person's back. When the giver sits down, everyone says together, "Who gave?" Then the "getter" has to guess who set the gift down. He tries to guess by looking at faces to see if anybody looks like he or she did it. Remember that you can't always tell by the way it looks. If the "getter's" guess is right, the "giver" becomes the "getter."

across. There were lots of people, so there would have to be lots of boats!

But things are not always the way they seem. God told the priests to walk right into the river. When they did, the water moved back. God's people were able to walk across the river on dry ground.

To us it may look like there is no way something can happen. But "there is nothing that God can't do" (Luke 1:37).

"Dear Father God, when things look like they can't be done, help me remember that you can do anything."

WEDNESDAY

 Read "An Angel at the Altar," page 503 in *God's Story*. Or read this part of the story:

Herod was the king of Judea. At that time, there was a priest named Zechariah. He had a wife named Elizabeth. But they had no children, and they were growing old.

One day Zechariah was at the worship house. It was his turn to help with the worship. He left the people worshiping and praying outside. He went inside.

What Zechariah saw there surprised him. He saw an angel! . . .

"Don't be afraid, Zechariah," said the angel. "God heard your prayer. Your wife, Elizabeth, will have a baby boy. You'll name him John. . . .

"John will help many people turn back to God. He will come before the Lord comes," said the angel. . . .

"How can I be sure that what you say . . . is true?" asked Zechariah. . . .

"My name is Gabriel," said the angel. "I come from God. He sent me to tell you this good news. But you did not believe me. So now you won't be able to talk. You'll be quiet until the day this happens."

Soon it was time for Zechariah to go home. . . . It wasn't long before the angel's words came true.

Luke 1:5, 7-13, 16-20, 23-24

First of all, Zechariah was surprised to see an angel. He had never seen an angel before. The next surprise was the angel's message. Zechariah thought he and Elizabeth were too old to have children. But things are not always the way they seem. And the angel's message was right. They did have a baby!

God is always doing things that look like they can't be done. It looked like God's people would die in the desert. But God sent water from a rock. It looked like Gideon's army was too small to win. But God scared the enemy away. It looked like Peter would be killed in jail. But God opened the jail doors and led him out. So when problems don't look like they'll work out, look for God. He does things that look like they can't be done.

"Dear Father God, I'll trust you to take care of me no matter what happens. I'll trust you because you can do anything."

THURSDAY

 Read "A Trip to Bethlehem," page 506 in *God's Story.* Or read this part of the story:

Joseph went to Bethlehem to be counted. He took Mary with him.

While they were in Bethlehem, the baby was born. It was a boy. Mary wrapped him in warm cloth. But she had to put him in a feed box for animals. That's because there was no place to stay at the inn. The rooms were full. . . .

That night, some shepherds . . . were taking care of their sheep.

God sent an angel to the shepherds. . . . "Don't be afraid," said the angel. . . . "Today, in the town of Bethlehem, a baby was born. He is Jesus Christ the Lord, and he has come to save you. Here's how you can know it's him. You'll find him in a feed box."

The shepherds hurried into town. There they found Mary and Joseph and the baby. The baby was in a feed box for animals.

The shepherds went back to their fields. They cheered for God. *Luke 2:4-12, 16, 20*

Where do kings and queens and princes and princesses stay when they travel? They stay in big, beautiful hotels. Sometimes they stay in rich people's houses. Servants bring them whatever they need. People make sure that the places they go are clean and pretty. If a queen were coming to visit your town, where do you think she would stay?

Even before he was born, Jesus was greater than any king. He is called the King of kings. We would want to give the greatest king the best place to stay. But little Jesus was staying in a dirty barn with animals all around. When the shepherds came to the barn, what

did they see? Just a new baby in a feed box of hay. But things are not always what they seem to be. The shepherds were really looking at the greatest King of all.

What else made Jesus look like he was not a king? Why do you think God planned for Jesus to seem like a plain person?

"Dear Father God, thank you for sending Jesus to be like us in so many ways. He is a wonderful King!"

Friday

 Read "Up in a Tree," page 593 in *God's Story.* Or read this part of the story:

Jesus came to the town of Jericho. A man named Zacchaeus lived there. He was a tax man. He was very rich.

Zacchaeus . . . was a short man. . . . So he ran ahead of the crowd. He climbed up into a tree. He wanted to make sure he could see Jesus.

Jesus . . . looked up. "Zacchaeus!" he called. "Come down right away. I need to stay at your house today."

So Zacchaeus came down. He was glad to welcome Jesus into his house.

The other people began to fuss. . . .

But Zacchaeus was making things right. "Look, Lord," he said to Jesus. "I'll give half of everything I own to poor people. Did I trick people into giving me too much? Then I'll pay them back. I'll pay four times what I took!" *Luke 19:1-8*

He took tax money from people. So he didn't have many friends. Who cared whether this short little man got to see Jesus or not? Zacchaeus wasn't important to anybody. He wasn't important to anybody but Jesus.

Did you ever feel dumb or plain?

Did you ever think that your nose was too big? Or that your arms were too long? Did you ever think that your hair looked funny? Or that you said stupid things? Everybody feels bad about themselves once in a while. But remember. Things aren't always the way they seem to be.

God made us all different. But he doesn't think of any of us as being dumb or plain. We are all very special to God. He loves each of us in a very special way. And he has a very special plan for each of us.

If you start feeling bad about yourself, think about Jesus. Remember that you are very important to him.

"Dear God, thank you for making me special to you. Help me to remember that you love me just the way I am."

Putting God First

Put God first in your life. Then he will make sure you have everything you need. *Matthew 6:33*

MONDAY

Read "Trusting" and "God's Care," pages 232 and 233 in *God's Story*. Or read this part of the stories:

Trust in God with your whole heart.
Don't count on the way you understand things.
Always remember to let God be in charge.
Then he will show you what to do.

Let God be in charge of whatever you do.
Then your plans will work out for good. . . .

We can make plans. But God decides what we'll do.
Proverbs 3:5-6; 16:3, 9

Have you ever gone to a county fair or a state fair? There are rides and shows. You can walk through the long buildings and see things people have made, like pies and cakes and paintings. Or you can see the animals they have taken care of. There are all kinds of chickens and cows and horses and sheep and pigs. Judges look at them and say which ones are the best. Everyone wants the blue ribbon. That means the person won first place. Maybe someone in your family has won a blue ribbon.

What does it mean when something wins first place? That means it's the best. You can give

God first place in your life. You can let him be in charge. That means you know God is better than anything else. He is the most important. He promises that if you give him first place, he will make sure you have all you need.

"Dear Father God, I choose to give you first place in my life. You are the most important. You're the best."

TUESDAY

Read "Twins," page 21 in *God's Story*. Or read this part of the story:

Rebekah had . . . twin boys. The first one looked red. His body was hairy. They called him Esau.

The next baby was holding on to Esau's heel. They named him Jacob.

One day Jacob cooked some soup. Esau came in from his time in the fields. And he was hungry. "I'm so hungry, I'm about to die!" said Esau. "Hurry and give me some of that red soup!"

"First you must promise me something," said Jacob. "When

our father dies, he will leave most of what he owns to you. Promise me that you'll let me have it all."

"All right," said Esau. "After all, I'm about to die of hunger!"

"Promise!" said Jacob.

So Esau promised.

Genesis 25:24-26, 29-33

In the days of Jacob and Esau, every father made a promise to his oldest son. The father promised to give most of what he owned to this son. This oldest son would get the gift when the father died.

Esau and Jacob were twins. But Esau was born first. So Esau was called the oldest son. He would get most of what his father owned. That was called his "birth right." But Esau didn't think his birth right was very important. He gave it to Jacob by trading it for some soup.

You have a birth right from your Father in heaven. Jesus is God's only Son. But he came to earth so you could be part of God's family too. Everything God has will belong to you someday. It's your birth right.

So put God first. Make him the most important. If you do, you can be sure that you will have everything you need.

"Dear Father God, thank you for letting me be your child. I will put you first. I will trust you to give me what I need."

WEDNESDAY

Read "A Sad Prayer and a Happy Answer," page 121 in *God's Story.* Or read this part of the story:

Hannah . . . was very sad. So she went to the worship tent to pray. She cried to God. She asked God for a baby boy. She promised she would let her son serve God.

The next morning the family got up early. They worshiped God. Then they went back to their home in the hills.

God remembered Hannah's prayer. She had a baby boy. She named him Samuel. . . .

Hannah's husband went to the worship tent that year. But Hannah didn't go with him. "I'll go when the baby is older," she said. "I'll take him with me. I'll give him to God. He can live there and serve God all his life."

Samuel grew a little older. Then Hannah took him to the worship tent. She took him to Eli, the priest.

"I'm the woman who was praying here," said Hannah. "I prayed for this boy. God gave me what I asked for. So I'm giving my boy, Samuel, to God now. My son will serve God all his life."

Samuel's mother made him a new robe every year. She and the boy's father came to the worship tent once a year. That's when she brought the robe to Samuel.
1 Samuel 1:9-11, 19-22, 24-28; 2:19

When Hannah was sad, who did she talk to? She talked to the ones who were the most important to her. She probably talked to her husband, and we know she talked to God. When Hannah talked to God, she made a promise to him. She asked for a baby boy. But she promised she would let her son serve God. Hannah kept her promise when she took Samuel to live with Eli. Hannah showed that God was the most important to her.

How can we show God that he is

SOME THINGS YOU CAN DO THIS WEEK

☐ **Play "Solomon Says."** Play it like "Simon Says." Choose a leader. The leader tells the other players what to do. If he says, "Solomon says," first, they must do what he says. But if he doesn't say, "Solomon says," first, they must *not* do what he says. Remember Solomon's wise words about trusting. *(See Monday's reading.)*

☐ **Make a Bible marker.** Cut out a piece of paper about two inches wide and six inches long. Write this week's verse on it, and color it. Put clear self-stick paper around it if you want to make it last longer. Put it in your Bible to help find the place where you will read each day.

☐ **Draw the first six words of this week's verse** on a piece of paper. Make each letter look like a person.

☐ **Make a blue-ribbon banner.** Tape two pieces of typing paper together so you have a big piece of paper. Across the paper, write "Put God in First Place." Tape blue crepe-paper streamers along the bottom of the banner. That will make it look like blue ribbons are hanging down from it. *(See Monday's reading.)*

☐ **Make chicken noodle soup.** Ask an adult to help. Put chunks of cooked chicken meat (a pound or less) into a big pot. Add five cups of water and five teaspoons of instant chicken bouillon. Add two carrots, cut up, and half of an onion, cut up. Bring it to a boil, and cook it for 20 minutes. Add four ounces of noodles, and cook it for 20 more minutes. Remember how Esau traded his birth right for soup. *(See Tuesday's reading.)*

the most important one? How can we put him first? We can choose what's right by doing things that make God happy. We can think about him and take time to talk to him. We can tell other people about him.

How will you show God that he is the most important to you?

"Dear God, you are the most important one to me. Help me do the things that make you happy."

THURSDAY

 Read "Wake Up the Morning," page 189 in *God's Story*. Or read this part of the story:

My heart will stay with you, God.
I will sing. I will make music with all my soul.
Wake up, harp!
I will wake up the morning.
I will praise you, God.
Your love is higher than the sky.
Be praised above the sky.
Show your greatness over all the earth. Psalm 108:1-5

Some people put God first by talking to him first thing in the morning. Before they do anything else, they read from their Bible and pray. That's one way they show God that he is the most important one of all. David must have gotten up very early. He said "I will wake up the morning. I will praise you, God."

There are many things that we could choose to put first in our lives. What are some things that boys and girls put first? Some might think school is the most important thing. Some might think friends are the most important. Some might think TV is the most important. Some adults think their jobs are the most important.

But there is only one who can be with you all the time. There is only one who can make everything turn out for your good. There is only one who can give you life forever. It's God. He is the most important.

"Dear Father God, you are the most important one of all. I will put you first in my life. I will take time to be with you."

FRIDAY

Read "A Message for Mary," page 504 in *God's Story*. Or read this part of the story:

God sent the angel Gabriel . . . to the town of Nazareth.

Gabriel went to a young woman. . . . Her name was Mary.

"Hello!" said Gabriel to Mary. "You are very special. God is with you!"

Mary was afraid. She . . . wondered what the angel meant.

"Don't be afraid," said Gabriel. "God is happy with you. You are going to have a baby boy. You are to name him Jesus."

"How can this happen?" asked Mary. "I've never slept with a man the way a wife would. I'm not even married yet."

"The Holy Spirit will come to you," said Gabriel. "God's power will come over you like a shadow. So the baby will be special. He will be holy. He will be God's Son."

"I'm God's servant," said Mary. "Let this happen just the way you said it would."
Luke 1:26-31, 34-35, 38

Mary was very surprised when she heard the angel's message. She didn't understand how she could have a baby. And she didn't understand how the baby could be God's Son. But God let Mary choose. She could have said no. But she said yes. She put God first. She let things happen the way God wanted them to.

We can choose too. We can learn how God wants us to act. We can learn how God wants us to talk. Then we can choose to do things God's way or not. When we choose God's ways, we are putting him first.

How can you put God first?

"Dear God, teach me more about how to act and talk the way you want. I choose to do things your way. I will put you first. Thank you for your promise to make sure I have everything I need."

Wise Thinking

Nothing you want can be better than being wise. *Proverbs 8:11*

MONDAY

 Read "What Is Wise Thinking?" and "Hidden Riches," pages 230 and 231 in *God's Story*. Or read this part of the stories:

*"Listen. Choose to learn from what
    I say.
Nothing you want can be better
    than being wise.*

*"Thinking what's wise and doing
    what's wise go together. . . .
If you look for wise thinking, you'll
    find it."*

*My child, listen to what's wise.
Try to understand. Ask for help
    with all that you need to know.*

*Then you'll understand how to look
    up to God.
You'll find out how to know God.*

*Wise thinking will help you be safe.
You won't be afraid when you lie
    down.
You will have a good night's sleep.*
Proverbs 8:6, 10-12; 2:1-3, 5; 3:21-24

King Solomon knew he was *not* wise. And he knew he would need to be wise to rule God's people. So he asked God to give him a wise mind. God did. Solomon's wise thinking helps us become wise too. That's because of one of the wise things Solomon did. He wrote down what he knew about being wise.

So how can you be wise? "You can begin to be wise by looking up to God," wrote Solomon (Proverbs 9:10). Some people might say, "Put first things first." Since God is the most important, that means putting God first. That's the first wise thing to do!

"Dear Father God, thank you for the wise sayings that Solomon wrote. I will put you first so I can begin to be wise."

TUESDAY

 Read "Wise Men from the East," page 508 in *God's Story*. Or read this part of the story:

It was some time after Jesus had been born in Bethlehem. . . .

Wise men from the East came to Jerusalem. They began asking about Jesus. "Where is the child who was born to be King of the Jews? We saw a star in the east. It was his star. We have come to worship this baby king."

King Herod heard about their questions. He was upset.

King Herod called a secret meeting with the wise men. . . . "Look carefully for this baby," he said. "When you find him, report back to me. . . ."

The wise men . . . followed the star. It went ahead of them and then stopped.

The wise men saw that the star was over a house. They were full of joy. They went into the house. There they saw the child Jesus. He was with his mother, Mary.

The wise men bowed down and worshiped Jesus. Then they . . . gave him gold, sweet-smelling incense, and myrrh.

Now God talked to the wise men in a dream. He told them not to go back to King Herod. So they took another road back to their own land. *Matthew 2:1-3, 7-12*

We don't know for sure who the wise men were, but they came from the East. That means they may have come from the land of Persia. Why are they called wise men? Were they really wise? We know that they watched the sky carefully. They knew where all the stars were. So it's likely that they knew a lot and enjoyed learning about many things.

People who enjoy learning often become wise. They watch the world around them. They listen. And they think about what they see and hear. They also learn from what they do. If they make a mistake, they learn what's *not* good to do. If they do something right, they learn what *is* good to do.

Children learn in school. But that's not the only place they learn. And they keep learning all their lives. So the older people get, the wiser they can be.

The wisest thing the wise men did was to take time to be with Jesus. The wisest thing you will ever do is to take time to be with Jesus too.

"Dear God, thank you for all the things we can learn. Help me to learn more and to become wise."

WEDNESDAY

Read "Ten Lamps," page 604 in *God's Story*. Or read this part of the story:

Jesus told a story. . . . "The kingdom of heaven will be like 10 young people," he said. "They . . . were going to a wedding party. They were going to be with the groom.

". . . Five of these young people were foolish. They didn't bring any oil to keep their lamps lit up. Five of them were wise. They brought oil in jars.

"It took a long time for the groom to come. . . .

"In the middle of the night, a voice called out. 'Here comes the groom! Come and meet him!'

"All the young people woke up. They lit their lamps. But the foolish ones had run out of oil. They . . . went to the store. While they were gone, the groom came. The young people who were there went with him. . . . The door closed behind them.

"Sometime later, the other young people came back. They called, 'Open the door. Let us in.'

"But the groom said, 'I don't know you.'

"So watch. You don't know when I'll come," said Jesus.
Matthew 25:1-13

Part of being wise is *thinking ahead.* That means we try to think about what will happen if we do something.

Let's say you are reading outside. Your friend comes over to play ball. You don't want to take time to put the book inside your house. But you are wise. So you think ahead. You think, *If I leave my book here in the grass, I might forget it. If I forget it, it might get rained on. If it gets rained on, the pages might curl up. If the* *pages curl up, then nobody can read it.* That's thinking ahead! Being wise, you choose to take the book inside.

Five of the young people in Jesus' story were not wise. They didn't think ahead.

When you read about other people's mistakes, you can learn from them. You can learn from your own mistakes too. Then you'll think ahead next time. And you will have grown wiser!

SOME THINGS YOU CAN DO THIS WEEK

☐ **Make star cookies.** Get a roll of sugar cookie dough. Cut star shapes out of the dough. Bake them and frost them. Think about the wise men who followed the star. *(See Tuesday's reading.)*

☐ **Play "Copy Cat."** Get a friend or someone from your family to stand face-to-face with you. Choose which one of you will go first. Stay facing each other. The first person moves, and the other person copies him like a shadow. Try to copy as quickly and smoothly as you can. After the first person has led, let the second person lead. Think about copying wise people.

☐ **See how fast you learn.** Ask a friend to hold a yardstick so that it's hanging down in front of you. Hold one hand out around the yardstick, but don't touch it. See what number your hand is close to. Ask your friend to drop the yardstick. Try to catch it with the hand that's around it. Look at the number where you caught it. See how far it fell. Try it a few more times. See if your hand learns to catch it faster. Think about learning to be wise.

☐ **Make a lamp.** Get a gallon plastic milk jug. It should be empty and clean and have its lid on. Cut a hole in the side big enough for a flashlight to go in and out of. Leave the handle on the milk jug. Put rocks, clay, or play dough in the jug to help it stand up. Put the flashlight in the hole, and turn the light on. Now you have a lamp. Think about the 10 young people who had lamps. *(See Wednesday's reading.)*

How can you think ahead?

"Dear God, thank you for giving me a mind to think. Help me to think ahead and be wise. When I make mistakes, help me learn from them and do better next time."

THURSDAY

Read "The King's Dreams," page 36 in *God's Story*. Or read this part of the story:

"I had a dream," said the king. ". . . I heard that you can tell what dreams mean."

"I can't," said Joseph. "But God can."

So the king told Joseph about the fat and thin cows. He told Joseph about the fat and thin wheat.

Joseph said, ". . . The seven fat cows and the fat wheat . . . mean seven years. Lots of food will grow in those seven years.

"The seven thin cows and the thin wheat . . . mean seven more years. No food will grow then.

"So first this land will have seven years with enough food. Then there will be seven years of no food. This will happen right away. So you should find a wise man. Put him in charge of Egypt. Save food that grows in the good years. Then later the people can eat the food they saved."

The king liked Joseph's idea. He said, "God has told this to you. You are the wisest of all. So you will be in charge of my palace."
Genesis 41:15-40

Joseph told the king what his dreams meant. Then Joseph said that the king would need to put a wise man in charge. So the king put Joseph in charge. Do you think that surprised Joseph? The king said, "You are the wisest of all."

Think about what made Joseph wise. He had been taught about

God when he was young. But then his brothers sold him. He had to be a servant in Egypt. He had to work very hard. He had to learn to trust God no matter what happened. Those hard times made Joseph grow wiser.

Have you ever had hard times? If you have, how did they help you grow wiser? When you have hard times, do what Joseph did. Learn from those times. And trust God no matter what happens. Then you will grow wiser.

"Dear Father God, I know that hard times can make me grow wiser. I will trust you no matter what happens."

FRIDAY

Read "The Fingers That Wrote on the Wall," page 453 in *God's Story.* Or read this part of the story:

Now King Belshazzar had a great dinner for 1,000 leaders. They were in the palace. They ate, and they drank wine. The cups were from the worship house in Jerusalem. . . . While they drank, they cheered for their fake gods.

All of a sudden the fingers of a man's hand showed up. The fingers wrote on the wall by the lamp stand.

The king watched. His face lost its color. He was . . . scared.

The queen . . . came into the great hall where they had dinner.

"Live forever, my king!" she said. ". . . There is a man in this kingdom who is . . . as wise as a god. . . . His name is Daniel. . . . He will tell you what the writing says."

So Daniel came to see the king. "You didn't worship God," said Daniel. "He holds your life in his hands. So God sent the hand that wrote on the wall. These are the words.

"MENE, MENE, TEKEL, PARSIN

"Here's what the words mean.

"MENE means God has counted the days of your kingdom. He has ended it.

"TEKEL means you've been tested, and you weren't good enough.

"PARSIN means two other nations will share your kingdom."
Daniel 5:1, 3-6, 10-13, 23-28

The king needed help. The queen told him that Daniel could help. She said Daniel was wise. How did Daniel get so wise? First of all, he looked up to God just as Solomon said to do. He put God first. Then God began to make him wise. Daniel and his friends also obeyed God. They wouldn't even eat food that God didn't want them to eat. So God let Daniel and his friends know and understand all kinds of things.

James wrote, "Do you need to be wise? Ask God. He gives plenty of wisdom to everyone. He doesn't blame you for asking. God will make you wise" (James 1:5). Do you remember someone who asked for wisdom? Solomon did!

So how can you grow wise? Put God first the way Daniel did. Trust him and obey him. And ask him to make you wise, just like Solomon did.

"Dear Father God, I will put you first. I will trust you and obey you. Please make me wise."

God's Plans

God will do what he planned for me. *Psalm 138:8*

MONDAY

Read "Moses' Song," page 94 in *God's Story*. Or read this part of the story:

God told Moses, "These people will forget me. So write down this song. Teach it to the people."

So Moses wrote the song down. Then he taught it to the people.

I'll tell about God's name. Praise God's greatness!
He is like a Rock for us. Everything he does is right.
He keeps his promises. He doesn't do anything wrong.

Remember the old days. Ask your fathers. They'll tell you.

God will be kind to people who serve him.
He will save his land and his people.

That day God told Moses, "Go up on the mountain." So Moses climbed up the mountain. God showed him the Promised Land. Then Moses died.

God's people cried when Moses died. There has never been another prophet like Moses. God talked with him in a special way. Moses did many wonders. Nobody else ever showed as much of God's great power.

Deuteronomy 31:16, 19, 22; 32:3-4, 7, 36, 43, 49; 34:1, 5, 8, 10-12

Think about how God worked in Moses' life. God saved Moses when he was a baby. Moses grew up learning about the kings of Egypt. He learned to lead by being a shepherd. He showed God's wonders to the leaders of Egypt. He led his people through the desert. God gave his laws to Moses and talked to Moses like a friend. All of this was God's plan for Moses. Moses obeyed and followed God. So God worked his plan out.

God loves you just as much as he loved Moses. And God has a plan for your life too. God is getting you ready to do great things. So get to know God better. Love him and obey him. Watch to see how he works out his plan for you. It will be better than anything you can think of!

"Dear God, thank you for loving me and having a plan for me. I will love and obey you. You are a great God!"

TUESDAY

Read "The Holiday," page 483 in *God's Story.* Or read this part of the story:

So the Jews got . . . ready to fight people who would fight them.

Nobody could win against the Jews. . . . Even the leaders helped the Jews. They were afraid of Mordecai. Mordecai was now an important man at the palace. . . .

So the Jews killed their enemies that day. The king told Queen Esther about it. "Now what would you like to have?" he asked. . . .

"Let the Jews keep fighting their enemies tomorrow," Esther said. . . .

So the king gave the order. The Jews fought against their enemies the next day.

The day after that, the Jews rested. It was a day of big, happy dinners. . . .

Mordecai . . . sent letters to all the Jews in the land. The letter told them to have a two-day holiday. . . .

They call these days Purim. . . .

Queen Esther and Mordecai wrote a letter. It said that Purim would be a holiday. Mordecai sent the letter to all the Jews in the land. It cheered up all the Jews.
Esther 9:2-5, 12-14, 17-31

Do you remember the story of Esther? Think about how God worked in her life. Esther was taken to

SOME THINGS YOU CAN DO THIS WEEK

☐ **Play "Grow a Man."** Play this like "Hangman," but *grow* the man instead of *hanging* him. Choose a word, and tell the players whether it is a person, place, or thing. Draw lines on a piece of paper to show how many letters the word has in it. Let players take turns guessing a letter they think is in the word. If the person is right, print the letter on the line where it goes in the word. If the person is wrong, draw a circle for the head of his or her person. Keep going, adding lines for a body, arms, and legs. Once a player's person is all drawn, he has no more turns at guessing. Think about how God is growing you and has plans for you.

☐ **Make a picture all about you.** Cut pictures from magazines of things that you like. Glue them onto a piece of paper. Talk about how you are going to do things for God with all that you are learning.

☐ **Print the letters of your name** very large on a piece of black paper. Cut out the letters carefully, leaving the paper around the letters in one piece if you can. Glue your cut-out name onto a piece of white paper. Glue the paper that you cut the letters from onto another piece of white paper. Talk about God's plan for you.

☐ **Make hand prints.** Pour a little finger paint onto a paper plate. Press your hand into the paint to get paint onto your palm and fingers. Then press your hand onto white paper. Remember that as you grow, your hand will grow too. After you wash off your hand, print on the paper: "God is growing me up to be like Jesus."

the palace with other young women. The king chose Esther to be his queen. She was brave and went to see the king even though he had not called her to come. She told the king that the Jewish people who were going to be killed were her people. Soon after that, her cousin Mordecai became an important man at the palace. He wrote a law to save the Jews.

God put Esther and her cousin in the right place at the right time. He had a plan for them. God has a plan for you, too. God loves you just as much as he loved Esther and Mordecai. So trust and obey God. Follow him no matter what happens. He has promised that he will work out his plan for you. And he will make everything turn out for your good.

"Dear Father God, thank you for having a plan for me. I will follow you. Thank you for making everything turn out to be good."

WEDNESDAY

Read "On the Wings of the Wind," page 162 in *God's Story.* Or read this part of the story:

I love you, God. You make me strong.

God is like a strong rock to me. He is like a fort around me.
He saves me. He is like my guard.
I pray to God. I want to praise him.

When everything was going wrong, I asked God for help.
God heard me. . . .

God opened heaven and came down.
His feet stood on dark clouds.
He flew on the wings of the wind.

God reached down and saved me.
When everything seemed lost, God helped me.
He was happy with me.
Psalm 18:1-10, 16-19

Think about how God worked in David's life. God let David be a shepherd boy. He had to lead. He also had to fight lions and bears. He had time to think about God and sing songs to God. Then God helped David kill Goliath. He let him serve Saul with his songs. At last, David became the king of all God's people. With God's help, he won many fights against his enemies.

God had a plan for David. And God has a plan for you. God loves you just as much as he loved David.

David loved God and followed God with his whole heart. You can love God and follow him with your whole heart too. God will do what he planned for you. Then you will say what David said. "I love you, God. You make me strong" (Psalm 18:1).

"Dear Father God, I do love you. I know you will make me strong. Thank you for loving me and having a plan for me."

THURSDAY

 Read "Daniel's Prayer and God's Answer," page 455 in *God's Story*. Or read this part of the story:

I, Daniel . . . prayed. . . . I said, "Lord, you are a great, wonderful God. You keep your promise of love to everyone who loves you. You keep your promise to everyone who obeys you.

"God, you do what's good and right. . . . Jerusalem is your city. . . . Now, God, hear my prayers. Be kind to your city.

"We don't ask you because we are right and good. We ask because you are kind. Listen, God! Forgive us! Hear and act!"

Gabriel said, "Daniel, I came to help you understand. An answer was ready for you right when you began praying.

"There will be a law made to build Jerusalem back again. . . . The city will be built back up. But it will be built in a time of trouble."
Daniel 9:2, 4, 16-19, 21-23, 25

Do you remember the story of Daniel? Think about how God worked in Daniel's life. Daniel was a young man when the enemy came to his land. They took Daniel and his friends to their country to live. God made Daniel and his friends wiser than all the other wise men. God let Daniel understand dreams, too. Daniel never stopped trusting God. God used Daniel to talk to the kings of this nation far away.

God had a special plan for Daniel's life. Daniel knew that God was with him everywhere he went, even in the enemy's country. God is also with you everywhere you go. You can follow and obey God no matter where you are. God will take care of you. That's because he loves you just as much as he loved Daniel.

God has a special plan for you too. You can pray Daniel's prayer, too, thanking God for keeping his promises.

"Dear Father God, you are a wonderful God. Thank you for loving me and taking care of me. Thank you for being with me everywhere I go."

FRIDAY

Read "Tossing Dust into the Air," page 721 in *God's Story*. Or read this part of the story:

"Listen to me," said Paul. . . . "I'm a Jew. . . . I grew up in this city. I went to school here. . . . I worked hard for God and his Law. . . .

"I was on my way to Damascus," said Paul. "About noon, a bright light shone down on me from heaven. . . ."

Paul told the crowd his story. He told them how Jesus had talked to him. . . . He told how he had gone back to Jerusalem.

"I was praying at the worship house," said Paul. . . . "The Lord talked to me again. 'Go. I'm sending you far away to people who aren't Jewish,' he said."

The crowd listened to Paul until he said that. Then they yelled, "Get rid of him. . . ." They tossed dust into the air. . . .

The captain said to beat Paul. . . . But Paul said, "Isn't it against the law to beat a Roman? . . ."

The captain went to Paul. "Are you really a Roman?" he asked.

"Yes," said Paul. "I am. . . ."

The guards had planned to ask Paul questions. But now they left right away.
Acts 22:1-9, 17-29

Do you remember the story about Paul? Think about how God worked in Paul's life. Paul's family was Jewish. Paul had good Jewish teachers. But his family was also Roman. So Paul could not be beaten by Roman guards. When Paul believed something, he let everyone know.

He stood up for what he believed. So when Paul met Jesus, he followed Jesus with his whole heart.

You can follow Jesus with your whole heart too. You can stand up for what you believe. God loves you just as much as he loved Paul. God has a plan for you. So you can say these words along with Paul: God "chose us so we could praise him. He chose us so we could show how great he is" (Ephesians 1:11-12).

Moses, Esther, David, Daniel, and Paul couldn't see God's plan when they were your age. But they took time to get to know God better each day. They trusted him. They followed God no matter what happened. And you can do the same thing.

"Dear God, help me get to know you better each day. I will follow you no matter what happens. I love you. You are my great, wonderful, loving Father in heaven."

Index of Bible Stories

Old Testament

New Testament

Index of Weekly Theme Verses